An OPUS Book

Twentieth-Century South Africa

William Beinart is Reader in History at the University of
Bristol. He studied at the Universities of Cape Town and
London, and the School of Oriental and African Studies,
and has held posts at Yale and Oxford Universities. He
was joint-editor of *The Journal of South African Studies*
from 1982 to 1987 and Chair of its editorial board in 1992.
His publications include books and edited collections on
modern South African history.

Twentieth-Century South Africa

WILLIAM BEINART

Oxford   New York

OXFORD UNIVERSITY PRESS

1994

Oxford University Press, Walton Street, Oxford OX2 6DP

Oxford New York Toronto
Delhi Bombay Calcutta Madras Karachi
Kuala Lumpur Singapore Hong Kong Tokyo
Nairobi Dar es Salaam Cape Town
Melbourne Auckland Madrid

and associated companies in
Berlin Ibadan

Oxford is a trade mark of Oxford University Press

First published 1994 as an Oxford University Press paperback

British Library Cataloguing in Publication Data

Data available

Library of Congress Cataloging in Publication Data

Beinart, William.
Twentieth-century South Africa / William Beinart.
p. cm.
'An OPUS book.'
Includes bibliographical references and index.
1. South Africa—Politics and government—1836–1909. 2. South
Africa—Politics and government—20th century.   I. Title.
II. Title: 20th-century South Africa.
DT1848.B44   1994   968.05—dc20   93–50619

ISBN 0–19–289239–8

1   3   5   7   9   10   8   6   4   2

Typeset by CentraCet Limited, Cambridge
Printed in Great Britain by
Biddles Ltd.
Guildford and King's Lynn

Preface and Acknowledgements

This book is not intended as a general history but as an introductory essay accessible to undergraduate students. The Editors of the OPUS series were generous in allowing so much space. Nevertheless a good deal of material in the early chapter drafts had to be omitted and the book makes no pretence at completeness.

My aim has been to maintain a central political narrative in plain language, placed firmly in the context of the country's economic, social, and cultural history. I have drawn heavily on the rich new historical writing, largely in English, of the last couple of decades. There is no longer one 'school' of 'revisionist' or radical history, but most authors have shared an opposition to apartheid and a commitment to discovering the history of black people. I have not been able to expand on historiographical debates, nor on the exciting developments in local history, as much as I would have liked. The southern African region is also neglected because of constraints on space. In a short book without footnotes, it has not been possible to acknowledge everyone's work adequately. I hope those who recognize their material and ideas will feel that they are reasonably used. There is a bibliographical guide to each chapter at the end of the book.

My teaching experience, largely with British undergraduates at the University of Bristol—who have no background in South African history but have raised many interesting points over the years—shaped my approach to the book. The first half is based around a Special Subject seminar course on South Africa, 1880–1930. Most of my own research has been on the rural areas; I have tried to give more emphasis to their significance than is often the case in general works. Editing the *Journal of Southern African Studies*, an important repository of new historiography, has influenced the contents both of my memory and of the book. Lastly, writing was done in the British summers of 1991 and 1992 as South Africa lurched between political settlement and violence. The uncertainty of these years is probably reflected in my analysis and has made it difficult to bring the coverage as close to the present as OUP requested. Like many South Africans I wish to be optimistic about a peaceful, non-racial, and democratic future, but as a historian cannot lose sight of the forces of division.

In an attempt largely to explain twentieth-century developments, I deal with a long twentieth century, drawing copiously on earlier material for background and context. The first half, 'A State without a Nation', is arranged around four initial thematic chapters, dealing with the period roughly from the 1880s to the 1920s, followed by one chapter in which various strands are drawn together up to 1948. The advent of the Afrikaner Nationalist government in that year seemed an obvious dividing line although continuities are noted. The second half of the book, 'Afrikaner Power and the Rise of Mass Opposition', begins with a general chapter on the introduction of apartheid and then juxtaposes political, economic, and social developments in three chapters covering the period from about 1961 to 1984. The concluding chapter explores the changing political balance up to 1992. There are bound to be disadvantages in a thematic approach, but I have tried to show the dynamic links between economics and politics and between white and black communities.

I would like to thank Catherine Clarke and Simon Mason, editors of the OPUS series, for suggesting the book and for their encouragement and patience. Richard Evans, General Editor of the series, as well as readers for the publishers—in particular Martin Legassick—made a number of valuable comments. Colin Bundy and Saul Dubow responded helpfully to the typescript in its penultimate form. My primary debt is to Troth Wells for her support, her interest in the work, and her careful reading of the text which has undoubtedly made it clearer and more accessible.

W. B.

May 1993

Contents

Preface and Acknowledgements   v

Maps, Tables, and Figures   x

Abbreviations   xi

Chronology   xiii

Introduction: Conquest, Control, and the State in South
   Africa   1

PART I: A State without a Nation, 1880s–1948   7

1   *African Rural Life and Migrant Labour*   9
    The Division of Land   9
    The African Heritage   15
    African Peasantries   20
    Mining and Labour Migration   25

2   *Economic and Social Change on the Settler
       Farmlands*   35
    Agrarian Worlds in the Cape   35
    Natal and the Highveld   43
    The Fate of Tenants   51

3   *War, Reconstruction, and the State from the 1890s to
       1920s*   59
    War, Reconstruction, and the Logic of the Mines   59
    Social Policy and Urban Growth in the Reconstruction
       Era   67
    Afrikaners Re-emergent   74

4 *Black Responses and Black Resistance*   84
   The Black Élite and African Nationalism   84
   Chieftaincy, Ethnicity, and Rural Protest   92
   Popular Struggles in the 1920s   98

5 *The Settler State in Depression and War, 1930–*
      1948   109
   The Settler State and Afrikaner Politics   109
   Segregation and Urbanization   117
   African Urban and Rural Life   122
   The Demise of Smuts   131

   PART II: Afrikaner Power and the Rise of Mass
      Opposition, 1948–1992   135

6 *Apartheid, 1948–1961*   137
   The Nationalist Mission   137
   Legislation and Reaction   142
   Apartheid, Labour Control, and the Homelands   149
   Sharpeville and the Republic   159

7 *Economy and Society in the 1960s and 1970s*   163
   Apartheid and Economic Growth   163
   White Society and Culture   171
   Class and Social Change in African Urban
      Communities   180

8 *Farms, Homelands, and Displaced Urbanization,*
      1960–1984   188
   The Demography of Change   188
   The White-Owned Farmlands   192
   Displaced Urbanization   197
   Social Division and Politics in the Homelands   203

9 *Black Political Struggles and the Reform Era of P. W.
      Botha, 1973–1984*   212
   The ANC and the Politics of Exile   212
   Internal Remobilization: Black Consciousness   216
   Trade Unions   222
   Crisis, Reform, and the UDF   225

10 *Insurrection, Fragmentation, and Negotiations,
       1984–1992*   236
    Urban Government and the 1984–6 Insurrection   236
    The State: Militarization, Vigilantes, and Retreat   244
    Violence and Negotiation   250

    Appendix 1. *Tables*   261
    Appendix 2. *Figures*   265
    Bibliography   268
    Index   282

List of Maps

1. Union of South Africa, c.1910   12
2. Homelands and Urbanization   200
3. Townships in the Pretoria–Witwatersrand–Vereeniging
    Region   240

List of Tables

1. Total population and percentage by race as designated in
    census   261
2. Average annual increase over previous census
    year   262
3. Proportion of population in urban areas   263
4. Motor vehicles   264

List of Figures

1. Urban growth, 1911–2000. Main metropolitan
    areas   265
2. African employment in Transvaal mines   266
3. Age structure of population, 1980   267

Abbreviations

AAC	All Africa Convention
AMEC	African Methodist Episcopal Church
ANC	African National Congress
APLA	Azanian People's Liberation Army
APO	African Political Organization
BAABs	Bantu Affairs Administration Boards
BAWU	Black Allied Workers' Union
BOSS	Bureau of State Security
COSAS	Congress of South African Students
COSATU	Congress of South African Trade Unions
CP	Communist Party
CUSA	Council of Unions of South Africa
ESCOM	Electricity Supply Commission
FOSATU	Federation of South African Trade Unions
FRAC	Franchise Action Committee
HNP	*Herenigde* National Party
ICU	Industrial and Commercial Workers' Union of South Africa
ISCOR	Iron and Steel Corporation
JAH	*Journal of African History*
JSAS	*Journal of South African Studies*
KWV	Koöperatiewe Wynbouers Vereeniging
MAWU	African Metal and Allied Workers' Union
MK	Umkhonto we Sizwe
NAD	Native Affairs Department
NEC	Native Economic Commission
NECC	National Education Crisis Committee
NEUM	Non-European Unity Movement
NRC	Native Recruiting Corporation
NUSAS	National Union of South African Students
OB	Ossewabrandwag
PAC	Pan Africanist Congress
Putco	Public Utility Transport Corporation
SAAU	South African Agricultural Union

SAAWU	South African Allied Workers' Union
SACTU	South African Congress of Trade Unions
SANAC	South African Native Affairs Commission
SANC	South African Native Congress
SANNC	South African Native National Congress
SAP	South African Party
SASM	South African Students Movement
SASO	South African Students Organization
SPP	Surplus People Project
SWAPO	South West African People's Organization
TNIP	Transkei National Independence Party
TUCSA	Trade Union Congress of South Africa
UDF	United Democratic Front
UP	United South African Nationalist Party
WNLA	Witwatersrand Native Labour Association
ZANU	Zimbabwe African National Union
ZCC	Zion Christian Church

Chronology

1877–80	British conquest of Transvaal, Sekhukhuneland, Zululand; rebellions quelled in Lesotho, Transkei, and Bechuanaland. Afrikaner Bond founded in Cape.
1881	South African Republic in the Transvaal reasserts independence.
1880s	Cape African peasantry flourishes; J. T. Jabavu starts newspaper *Imvo Zabantsundu*.
1886/8	Discovery of gold on Witwatersrand; De Beers monopoly of Kimberley diamond mines under Cecil Rhodes.
1890–6	Rhodes Prime Minister of Cape.
1895	Jameson Raid—abortive forcible take-over of Transvaal.
1896–7	Rinderpest epizootic—cattle disease.
1899–1902	South African War.
1905	Report of the South African Native Affairs Commission—Reconstruction government's programme for segregation.
1906	Bambatha rebellion in Natal.
1904–11	Johannesburg overtakes Cape Town as region's largest city; African employment on mines exceeds 200,000.
1910	Union of South Africa formed including the Cape Colony, Natal, Transvaal, and Orange River Colony (Orange Free State); South African Party government led by Generals Louis Botha and Jan Smuts.
1912	Foundation of the South African Native National Congress (later ANC).

1913   Year of crisis: Natives Land Act passed;
                Gandhi's march to the Transvaal and Indian
                sugar workers' strike; African women march
                against passes in Bloemfontein; white workers
                strike in gold mines.

1914/15   National Party founded under General J. B. M.
                Hertzog, based in Orange Free State; Afrikaner
                rebellion, coinciding with outbreak of First
                World War; *Die Burger* newspaper launched.

1918   Influenza epidemic.

1919   Botha dies; Smuts becomes Prime Minister.

1918–20   Strikes and boycotts on the Rand culminating in
                first major African mine-workers' strike.

1922   Rand Rebellion of white workers.

1923   Drought Commission Report highlighting
                environmental degradation; Natives Urban
                Areas Act tightens urban segregation.

1924   Hertzog's National Party wins election in
                alliance with white Labour Party.

1925–30   Industrial and Commercial Workers' Union,
                founded in Cape Town 1919, becomes mass
                movement and spreads to rural areas.

1927   Native Administration Act extending
                recognition of chieftaincy and forming basis for
                decentralizing authority in African reserves.

1930–1   Small stock numbers peak at over 50 million.

1930   White women enfranchised.

1926–30   Imperial conferences give South Africa
                enhanced independence as a Dominion.

1930–4   Depression and drought; *Native Economic
                Commission* report, 1932, provides guide-lines
                for development of reserves.

1933–4   Hertzog and Smuts form Fusion government and
                United Party in response to Depression;
                National Party (purified) breaks away under
                D. F. Malan.

1932–40	South Africa leaves gold standard; gold-mining expands rapidly and employment exceeds 400,000; manufacturing boom begins.
1936	Native Trust and Land Act passed; remnant African common roll vote in Cape terminated.
1939	South Africa votes to enter Second World War. Hertzog resigns; Smuts governs as Prime Minister to 1948.
1940	Ossewabrandwag, Afrikaner paramilitary movement, founded.
1940–6	Wartime industrial expansion; employment in manufacturing industry overtakes that in mining; rising level of African militancy culminating in 1946 black mine-workers' strike and launch of squatter movements on Rand.
1948	Malan's Nationalists win election on apartheid slogan.
1950–3	Major apartheid legislation passed: Population Registration; Suppression of Communism; Group Areas and Prevention of Illegal Squatting; Separate Representation of Voters; Bantu Authorities; Bantu Education.
1952	ANC leads Defiance Campaign.
1955	Freedom Charter.
1956	Tomlinson Commission report on homelands.
1958	H. F. Verwoerd becomes Prime Minister.
1958–60	Black opposition peaks: Pan Africanist Congress splits from ANC; Natal and Transvaal rural resistance; Sharpeville massacre; Pondoland revolt and mass stay-aways; march on parliament in Cape Town.
1960–1	Referendum on the Republic; South Africa becomes Republic outside the Commonwealth; ANC and PAC banned and go underground.
1962–3	ANC leadership including Nelson Mandela captured and imprisoned.
1966	Verwoerd assassinated; J. B. Vorster becomes Prime Minister.

1960s	Years of rapid economic, especially industrial growth; white incomes increase as apartheid entrenched; homelands and forced removals policies implemented; black population growth increasingly outstripping white.
1972	Black People's Convention launched.
1973	Durban strikes; independent trade unions launched.
1975	Inkatha—Zulu cultural and political movement relaunched; Portuguese colonies of Angola and Mozambique achieve independence.
1976	Soweto students protest; Transkei becomes first 'independent' homeland; television introduced.
1977	Steve Biko killed.
1978	P. W. Botha Prime Minister.
1970s to mid-1980s	Rural removals and displaced urbanization peak.
1979–80	Nation-wide strikes, student and community protests; African government in power in Zimbabwe.
1982	Conservative Party formed.
1983	Tri-cameral parliament and new presidential government launched; United Democratic Front initiated in protest.
1984–6	Insurrection and State of Emergency.
1985	COSATU trade union federation founded.
1986	Rescinding of pass laws as population of major cities explodes with informal settlements.
1989	F. W. de Klerk becomes President.
1990	Nelson Mandela released; ANC and other movements unbanned; rescinding of apartheid laws gathers pace.
1991	Convention for a Democratic South Africa meets to negotiate constitution for a new South Africa.
1990–2	Violence in black townships spreads.
1992	Boipatong massacre; talks suspended but relaunched at end of year.

Introduction: Conquest, Control, and the State in South Africa

By the early 1870s the area that became South Africa had been washed by successive waves of European expansion, notably the Dutch maritime empire of the seventeenth and eighteenth centuries and British imperialism in the nineteenth. Four settler states had been established. The original Cape Colony, which passed finally to Britain in 1806, boasted the largest area and settler population. It had recently acquired a parliamentary system and a measure of self-government. Natal remained a British Colony. The Boer states of the Orange Free State and South African Republic on the interior highveld of the country struggled to maintain their independence from British and Cape influence.

The African people of the region had been deeply affected by colonization over two centuries. In the Cape, the San and Khoikhoi had been decimated and largely displaced; they survived as farm-workers or on mission stations and settlements around the peripheries of white control. The Xhosa on the eastern frontier and the Sotho on the highveld had been conquered and partly incorporated. Yet the colonial impact was uneven. Between the settler states and to their north a number of African polities remained, by reason of their power and size or their geographic position, relatively independent. The Zulu kingdom on the East Coast, north of Natal, was the largest; the Swazi, Tswana, Pedi, Venda, Mpondo, and Thembu remained substantial chiefdoms. Within the next couple of decades, however, they were drawn decisively, with more or less force, under British or settler rule.

In the decades around the turn of the twentieth century, South African society was deeply moulded by the British imperial presence. Not only did imperial armies, together with the commandos and cavalry of the settler states, finally com-

plete the conquest of African chiefdoms, but a huge investment
of European capital made the mining industry into the new
economic motor of the country. Settler and African agrarian
economies were fundamentally reshaped. Between 1899 and
1902, Britain fought perhaps its greatest colonial war to annex
the Boer republics.

As ox-wagons trundled across the veld, moving Lord
Kitchener's giant army, so the tracks were laid for a coherent
single state in South Africa. The country was locked together
in war. Ox-wagons had carried the Boer settlers into the
interior; wagon-routes were the sinews of the trading economy
which, spreading from the major colonial ports in the nineteenth century, clutched both black and white societies into its
grasp. The ox-wagon, so potent a symbol of Afrikaner identity
in the twentieth century, was previously a vehicle of imperial
conquest.

British power, which had ebbed and flowed in southern
Africa through the nineteenth century, projected itself as an
essentially peaceful force. Though Britain honoured its military
heroes with graves in St Paul's Cathedral, it conceived of
violence as provoked by uncivilized 'hordes' and 'tribes', or by
semi-barbarized Boers. The British duty to civilize them all
both explained and justified conquest. But in nineteenth-
century South Africa, empire and its colonial agents were
harbingers of a great deal of bloodshed which was not simply
incidental to expansion. Most of the major battles were fought
on the territory of Britain's opponents. While there were
periods of indecision in the conquest of this corner of the
Empire, there was no absence of mind. Britain's economic and
strategic imperatives made it determined to defend and expand
its interests in the subcontinent. This required war with the
Zulu, the most powerful remaining African state, and with the
Afrikaners. Had the South African War of 1899–1902 not been
dwarfed by the First World War, it would have studded world
history even more sharply.

British expansion in the nineteenth century had by no means
been the only trigger of conflict. The settler states were often
themselves key agents of expansion and conquest. African

chiefdoms were trying to consolidate their authority and defend
their boundaries against black and white challenges. It is very
difficult to write nineteenth-century South African history
without constant reference to violence and military engage-
ments. All these nodes of power had competed for land, labour,
natural resources, and political space. Guns poured into the
subcontinent, intensifying its conflicts. But British interventions
greatly increased the scale of violence in the late nineteenth
century.

Ironically, British intervention also resulted in the imposition
of a colonial peace which ended more than a century of war.
The economic muscle and bureaucratic sophistication of an
advanced capitalist country was transferred to the region and
helped to bequeath a powerful state structure. Twentieth-
century conflicts were civil rather than military. The *impi*, the
redcoat regiment, and commando moved to the background;
conflict had its locus in the mines, the streets, and on the farms.
For seventy years, until the waves of decolonization swept
downwards across the subcontinent, and a resurgent mass
opposition burst through internally, the state established at the
turn of the century held sway and remained militarily secure.
Even the guerrilla wars of the 1960s to the 1980s, the rearming
of the subcontinent, and internal insurrections of the 1980s
have not quite dislodged it.

The very solidity of the state provided the stepping-stones
for whites, both English and especially Afrikaans-speaking, to
take power and entrench a system of racially based dominance
that was unique in its rigidity. Segregation to 1948, and
apartheid afterwards, were policies aimed not simply at separating white from black, but at regulating the way in which the
indigenous population was drawn into a new society. Economically, blacks were essential as peasants, workers, and farm
tenants; politically the settler state tried to exclude them. The
country's relative peace for nearly three-quarters of a century
was achieved at the cost of deep divisions of power, race, and
wealth. White power in South Africa was more efficient and
often more uncompromising than in many other colonial
contexts.

White power has deep foundations in the region and no doubt it will have a long legacy. But even at its height in mid-century, the settler state was shaped by its African context. Moreover, the twentieth century has surely seen the apogee of a form of rule where the privileges of race and class could be made congruent. In Africa as a whole, colonial rule, though far-reaching in its consequences, was a short-lived phase. In South Africa this phase has been longer. More radical social transformations—industrialization, urbanization, and agricultural expansion—have been effected. If African people gain power, it will be in a country which is overwhelmingly urban and wage dependent, rather than rural. Yet it is important to understand that South Africa remains part of the African continent.

In the early twentieth century a single state was forged but not a single nation. Economic change and new forms of government overlaid but did not fully subsume what went before. The old identities and social geography of African chiefdoms remained partly intact and a dynamic factor in the country's development. Old layers of settler society also continued to exercise a deep influence on the political trajectory of the region.

Liberal and radical historians of South Africa have often focused on the rapidity with which a common economy and society emerged, arguing that the reality of interaction was stopped in its tracks by politically enforced segregation. Mining and industrialization have recently been the organizing historical themes, together with the rise of new nationalisms, both Afrikaner and African. These must remain central and persistent historiographical concerns. But we need to find a method which will allow analysis of these forces, together with the remnant identities and particularisms which have been so powerful in shaping the ideas of the mass of people in the country. The history of political opposition, for example, cannot be reduced to the rise of African nationalism or the working classes. A means has to be found to express also the vitality of discrete rural localities, the salience of ethnicity, the fragmented patterns of urban social life, the multiplicity of religious expression. These are all forces, both dynamic and destructive, which have stalked and enlivened twentieth-century history.

South Africa differed from much of colonial Africa in that its climate, its diseases, and natural resources allowed for substantial early European settlement. The Khoisan population of the Cape was highly susceptible to new diseases such as smallpox. In this area, the colonial experience in South Africa was more like Australasia or the Americas than Africa. Elsewhere southern Africa differed from 'new world' colonies of settlement in that the settler thrust was weaker and the indigenous response stronger. The further the settlers penetrated the interior, or into areas of dense African settlement, the more dilute their influence became. No land, in any colonial context, has been 'vacant'; all myths of vacant lands are precisely that. But unlike North American, or the Australian coast, land in South Africa beyond the old Khoikhoi areas could be taken over only with great difficulty.

The area of modern South Africa was, to a significant extent, shaped by the zones of effective white settlement in the nineteenth century. Yet even in the census of 1904, which was taken when the white population was probably at its highest relative to the black, the country was demographically speaking largely African (Table 1). A little under 5.2 million people were counted in the states that became South Africa. By this time the racial categories of European, Asiatic, Coloured, and Native were firmly established. Roughly one fifth (21.5 per cent) of the total, or 1.1 million people were counted as Europeans; 8.6 per cent were counted as 'coloured', overwhelmingly in the Cape, descended from the Khoikhoi, slaves, and settlers. About 2.4 per cent were Asiatic, largely Indian workers on the Natal sugar estates and their descendants. And around two-thirds, or 3.5 million people, were counted as Africans. If Lesotho, Swaziland, and Botswana—all part of the same economic and political zone—were included, the proportion of the white population would have been smaller.

C. W. de Kiewiet, author of the most exciting single-volume history of South Africa, published in 1940, expressed the particularity of the South African experience by arguing that South Africa was not 'a romantic frontier like the American West' (de Kiewiet, 48): 'Legend has denied the Pondos, for example, a place beside the Pawnees . . . The stuff of legend is not easily found in a process which turned the Ama-Xosa, Zulus, or Basuto into farm labourers, kitchen servants, or messengers.' De Kiewiet was surely wrong. It was the very fact that South Africa remained part of Africa and that its black population survived conquest and made the transition from warrior to wage slave which has been the core of the South African black legend. De Kiewiet's romanticization of the native Americans was a celluloid picture, made in Hollywood, which could be recreated by the dominant culture precisely because the people on whom it was based had almost been exterminated. His alliterative choice of the Pawnee, who tended to side with the colonists and still lost their land, was hardly appropriate.

The romance of Mpondo history—or that of the Sotho or Xhosa or Zulu—was that they survived and retained some of their land and their culture. The Mpondo survived well enough to stage one of the last major rural revolts against white authority in 1960. It was the capacity of black peasants and workers to adapt, increase demographically, educate themselves, and strike back politically that has been at the heart of twentieth-century South African history. Their experience is now also, like the demise of the Pawnee, the subject of celluloid celebration in films such as *Cry Freedom*.

South Africa was part settler state and part African colony in the early twentieth century. It included diverse recently conquered African polities as well as a divided white population. The strength and unity of the African population is only now being fully asserted. Whether these various elements can be amalgamated into a distinctive national culture, and become the basis for a new and stable state, remains uncertain.

PART I

A State without a Nation,
1880s–1948

1 African Rural Life and Migrant Labour

The Division of Land

Any author writing a general book on South Africa must decide whether to start with whites or blacks. For reasons both of accuracy and ideology, most historians writing recently have abandoned 1652, date of the first Dutch station at the Cape, and begun instead with pre-colonial African societies. It is more difficult to start with African people in a book which deals largely with the last hundred years. Markets, empire, industry, capital, railways, and political union in 1910 were the new motors of change. None of these forces had to do simply with white or black, but in dealing with them the agency of the settler and metropolitan worlds must be emphasized.

One way out of the dilemma is to address the last century initially from the vantage-point of the varied agrarian worlds which were being consolidated into a single state. There is a demographic argument for this approach in that the great majority of people still lived in the countryside at the turn of the century. There is also an explanatory logic: by starting with different rural zones it will be easier to keep the diversity of the country in mind as other themes are developed. And by focusing most of the first two chapters on the rural areas, it is also possible to begin with African people. Although a majority (53 per cent) of whites lived in towns by 1904, only 15 per cent of blacks and 10 per cent of Africans, including migrant workers, did so (Table 3). The bedrock of settlement and population in the country, well over three million people, were Africans who lived in villages and dispersed homesteads on reserved lands and farms.

The division of ownership and possession of rural land by race in South Africa, which had deep historical roots, was formalized and consolidated in the 1913 Natives Land Act. It is often said that 87 per cent of land was reserved for whites and 13 for blacks. These figures are not quite accurate for the first few decades of the twentieth century. Whites have never owned quite so much land and rather less was initially reserved for Africans. About three-quarters (77 per cent) of the country's surface area was demarcated for private owner-ship by white individuals or by companies; around 8 per cent was reserved solely for African occupation, and a little more was privately owned by Africans or for them by institutions such as missions. Perhaps 13 per cent was crown or state land. Much of it was demarcated for game reserves, forests, or other uses and only lightly occupied, but some was rented out to tenants. Only after the 1936 Native Trust and Land Act did the area reserved for African occupation gradually increase to 13 per cent.

Whatever the exact numbers, this was a degree of land alienation unrivalled in any sub-Saharan African context. In neighbouring countries with large areas of private farmlands, such as Zimbabwe, Swaziland, and Namibia, under 50 per cent of the total area fell into the hands of settlers. But these stark South African figures require more detailed explanation. They disguise a pattern of land occupation and distribution which initially allowed Africans to retain a more significant stake in the land than the raw percentages might suggest.

The land area that came to comprise South Africa is divided roughly in half by the 20-inch or 500 mm. rainfall line, which runs from Port Elizabeth in the eastern Cape through the western Orange Free State into the western Transvaal. Over half the country, most of it to the west of this line, receives so little rain that it was very difficult to grow crops. The dense settlements of iron-using, cultivating, Bantu-speaking African people, who have for centuries made up the bulk of the country's population, lived mostly to the east. They did not penetrate into the one better-watered pocket of the west around the Cape Peninsula. In pre-colonial times both the western Cape and the drier parts of the interior were occupied largely by Khoisan hunters, gatherers, and herders. The major exception has been the Tswana chiefdoms whose territories, based around pre-colonial towns, straddled semi-arid highveld zones. Xhosa communities also penetrated to the dry northern Cape in the early nineteenth century.

The land reserved for African occupation in the twentieth century was largely within the higher rainfall zone. Some of it may have become very poor, but initially it was not the worst land. Africans tended to retain reserves in the heartlands of their old, conquered chiefdoms—the areas most suitable for their systems of agricultural and pastoral production. They certainly lost a great deal of land and were severely disadvantaged in the competition for new areas made possible by new technologies such as the plough and the windmill. But over 20 per cent of the land which they had effectively used was initially reserved for them. Within the eastern half of the country, a majority of African people lived in the relatively narrow strip of land between the Kahlamba (things cast down in a heap) or Drakensberg (Dragon) mountain range and the Indian Ocean. It was here also around the old Xhosa, Thembu, Mpondo, and Zulu chiefdoms that the bulk of African reserve land was situated. Most East Coast chiefdoms retained a far higher percentage of their land.

Another reason for caution when discussing the racial division of land is that many Africans stayed on white-owned land. It would be a mistake to draw too hard a dividing line between types of land at the turn of the century. Land alienation was part of the process of military conquest only recently completed. It proved more difficult for whites to control land than to defeat African armies. Private property was sometimes imposed over areas which were still occupied by African communities. Whereas in Natal and the Cape reserve policies were instituted from the middle of the nineteenth century, Boer ideas led them to demarcate private property more generally, whether or not this could be enforced. In all areas, farms were held for speculative purposes. African settlements could straddle the boundaries of private and reserved land. The rural African population of the Orange Free State, and especially the Transvaal, concentrated around the old Sotho, Tswana,

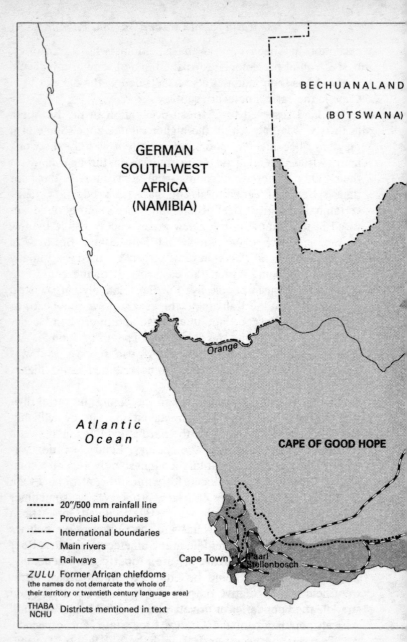

BECHUANALAND

(BOTSWANA)

GERMAN
SOUTH-WEST
AFRICA
(NAMIBIA)

Orange

*Atlantic
Ocean*

CAPE OF GOOD HOPE

········· 20"/500 mm rainfall line
-------- Provincial boundaries
·—·—·— International boundaries
⌒⌒ Main rivers
▬▬▬ Railways
ZULU Former African chiefdoms
(the names do not demarcate the whole of
their territory or twentieth century language area)
THABA
NCHU Districts mentioned in text

Cape Town Paarl
          Stellenbosch

MAP I. *Union of South Africa, c.1910*

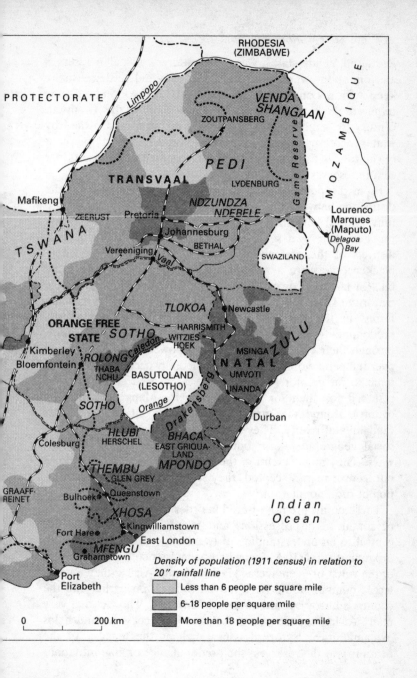

RHODESIA (ZIMBABWE)

PROTECTORATE

Limpopo

VENDA
SHANGAAN

ZOUTPANSBERG

PEDI

TRANSVAAL

LYDENBURG

Mafikeng

Game Reserve

MOZAMBIQUE

ZEERUST   Pretoria

NDZUNDZA
NDEBELE

Lourenco
Marques
(Maputo)
Delagoa
Bay

Johannesburg

TSWANA

Vereeniging   BETHAL

SWAZILAND

Vaal

TLOKOA   •Newcastle

ORANGE FREE
STATE   SOTHO

HARRISMITH
WITZIES
HOEK

MSINGA

ZULU

Kimberley

ROLONG

Caledon

NATAL

Bloemfontein   THABA
NCHU

BASUTOLAND
(LESOTHO)

UMVOTI

INANDA

SOTHO

Orange

Drakensberg

Durban

HLUBI
HERSCHEL

BHACA
EAST GRIQUA-
LAND

Colesburg

THEMBU
GLEN GREY

MPONDO

GRAAFF
REINET

Bulhoek•   Queenstown

XHOSA

Indian
Ocean

Fort Hare•   •Kingwilliamstown

MFENGU   East London
Grahamstown

Port
Elizabeth

Density of population (1911 census) in relation to
20" rainfall line

Less than 6 people per square mile

6–18 people per square mile

More than 18 people per square mile

0   200 km

Pedi, and Venda states, was thus scattered in smaller reserves and on white-owned farmlands. Not only did settlers usually keep Africans on their farms as tenants and workers but they required more. Throughout the first half of the twentieth century the number of black people on rural land owned by whites increased rapidly. In the 1936 census about 37 per cent of the total African population were counted on farms, 45 per cent in reserves, and 17 per cent in towns.

From the point of view of some African communities, the distinction between different sorts of land was only being more fully infused with meaning at the turn of the century. Many retained their own sense of social geography—the phantom districts of the pre-conquest chiefdoms. Almost everywhere black people were a majority in farming districts where the bulk of land was owned by whites; in some they were a large majority. There never was a 'white man's country' nor 'white farms' in the sense that these were zones of numerically predominant white occupation, only in the sense that whites, through their economic and political power, exercised control over the people on them. Africans actually occupied, mostly as tenants, far greater swathes of the countryside than the land reserved for them or owned by them. Maps depicting the country around the turn of the century fail to reflect this fundamental reality. They report graphically the new colonial social geography—farm boundaries, towns, roads, and railways. They might mention the names of a few old chiefdoms but, census maps excepted, they seldom illustrate the distribution of rural population.

These points are not offered in order to minimize the impact of conquest, dispossession, and racial legislation. They are central to an understanding of twentieth-century history, both urban and rural. If Africans had been restricted to 10 per cent of the worst or even average land in South Africa, then a much larger number would have moved to town far earlier and the country's history would have been different. The fact that very many Africans were able to retain some access to land helps explain critical historical issues such as the tenacity of the peasantry in the reserves; the predominance of migrant labour as a form of proletarianization; the importance of tenancy on the white farms; and the character of African political struggles.

The African Heritage

The African reserves and tenanted farmlands of the eastern half of the country were the most densely populated parts of rural South Africa in the early twentieth century. Although their inhabitants were involved in deeply rooted patterns of agriculture and social life, they found their lives transformed in increasingly fundamental ways: what patterns of authority and power they recognized and how they sought to alter these; what they produced and consumed; how they worked and for whom; and which gods they looked to. The term peasant has been used widely by historians attempting to describe and analyse these broad changes. On the one hand it affirms the point that most Africans depended on their homesteads, agricultural production, and family labour for subsistence; on the other that most were no longer part of independent chiefdoms, but incorporated in some way into a broader colonial economy and society.

Debates about the causes and nature of these changes have been central in recent historiography. Bundy's *Rise and Fall of the South African Peasantry*, which suggested a relatively positive African response to the new opportunities, markets, and faiths of the nineteenth century, remains a trenchant text. Some historians have emphasized the more coercive elements of incorporation. They have seen fewer economic benefits for Africans in the early stages of colonial rule and a more continuous decline in standards of living after conquest. Others have detected pockets of powerful African traditionalism. Case-studies illustrate considerable diversity in African responses to social and economic change. The idea of a peasantry can be a blunt analytical instrument in distinguishing the experiences and fate of local African communities from different pre-colonial chiefdoms, on different types of land, subject to different patterns of colonization. It nevertheless remains a useful term to describe the broad processes involved.

Any discussion of African societies in the late nineteenth and early twentieth centuries must include an analysis of their subjection. But an understanding of African responses must also recognize the powerful social legacies of pre-colonial societies. First, there was no single African political or economic system in that period. The chiefdoms were independent before colonization and while alliances were possible between them in the face of colonial encroachments, there never was a unified political or military response. Historically, the shape and size of African chiefdoms had not been static. The rate of change accelerated in the early nineteenth century when the rise of the Zulu kingdom was accompanied by fundamental restructuring of political authority and settlement. The Sotho, Swazi, and Mpondo, amongst others, conquered or absorbed smaller polities and clans so that their size grew to over 100,000 people by mid-century—and the Zulu state twice that. But a common African identity was still to be forged.

The East Coast, where Zulu and Xhosa-related languages predominated, and the Sotho- and Tswana-speaking interior highveld were to some degree culturally distinct. Environmental influences, such as the availability of water, combined with social and political institutions to shape different patterns of life. A web of rivers flowed eastwards from the Drakensberg mountains to the sea. Not only was rainfall generally higher on the East Coast, but water was widely distributed through the broken, hilly countryside. Settlement tended to be in dispersed homesteads rather than villages, often on ridges above valleys where women collected water from the streams. Homesteads were large, housing three generations, including a number of married men (brothers and sons), their wives and children.

By the early twentieth century, the old wicker 'beehive' huts had been displaced by 'wattle and daub' structures where a framework of poles and laths was plastered with mud. Almost everywhere, and especially in the deep reserves of Zululand and Transkei, local materials were still used for building, huts were circular, and their conical roofs were thatched. Many families still arranged their huts in a semicircle around the cattle kraal where the animals were brought home from the pastures for protection each night. Square houses, usually of mud-bricks, had appeared on mission stations and were a mark of Christianity elsewhere. Pastures, fields, and buildings though changing in form were the result of centuries of settlement, leaving only pockets of indigenous forest. This countryside of rolling hills, green and lush in summer after the rains, brown and dry in winter, had a beauty which was noted by colonial observers. Remnants of this pattern of settlement and efficient resource use still survive and have lessons to teach.

Across the Drakensberg mountains, in the interior, rainfall tended to be lower and more sharply concentrated in dramatic afternoon storms. In a flatter world, water flowed in fewer streams and large river systems—such as the Orange, Caledon, Vaal, Limpopo, and their tributaries—were more important lifelines. Springs and vleis (shallow depressions) were also critical as water-sources. Settlement tended to be clustered in villages both for water and defence. Pre-colonial towns were most developed on the extreme west of African occupation where they reached over 10,000 people; some have provided the basis for later urban development in Botswana. Where wood was scarce, as in Lesotho, stone building was developed by mission-trained masons. Cattle could not be grazed so close to home in these chiefdoms and they were often taken to cattle posts for long periods.

Africans' capacity to contain the impact of settler incursions, trade, and demands for labour stemmed from their control of some land and also the strength of their productive systems. All except those in the driest regions had added maize, originally from America, to sorghum as a staple crop in the eighteenth and nineteenth centuries. All except those whose lands merged with the tsetse-fly belt in an arc around the north-eastern boundaries of the country were cattle-keepers. Cattle supplied milk, meat, and skins as well as oiling the wheels of exchange. A good herd could be the basis of economic independence after colonization, just as it had been the primary object of accumulation before. Although the resources of individual homesteads were being squeezed, many rural families still produced much of the food they consumed and maintained complex economic and social links between homesteads.

Some of the pre-colonial political hierarchies around the major chiefs, especially in larger reserves of the Transkei, Natal, and the Transvaal, remained significant. Chiefs and headmen had to work under magistrates and they could no longer command regiments or the labour of large numbers of men. But their income from court fees, fines, and death duties did not immediately disappear. Nor did their capacity to distribute cattle as loans in return for labour service and to cement their status by polygyny. As guarantors of African land they had a powerful symbolic standing.

African patterns of marriage and bridewealth proved remarkably resilient. Bridewealth was paid by the husband's family to the wife's, often in the form of cattle. Women moved on their marriage to their husband's homestead where they did the bulk of the agricultural work as well as household labour and care of children. Patriarchy was symbolized by avoidance customs (*hlonipa* in Xhosa) which women had to obey: they could not use words which contained the names of their husband's male kin, or handle cattle or even drink milk in many situations. Cattle were the province of men: boys and youths herded them. The division of labour had never been rigid and taboos were breaking down in the early twentieth century. But women and children worked hard and ambitious men still strove to accumulate the resources in cattle to marry, procreate, extend their lineage and labour force. Though polygynous marriages were limited in number, they were not prohibited by colonial law.

Hierarchies of age, gender, and rank were the hallmark of the homesteads and villages. But these were inclusive institutions which provided food and security. The size, adaptability, and cohesion of the 'extended family' was a major ballast against deprivation. Though women carried many of the burdens of rural life, they could especially when older acquire some influence. The African homesteads, and the changing dynamic of the social relationships within them, remained a major force in twentieth-century South Africa. More extensive networks of clan were recognized by the use of clan names (*izibongo* in Zulu/Xhosa) in greetings.

The term 'communal tenure' has often been applied to African landholding systems. In so far as it indicates that land could not be bought and sold, it remains useful but it disguises great variation in patterns of tenure and control over land. To generalize: African systems involved rights to land which came from membership of a lineage, a family grouping or chiefdom. In the nineteenth century, there was enormous mobility between and within African political systems, which helped to define new identities and ethnicities. Land was acquired by *khonza*—to use the Zulu term—or recognition of the political authority of a chief or headman and the obligations which this entailed. Local political authorities would then grant specific sites; arable plots were usually assigned to married men who had the wives to work them. The number and size of fields was expanding rapidly and ploughs gave late nineteenth-century peasants profligate new powers of production. Thus the right to break new fields was as important as the right to keep a field within a family; again it was negotiated through the local headmen and council. Pasturage, the bulk of land in any African territory, was open to all those who possessed stock.

Specific pieces of arable land might be removed from families but chiefs could not generally disqualify their subjects from access to land. Even when individuals were absent, the homestead could maintain its rights. This differed from settler zones where land was more rigidly divided into private property. In the nineteenth century, Afrikaners who did not own farms or a share in them could often get access to land through tenancy and other relationships. When these came under pressure during the agrarian transformation of the early twentieth century, Afrikaners were driven off the land very rapidly. A larger proportion of Africans in the reserves, protected by communal tenure, was able to maintain access to land, but the system also greatly inhibited a transition to more capitalist forms of agriculture in the reserves.

African Peasantries

In many areas, especially in the eastern Cape, coastal and midland Natal, and the highveld of the Transvaal and Orange Free State, loss of land necessitated changes in the way that African families survived. Resources such as game—hunted out by settlers and Africans with firearms—became scarce by the late nineteenth century. Everywhere colonial taxes were, in Cecil Rhodes's ironic words, a 'gentle stimulus' to labour. Taxes in South African colonies were relatively high in comparison to the rest of the subcontinent. The hut tax, favoured in the Cape and in Natal before 1906, was levied on married men with land and could be met by the sale of produce. Poll taxes levied in the Transvaal, Orange Free State, and Natal on all adult men whether they had rural resources or not were designed more explicitly to push them into seeking waged work.

In the Cape, the Glen Grey Act of 1894 attempted to introduce a new labour tax, a form of individual (but not fully private) land tenure as well as segregated local councils financed by yet further taxes. In some senses this law, often cited as a corner-stone in the development of white domination, is a red herring in South African historiography. The labour tax proved so unpopular and difficult to collect that it was dropped; individual tenure spread through only seven districts out of about thirty-five occupied largely by Africans in the Cape. The most important legacy of the Act was the system of councils in the African districts, gradually extended through the country as a whole, which were later used as a basis for political balkanization.

Taxation and land loss were not the only forces at work in transforming African societies. Trade almost always pre-dated such processes. In the nineteenth century guns had been important imports. Muzzle-loaders in African hands did not delay the forward march of colonialism for very long, but they were seen as vital by African chiefs throughout the subcontinent both to claim a breathing-space against settler commandos and as defence against armed African neighbours. By the 1870s mounted cavalry with muzzle-loaders, even breech-loaders, rather than foot-soldiers with shields and assegais were the spearhead of a number of surviving African armies. However, investment into firearms became very difficult once conquest was completed.

Most ubiquitous of the trade items were cotton and woollen goods. Blankets almost completely displaced hides or *karosses* by the end of the nineteenth century and were in some communities giving way to Western-style clothes. Blankets initially saved time taken in preparation of skins. But they also reflected the flexibility of African taste. Africans used them to create new styles of dress appropriate to their needs and identities which later was called traditional or 'tribal' dress. They were thus able to contain and shape if not exclude colonial commercial forces in which textiles and clothes were often at the cutting edge.

All the African societies of southern Africa had iron-workers but the quantity and variety of goods available were limited and the cost high. British-made iron goods such as three-legged cooking pots, nails, hoes, and ploughs, became central to the life of Transkei peasants and Transvaal tenants alike. Ploughs also demanded an innovation in the use of oxen as draught animals. In the second half of the nineteenth century, African agriculture in southern Africa went through a revolution in technology probably unrivalled on the continent for its rapidity and scope as tens of thousands of ploughs poured into the country and new lands were brought into cultivation. Further north the scourge of tsetse fly, vector of the disease *nagana* (trypanosomiasis), inhibited the use of cattle as draught. Oxen, sometimes used as pack animals in pre-colonial times, now in teams transformed the capacity of African farmers to transport their goods. Some of the 'burdens borne on the heads of women' (Bundy, 55) were transferred to sledges, wagons, and carts, though women were still responsible for the collection of water and firewood. Introduced animals, such as wool-bearing Merino sheep which displaced the fat-tailed, hairy, indigenous variety, facilitated exploitation of marginal lands.

Missionaries and magistrates recorded these developments

with enthusiasm. Of Herschel, in the north-eastern Cape, one
wrote:

The extent of cultivation carried on is something surprising. *Ploughs*
were at work in all directions, and kaffir picks where ploughs could
not work. Wagons and even horse carts were to be seen at several of
the native establishments. The quantity of wheat, mealies, and kaffir
corn raised is such as to bring buyers from among the farmers on all
sides and even as far as Colesberg. Indeed, the 'Reserve' since the
Basuto war has been the granary of both the [Cape's] northern districts
and the Free State too.   (Bundy, 151)

The range of settlement was perhaps most markedly
extended in Sotho-speaking areas where Moshoeshoe's people
had experienced dramatic dispossession in the loss of rich
arable land in the Caledon valley. Sotho farmers introduced
wheat as a winter crop alongside maize. They had also been
amongst the first Africans to adopt horses, initially for military
purposes, and bred a hardy mountain pony. Together with
woolled sheep and their cattle, these adaptations greatly facilitated expansion into difficult mountain terrain towards the
Drakensberg. Others adapted new agricultural techniques to
move as tenants and sharecroppers on to the farmlands of the
Orange Free State. It was not least Sotho peasants who
supplied the bulk of food to the Kimberley diamond fields in
the early years—much of it carried by Boer transport riders.
To the north, Tswana chiefs and notables became involved in
commercial hunting and supplied timber to Kimberley before
the railways and coal arrived in 1884.

The far-flung routes of international trade and empire were
imprinted on the African peasants of South Africa whose very
material existence now centred around maize from Latin America, woolled sheep from Europe, cloth from Manchester, and
imported ploughs. The changes they experienced were not
markedly different from those of Afrikaners enmeshed in the
same expanding networks of trade. By the turn of the century,
Australian gum trees and wattles began to make their appear-
ance around homesteads in Natal and Transkei for fuel and
timber; the aloe agave from Mexico as fencing for kraals.

An intricate network of trading stations was established through the rural areas so that by the early twentieth century, wherever there were people, there was a trading store. In the Cape alone there were probably close on 1,000, usually owned and run by licensed whites. While they facilitated the growth of commerce, they also precluded the development of African markets. Traders became the conduit for migrant workers as well. Sales of grain, cattle, wool, or labour were vital for the purchase of commodities or to pay taxes, rents, and school fees. South Africa's settler frontier has been contrasted with West Africa where production was dominated by peasants. Yet South Africa had its moment of peasant expansion. Because of the plough, which was rare in West Africa, the productive capacity of South African black peasant farmers may have rivalled that of West African cash-crop producers.

The great majority of African homesteads were incorporated to some degree into the colonial world by the twentieth century, but some resisted the process. Especially in Zululand, the coastal Transkei, and the northern Transvaal, the combination of chiefly power, adequate land, and explicit traditionalism held commercial forces at bay. Those who most fully reconstituted their identities and consumption patterns tended to be most numerous where pre-colonial society was disrupted and along the major routes of Boer and British expansion. Mfengu communities, refugees in the eastern Cape from the conflicts in Zululand in the early nineteenth century, as well as Sotho-speaking tenants on the highveld and *kholwa* mission station families of Natal were striking examples. From amongst them emerged the vanguard of the African peasantry, the owners of private land, of wagons, and of square houses.

Colonial and settler intrusion did not simply create new classes. Those Africans called by traditionalists 'dressed', 'pierced', or *kholwa* developed their own sets of ideas about the colonial state and their rights within it. They hoped their loyalty to local magistrates and the ethos of an inclusive British Empire might protect them from the machinations of land-hungry settlers. They provided the levies for colonial wars, loyal headmen to displace recalcitrant chiefs as well as mission-educated ministers, teachers, and agricultural demonstrators who became the models and ideologues for a new African identity. Many were Christian, but there was no one version of Christianity. A multitude of denominations, from Anglicans and Methodists to Lutherans and Catholics, took root, reflecting the crowded and competitive mission field in South Africa. Although Christianity was still the religion of a relatively small minority in the early twentieth century, it was sufficiently deeply set to become the dominant, and still buoyant, faith of South African blacks as well as whites.

Black Victorian and Edwardian Christian culture flourished first in the eastern Cape, partly because it was earliest colonized and missionized. Mid-Victorian liberalism in Britain combined with local interests to produce a non-racial qualified franchise in the colony. Towards the end of the nineteenth century, African voting power became significant in some eastern Cape constituencies as did coloured in urban centres such as Cape Town itself. While Afrikaners and English-speaking farmers sought measures which discriminated against Africans, a more liberally minded settler minority of urban professionals, civil servants, missionaries, and merchants involved in the African trade, saw both moral justice and material advantage in trying to protect African civil rights, land occupation, and productive capacity.

For much of the 1880s and 1890s, a key figure in the African politics of the Cape had been J. T. Jabavu, editor of the first African newspaper *Imvo Zabantsundu* (Voice of the People), friend of white liberals and organizer of the African vote. He was reluctant to form a country-wide and assertive African organization, arguing that this would further alienate whites. Colonial courts and justice could provide protection. But African Christians were not simply the dependent clients of missionaries and liberals. Jabavu spearheaded a powerful challenge to settler ideas. And many African Christians throughout the region were rejecting the missionary version of Christianity for a new 'Ethiopian' church movement in the 1890s. The term was used not because of any direct connection with Ethiopia, but in a purely symbolic way to identify with a specifically

African Christian tradition in a country which had not been colonized. Methodism, perhaps the denomination with the largest African membership, produced the most dramatic splits when some of the first generation of black ministers left the mission church and affiliated with the American-based African Methodist Episcopal Church.

The first generation of African independent church leaders made no great innovation in the religious sphere and did not attract as many adherents as the mission churches which they left. Schooling, a major stimulus to conversion and the black demand for Christianity, remained essentially under mission control and this inhibited the growth of African churches. Established denominations were more financially secure. But independent churches made a powerful political statement about the capacity of Africans to manage for themselves and claim, in a slogan of the time, 'Africa for Africans'. They spread yet further the reach of Christianity and the profusion of churches.

Mining and Labour Migration

Africans were initially drawn into the colonial world through fighting it, trading with it, worshipping its gods, and paying its rents and taxes. By the early twentieth century the mining industry and other colonial enterprises increasingly influenced the pattern of incorporation. The awesome speed with which mining expanded after the discovery of diamonds in 1867 and the golden wealth of the Witwatersrand reef in the 1880s was not an accident. Industrialists and merchants in Europe were looking for overseas investments in the late nineteenth century. The gold standard had been widely adopted in the 1870s as the basis for currencies and the international markets for gold, based in London, were more than usually hungry. It was the age of the gold rush from the Klondike to Australia. A mobile population of prospectors, profiteers, and technicians followed the glint of minerals.

The sparkle of diamonds first attracted large quantities of capital and labour. Within twenty years about £3 million's worth was being exported annually, half of the Cape Colony's exports. Kimberley's 30,000 people made it the second city in southern Africa to Cape Town. When the labour force hit its early peaks, some 18,000 black workers were employed on the mines at any one time. Because the great majority of them were migrant workers from the Pedi chiefdom in the Transvaal, or from Lesotho or southern Mozambique, many more passed through the town annually.

The excitement of 'rushes', the charisma and hubris of Cecil Rhodes, and the extraordinary big hole covered with an intricate lace of ropes and pulleys all made Kimberley synonymous with money and wealth. In order to mine the deep pipes in which diamonds were found, capital, technology, and water were all-important. Mining of this kind lent itself to amalgamation. By 1888 Rhodes had created an effective monopoly through the De Beers company which displaced smaller companies as well as white and black diggers. A monopoly was also useful in order to prevent the market being flooded and diamond prices collapsing; control of marketing has been central to the twentieth-century diamond industry. Monopoly eased the enforcement of a racial division of labour which set the precedent for gold-mining and other industries. When Rhodes claimed that Kimberley was the 'richest community in the world for its size', he certainly did not include its black migrant workers; his aphorism was probably not true of whites either (Turrell, *Capital and Labour*, 57).

On the Witwatersrand the outcrops of gold-bearing rock could be mined by diggers with relatively little capital. But within a few years, it became clear that the deposits followed reefs deep underground sloping to the south. Successful exploitation needed well-capitalized companies prepared to make large investments. Diggers were again elbowed aside and control concentrated in six large mining houses which attracted between them external investments of perhaps £200 million over the first twenty-five years. Gold needed not only extensive underground works because of the depth and shape of the reef, but also more complex surface works than diamonds. Large quantities of rock had to be dynamited, taken to the surface, crushed, and then treated by chemical process. In 1899 the Rand produced 27 per cent of the world's gold and by 1913, 40 per cent—worth £30 million annually. By 1899, before the South African War, over 100,000 people worked in the mines alone; by 1910 well over 200,000. In 1911 Johannesburg's population had reached 240,000 and the Witwatersrand as a whole twice that. Between 1904 and 1911, by contrast, Cape Town's population actually declined a little from a peak of over 200,000 (Figure 1).

Such growth needs to be kept in perspective. American, Canadian, and Australian towns were expanding as rapidly and there were more of them. The 200,000 black workers recruited annually for gold-mining work throughout the whole region of southern Africa was still only twice that mobilized annually at the height of the Atlantic slave trade a full century before. But mining was a huge addition to the South African economy and mining interests asserted themselves forcefully in the political sphere. Rhodes, who controlled the diamond fields, had a major share in one of the gold conglomerates, and organized the colonization of Rhodesia, was the most influential politician of his age. As Cape Prime Minister between 1890 and 1896 he personified these forces.

Despite his blatantly imperial aims, he sought to realize his goals with the help of Cape farmers in the Afrikaner Bond (Chapter 2). Both mining companies and white farmers were more interested in increasing labour supplies than in African peasant production. Elijah Makiwane, a leader of the Cape African Christian community, noted that the influence of these 'money gentlemen' who were for 'repressing the native', was 'beginning to assert itself and sour the native mind all over South Africa' (Beinart and Bundy, 115). Legislation in 1887 and 1892 restricted the potential for growth in the Cape African franchise; the Glen Grey Act of 1894 provided for clearer political segregation. It was an alliance of diamonds, wine, and wool, which though shattered by the Jameson Raid and the South African War (Chapter 3), was precursor to the 'uneasy alliance between gold and maize' which characterized the pattern of dominance in the first half of the twentieth century.

Mining was central to South Africa's expansion. Black men became the core of its labour force at the heart of the economy thousands of feet underground. Their subterranean and compound existence was far removed from the leafy suburbs of South Africa's towns or the British home counties where much of the financial wealth from the mines was deposited. Perhaps, in a warped way, the stock exchange in the City of London recognized this contribution by calling South African gold-mining shares 'Kafirs'. In the early twentieth century, they were not, as in the period of conquest 'restless', but in stock-market parlance 'firm and active'.

Migrant labour, oscillating between town and countryside, was not unique to South Africa. It was a feature of many industrializing societies, signifying a transition from rural to urban life and agrarian to industrial work, especially where industrialization was in an enclave and not preceded by an agrarian capitalist revolution which destroyed the peasantry. Even in the peasant economy of Ghana, people from the north migrated south to work for African cocoa-growers. What was particular about southern Africa was the longevity of migrancy. For one hundred years it has been the dominant form of labour supply to the mines. It was extended to other industries and enterprises and became central to government policy. The practice of housing migrant workers in huge, single-sex compounds near the place of work, with all the associated controls, tensions, and personal frustrations was perhaps unique in its extent. In 1911 over 90 per cent of the black population of Johannesburg was male. It remained preponderantly so to the 1940s—with important consequences for African urban culture.

Male-only compounds for workers were initially entrenched in Kimberley. Mine owners argued that they were the only way to control diamond theft and illicit diamond buying. This most romantic of South African crimes, much favoured by novelists, was regarded as amongst the most heinous by budding South African capitalists in the same way that real or imagined stock theft traumatized settler farmers. Unlike gold, diamonds could be picked up; perhaps, as stories have it, some stones did get back to Pedi villages. But compounds were also a good way of reducing costs in housing and feeding workers, preventing absenteeism, and increasing control. Compounds were introduced during the first major recession on the diamond fields in 1884/5 and they were transferred to Johannesburg, even though gold theft was not possible. 'If the "dark satanic mill" was the abiding image of new social relationships in Britain, it was the repressive role played by the mine compound that came to symbolise the early development of capitalism in South Africa' (Turrell, *Capital and Labour*, 45).

One powerful explanation of the prevalence of migrant labour as a core institution of twentieth-century South Africa has concentrated on the demands of mining capital. The argument has rested on the point that mining required large quantities of cheap black labour and that migrant labour was particularly cheap. Employers did not have to pay wages which could meet the subsistence needs of the family as a whole in town because workers' families stayed in the rural areas and produced their own food. The costs of social security, or the reproduction of labour, would also be met by rural societies. Compounds enabled mine owners to put further downward pressure on wages as they provided cheap food and accommodation. In short, migrant labour gave capitalists a work-force without the full costs of supporting workers and their families in town.

The nature of gold as a commodity, and of the Transvaal gold-mines, has been invoked to strengthen this explanation. Gold prices were kept stable for many years from the 1870s to the 1920s as an underpinning for the international financial system. Yet Transvaal gold was expensive to extract and many mines had a relatively low grade of ore. Mine owners were faced with tight margins, particularly because they had little control over the costs of machinery, supplies, and skilled labour; it was easier to keep down wages for politically powerless unskilled black workers. A further element in the argument is that gold was not sold locally but exported on to markets which had an almost inexhaustible appetite for the commodity. Mine owners were unencumbered by the problem of domestic demand for their product. As long as they could get labourers, it was not in their interests to increase the purchasing power of workers.

In the long run, there is no doubt that the mining industry preferred migrant to settled workers and fought hard to maintain this system. However, explanations for the origins of migrancy have shifted. The mines were not the originators of long-distance migrant labour. Pedi workers from the eastern Transvaal had been walking 1,000 kilometres to Port Elizabeth for some decades before they went to Kimberley and the Rand. Mozambicans were established on the Natal sugar fields before they became the predominant group of workers on the mines. Moreover, migrancy was not initially cheap for all employers because of the costs of recruitment and because it inhibited the acquisition of skills; in the late nineteenth century, mine wages were relatively high. Employers were primarily concerned to get labour in whatever form it came. The origins of mass migrancy need to be sought as much in the dynamics of African societies as in the demands of the gold mines.

Although African participation in the labour market could from its very earliest phases be linked to dispossession, especially in the eastern Cape, this was not always the case. When long-distance migrancy began there were not yet bright lights in the city, nor were the streets of Johannesburg paved with gold, but there were particular commodities which African societies required. Pedi chiefs organized groups of young men to earn money to purchase guns to defend their political independence. Chiefs lost control over labour supply before the end of the nineteenth century. The wages which men received gave them more economic power, just as exchange with colonial traders loosened the economic bonds which held chief and subject together. But many migrants remained locked into rural society and determined to return there. Families tended to send out younger sons who were not essential for the maintenance of agricultural production. Fathers tried to control the wages of their sons, or to ensure that cash was invested in solid rural assets such as cows, ploughs, and wives. Even where married men continued to migrate to work, as became common in the early decades of the twentieth century, many saw wage labour as a means of establishing themselves more securely in the countryside. The persistence of forms of communal tenure in the reserves made this possible.

Southern Mozambique was the most important source of migrant workers on the Rand for many decades, providing over half the labour force in the first twenty-five years of gold production to 1910 (Figure 2). The Transvaal economy faced as much towards Mozambique's Delagoa Bay as to the Cape and it was President Kruger's intention to use the rail connection there in order to establish independence from British ports. In southern Mozambique, increasing rates of migrancy in the late nineteenth and early twentieth centuries were accompanied by rising rates of bridewealth. Young men going out to work were having to stay longer if they were to acquire rural assets. Similar patterns of bridewealth inflation, either engineered by elders in the society, who thus gained more control over wages, or merely as a result of demand because men could marry younger, occurred in Lesotho.

Elsewhere, as in Pondoland, families arranged advance payment of wages from local traders and recruiters before migrant workers left home. Cattle was given in exchange for a pledge of labour in much the same way as chiefs had cemented relationships with their followers before. This had the effect of drawing migrants home as they did not have the cash to establish themselves independently in town. Their immediate needs would be met in the compound while their families might meanwhile benefit from the use and increase of the animal. Rural traders, who often doubled as money-lenders and labour recruiters, also favoured systems of advance payment in cattle or cash as a means of increasing their turnover in competition with urban shops. Employers did not like advances because these facilitated desertion but they found them difficult to abolish until they developed a comprehensive system of deferred pay. Bridewealth inflation and advance payments suggest that rural societies worked hard to make sure that those who went to work—whether because of poverty or the desire to accumulate—returned and brought back their earnings. For these reasons, many rural people had an interest in maintaining a migrant system of employment.

African societies influenced the way in which labour was released to the expanding industrial sector in other ways. Male predominance in the mine labour force must largely be explained by the demands of employers. Although women and children had worked in the mines of Victorian Britain, by the turn of the century the British élite had clearer ideas about fit work for women. But the mines were not the only employers; there was great demand for domestic servants—probably the second largest sector of employment in early twentieth-century towns. In the newly colonized parts of South Africa, such as Natal and the Rand, the great majority of domestic servants were black men or youths. Employers did not always think them appropriate, but it was they who offered themselves.

The predominance of men in the labour market of South Africa in the early twentieth century can partly be explained by the division of labour within African rural society where women did the bulk of the field work. After boys had completed a phase of herding, they tended to have fewer responsibilities, especially as the calls of military service declined. Some African women, especially from Christian and tenant families, did themselves go to town, but this was a muted social development until the 1920s. Bozzoli has argued further that the strength of rural African patriarchy helped to ensure that women stayed at home and worked the land. Patriarchy may not have been the only influence. Evidence from rural women's political movements (Chapter 4) suggests that many were committed to the rural areas. Whatever the case, the division of labour in African families meant that it was least disruptive to send out youths.

By the early twentieth century, African peasant families were coming under increasing economic pressure in many districts—squeezed for land on which to expand agriculture, beset by taxes, disadvantaged in markets for agricultural produce, and in access to credit. Two devastating cattle diseases, the rinderpest in 1896/7 and East Coast fever, which moved slowly through the country from 1904 to 1913, each killed as much as 80 per cent of the herds in some districts. The diseases were not an intended cause of colonization, though some Africans believed them to be; rather they were part of a broader spread of new plagues consequent on more rapid mobility and international exchanges of people, plants, and animals. Cattle numbers recovered but at the cost of increasing rates of labour migrancy to pay for restocking. By the 1920s African small-scale farmers in the reserves and on the white-owned farms still produced nearly a quarter of the maize and held nearly half the cattle in the country. The Transkei—the largest single reserve area—probably imported only 10 per cent of its food by 1930. But fewer and fewer peasants were able to produce much surplus. Perhaps 30–40 per cent of the economically active men in rural reserve areas were away at labour centres at any one time. The character of migrancy also changed in that more married men were having to migrate over a long period in order to help meet the subsistence needs of their families. An increasing number were interested in moving to towns permanently and the state's role in controlling urbanization through wide-ranging pass systems became far more explicit.

Even then the drive to maintain a homestead was often important. One of the greatest ironies of early twentieth-century southern African history was that both the country's major industry and many rural communities favoured a system of labour mobilization in which male migrants worked only for a limited period and then returned with their wages to their homes. What became a highly exploitative pattern of employment appeared initially to many Africans to be less disadvantageous than a move to town. Many gave a high economic and social value to the rural assets which they held. Both parties also came to share an interest in maintaining reserved areas with inalienable land tenure where Africans would be free from the threat of further dispossession. For the mining industry, this was perceived to guarantee migrant labour in the longer term as further land alienation would drive more rural families to town. In some senses, there was agreement on this aspect of what became segregation policy. But by fighting to maintain reserves, rural Africans did not generally accept the terms of segregation as laid down in the 1913 Natives Land Act, nor their exclusion from other rights in society.

2 Economic and Social Change on the Settler Farmlands

Agrarian Worlds in the Cape

Commentators on the history of the white-owned parts of the South African countryside in the early decades of this century emphasized their backwardness. Colonial land policies and settler predispositions, so historians argued, combined to produce an extensive rather than intensive form of agriculture: pastoralism remained widespread, investment low, and improvement rare. The prevalence of African sharecropping and labour tenancy seemed to retard modernization and efficient use of labour. White impoverishment in the early twentieth century was seen as a result of isolation and outdated ideas, a barrier to economic growth, and a strong spur to racial protection and segregation. Agriculture in the settler Dominions, the USA, and Britain itself seemed to be developing more rapidly.

There is some substance in this view. South African farmers were not generally highly efficient and technical innovation lagged behind. But what is striking in retrospect is just how rapidly agricultural production grew in the late nineteenth and early twentieth centuries. Settlers had to confront severe ecological problems, and they did not have the freedom which the near genocide of the indigenous population had given those in North America and Australia. With the support of the state, they nevertheless wrought changes unique in their scale on the African continent. Moreover in parts of South Africa, production grew initially because of, rather than in spite of, African sharecroppers and labour tenants.

Claims to distinct and unique nationhood have been a powerful strain in twentieth-century white South African politics. But they should not disguise the way that the settler population was deposited in layers as successive phases of development in the world economy left their traces on the shores of the subcontinent. The Dutch empire brought both settlers and slaves; South Africa picked up Huguenots fleeing from France; the nineteenth-century post-slavery British plantation system supplied both planters and indentured workers. In the nineteenth century, when European imperial power made free international movement possible, Britons, Germans, Jews, and others poured out of their homes. People from all these groups found their way on to the land.

There were a number of discrete settler agrarian worlds at the turn of the century, each radiating out from a colonial port, each shaped by its ecology and climate, its pre-colonial heritage, distance from markets, and particular mix of crops. Farms in the longest established settler agricultural zone in the western and southern Cape produced wine, wheat, fruit, and pastoral products. At its heart was Cape Town, the seventeenth-century Dutch port which dominated trade with the Khoikhoi and settlers for two centuries and remained the largest city in southern Africa until 1904. The region was distinct from the rest of South Africa in its winter rainfall, 'Mediterranean' climate, and indigenous *fynbos* vegetation as well as its historical roots in the Dutch seaborne empire. Its products most closely resembled those of Europe; European oaks were a symbol of Dutch settlement. This made it attractive as a port supplying ships but also constrained its initial growth. In later years the fact that its seasons were the inverse of those in Europe helped launch exports. But Cape Town had no hinterland of subtropical sugar or cotton plantations which fuelled some other early colonial empires.

The western Cape was also distinct because the displacement of Khoisan peoples necessitated slave imports—many from Indonesia—as a source of labour. By the turn of the twentieth century, the working class, largely of Khoisan and slave origins, was called 'Coloured' rather than 'Native'. The predominant language of the farms and streets, the Cape vernacular, was a form of Dutch and a progenitor of Afrikaans. Islam, carried by those sections of the slave community which came from Asia

and revived in the nineteenth century, survived in the face of a
dominant Christianity. Though there were pockets of peasant
settlement, mainly around old-established mission stations, the
western and midland Cape had few reserves for black people.
Sharing the same agrarian and social world with Afrikaners,
coloured people moved more rapidly than Africans to town.
Especially in Cape Town, racial divisions were relatively fluid.
It is only in recent decades, with a huge inflow of African
people, that the city has come to share the demographic and
linguistic characteristics of most other South African cities.

The agrarian zone around Cape Town was losing its leading
role in the Cape by the mid-nineteenth century to the eastern,
sheep-rearing, parts of the colony. But it by no means stagnated. The power of its Dutch gentry was sufficient to withstand
the transfer of the colony to the British, the emancipation of
slaves in the 1830s, and the advent of representative government in 1854. Only a minority of Afrikaners joined the Great
Trek to the highveld (1836–8) to escape British authority and
most of them were from the eastern and northern frontier
districts. Ensconced in their whitewashed, Cape Dutch homesteads, the best of them beautifully gabled, some western Cape
families were able to hold on to their land and labour supply
through successive economic fluctuations. They did so with the
help of elaborate legal controls and the 'tot' system—partial
payment of wages to their workers in cheap wine which instilled
alcoholism and indebtedness. After the Cape received responsible government in 1872, its revenues swollen by wool and
diamond exports, the region's Dutch-speaking farming lobby
formed the Afrikaner Bond under J. H. Hofmeyr. Though
Hofmeyr refused to offer himself as Prime Minister, he became
the most influential broker in the Cape parliamentary system.

In the late nineteenth century, the growth of railways, ports,
and mines all sucked labour from the western Cape farms.
Recession in the 1880s was compounded by phylloxera, which
swept aside not only vines but many poorer farmers. Some of
those who displaced them had money from land speculation,
commerce, the law, and mining. They included John X. Merriman, the eloquent cabinet minister and Cape liberal, as well as

Rhodes himself who bought twenty-nine farms worth £250,000 in 1897, a year after he ceased to be Prime Minister. Wheat and dairy products were in strong demand for growing urban communities. Cape brandy held its own as a basic South African rot-gut to be found in colonial clubs and drink cabinets, in the hovels of workers on western Cape farms, and in the huts of African chiefs. Though wine production did not expand between 1891 and 1910, fruit became a promising option. Covent Garden in London was opened to refrigerated Cape fruit in 1893.

The western Cape remained not only an important agricultural region but a political and intellectual centre. Some of the earliest protagonists of Afrikaner nationalism came from these old agrarian heartlands which had lived longest in the imperial shadow. It was around Paarl and Stellenbosch that intellectuals defined the Afrikaans language as separate from Dutch and the first *Geskiedenis van Ons Land in die Taal van Ons Volk* (history of our country in the language of our people) was written in 1877. S. J. du Toit, its author, helped to found the Afrikaner Bond at this time but was ousted by the moderate Hofmeyr and went north to become Kruger's Secretary of Education in the Transvaal. Hofmeyr was more pragmatically concerned about empowering farmers in the colonial economy and content to achieve this in alliance with the arch-imperialist Rhodes until the Jameson Raid. Subsequently he worked with Cape liberals opposed to British jingoism.

Pragmatic Afrikaners were by no means immune to nationalist ideology nor unmindful of its potential economic advantages. Led by men such as Jan Marais, who had profited from diamonds as well as agriculture, they founded their own financial institutions, providing cheaper credit to farmers when British banks proved tight with loans. They also invested in educational and political ventures. In 1915 *De Burger* newspaper was launched as the leading voice of Afrikaner nationalism in the Cape. Soon afterwards the inappropriately named Victoria College became the 'Dutch-Afrikaans' Stellenbosch University, a centre of Afrikaner education, following a bequest of £100,000 in Marais's will. In 1918 Afrikaner insurance and trust companies were founded and wine-growers formed themselves into one of the earliest and most important agricultural co-operatives, the KWV.

Eastern and midland Cape agricultural expansion followed the in-migration both of British settlers after 1820 and Mfengu in the 1830s. Wool-bearing merinos shouldered aside the Khoikhoi fat-tailed sheep in a funnel of land between the 10- and 25-inch rainfall line; the least promising agricultural land became the new engine of the export economy. By the early twentieth century, probably over a third of South African land was dominated by sheep. Port Elizabeth, the major wool port, and East London—one hundred miles further up the coast, which also serviced the African districts—together overtook Cape Town as entrepôts. Graaff-Reinet, the only pre-British village in the east, became a busy commercial town with the largest concentration of Cape Dutch buildings outside the western districts. The imperially named Grahamstown, King-williamstown, and Queenstown all became important centres of administration, transport, and trade away from the coast. The settler population faced less towards the sea.

The history of sheep is often left in the 1860s, before the discovery of diamonds, when the value of wool exported was £1,700,000, or about three-quarters of the total of Cape exports. South Africa's significance as a sheep-holding country in the early twentieth century was overshadowed by gold. But while Australia always carried at least three times as many animals, South African flocks grew to rival those of the other major producers such as New Zealand, the USA, Argentina, Russia, and India. Small stock numbers finally peaked at nearly 45 million woolled sheep and 10 million others in 1930. The value of wool exports rose from £4 million in 1904 to a peak of £20 million in 1919, then stabilized at around £15 million annually. Markets for mutton and skins were not negligible: in the 1910s around 1.5 million carcasses were processed annually at the Johannesburg and Cape Town abattoirs alone. In these years, wool sometimes displaced diamonds as the country's second most valuable export.

Sheep transformed the frontier economy which depended

initially on the plunder of rich resources of wild animals, conquest of the Khoi, and the establishment of a mobile pastoralism. It was in this period of early expansion that the large farms of settler South Africa took shape. Trekboers on the frontier were never completely isolated from markets; their very existence depended on guns, ammunition, and wagons. The droving routes and outspans—a term derived from unyoking a team of oxen—were major channels of communication into the interior. But wool greatly intensified land use. In 1865 a third of the Cape settler population of about 180,000, considerably more than the whole of the Transvaal, lived in the main Cape sheep-farming districts. The land of the Khoikhoi became thirty or forty administrative districts, each with its small town, its magistrate, gaol, police post, shops, and services.

Migrant traders or *smouse* who moved from farm to farm were being displaced by wholesale and retail outlets linked to merchant firms such as Mosenthals in Port Elizabeth. As in African districts, Christianity and commerce were intertwined in the laying out of new towns, which became centres for churches and *Nagmaal*, the quarterly religious and social trek of far-flung farmers to a common meeting-point. Wool gave farmers cash and patterns of consumption changed as the need for self-sufficiency diminished. Country banks proliferated. Sixty newspapers were published outside Cape Town by the turn of the century, mainly in English but also in Afrikaans— from the *Graaff-Reinet Herald* to the *Colesberg Advertiser and Boerenvriend*. Newspapers helped to create a local civic identity and break the isolation of dispersed farmers, instilling on the one hand English-speaking ideas of progress and, on the other, the ethnic nationalism that enthused Afrikaners. The down-at-heel migrant tutor, or *meester*, immortalized in Olive Schreiner's *Story of an African Farm*, gave way to schools regularly inspected and staffed by trained teachers. In 1905 the Cape parliament legislated for compulsory primary education for whites.

Many of these districts had been sparsely populated; sheep did not 'eat' people in large numbers nor did they require much labour in the way of plantations. Migrants from the coloured mission villages or from African districts met the peak demand during shearing season. Thus population did not grow much after the turn of the century and railways, then lorries, reduced the economic significance of the villages. But sheep left their imprint on the rural environment in other ways. Unlikely stylish Victorian buildings dotted the semi-arid districts. Water rather than markets was the great constraint in expanding sheep numbers. Dams were one solution, but in the twentieth century boreholes, their pumps powered by windmills, became a popular alternative. Clanking metal windmills, originally imported from the USA, became a feature of the South African landscape. Prickly pear from Mexico, initially encouraged along with aloe agave as supplementary feed in dry districts, became a weed subject to desperate eradication programmes. These apparently isolated districts of South Africa became, like the African reserves, a crossroads for new animals and plants.

The spread of a more intensive pastoral economy had other important ecological effects. It spelt the end of wild game. Elephants had been hunted out of most of the country by the 1860s for their ivory. Buck were shot in sheep districts for their meat and skins and also because they competed for pastures. Springbok sometimes migrated in huge herds to escape drought. The last great migration of more than half a million 'as beautiful as it was wondrous' crossed the sparsely populated lands of the northern Cape in 1896. 'The Boers mounted a huge hunting operation to prevent them damaging the veld and hundreds of thousands were shot . . . the skin selling for 5d or 6d and the meat converting into large quantities of biltong [dried meat]' (MacKenzie, 115). The springbok became so powerful a settler symbol only when they came under threat. The South African rugby team adopted the name early in the twentieth century when rugby began to replace hunting as a major white sport.

Wool production drew civil authority into the countryside to police private property and settler accumulation. Farmers always perceived stock theft to be rife, just as they thought labour was always short. The state was also called in to deal with stock disease, especially scab—a major constraint on wool production. From the 1890s the Cape government enforced sheep-dipping, initially against some opposition from both white and black stock-owners. Cattle-dipping was introduced from 1904 when the tick-borne East Coast fever devastated herds. The colonial state took shape in the rural areas not least through the control of animals, their diseases, and the environment.

Cattle and sheep were grazed on the open veld well into the twentieth century. Some farmers continued to move their flocks and herds in search of seasonal grazing and water. As in African societies, animals were usually kraaled each night because of the danger of predators and theft. But as sheep numbers increased, kraaling and transhumance became the focus of concern. Officials argued in the 1920s that stock 'tramped out more than they ate', thus causing soil erosion. Dongas (eroded gulleys) scarred the South African countryside, raising fears of a 'newly created South African desert' (*Drought Commission*). They wanted farmers to adopt improved grazing techniques by fencing paddocks where animals could be left overnight.

Fencing Acts facilitated the supply of capital so that barbed wire—used both on the American prairies and in late nine-teenth-century warfare—began to snake across the country-side. Fences were not only a means of modernizing grazing. They were a physical mark of private property, defining bound-aries between farms and reserves, between black and white. As they restricted the free movement of people and animals, they were widely disliked by rural Africans. Fence-cutting, like stock theft, could be an expression of resistance. The state also acted against predators. Jackals, thought of as the epitome of stealth and wiliness, were estimated to take nearly the same number of sheep as were delivered to Johannesburg and Cape Town's abattoirs. A high bounty on 'vermin' from 1918 brought in over 300,000 jackal and wildcat pelts in the next six years. These interventions did not immediately solve grazing problems. When drought and depression hit the sheep-farming districts in the 1930s, nearly a third of animals were lost. Wool production never regained its former importance. Nor did it feed into a local textile industry. Although South Africa was one of the largest wool producers in the world it had no blanket factories till the 1920s; most wool went to Britain.

Natal and the Highveld

On the subtropical East Coast, the British settlement at Port Natal (later Durban) founded in the 1820s, depended initially on trade with Africans and settlers in the interior. Subsequently sugar, successfully established in the 1860s, fuelled Natal's growth. In the years up to 1911 British planters, unable to secure or coerce sufficient labour from local African people, turned to the imperial labour supply networks. A total of 150,000 Indian indentured workers came to Natal. They were followed by Moslem 'passengers'—traders and merchants who could pay their own fares. Not all stayed but a significant Indian population became established.

By the turn of the twentieth century Natal sugar production, with about 30,000 acres under cane, was relatively modest in international terms. But acreages expanded dramatically to 90,000 in 1920 and doubled again by 1940. Output rose even more rapidly from under 30,000 tons in 1900 to about 150,000 tons in 1920 and nearly 600,000 tons in the peak year of 1940. As in nineteenth-century Europe, sugar found favour with the growing urban and working-class populations, white and black, and the internal market underpinned expansion. Natal's agricultural economy diversified rapidly including bananas on the coast, dairying and stock-farming inland. Wattle plantations provided timber and their bark was used for tanning leather, one of South Africa's earlier coastal industries. Quick-growing wattles and eucalyptus spread through the country for use on farms and became a mark of habitation.

Sugar, unlike wool, was a crop which required relatively little land but a great deal of capital and labour both for agriculture and processing. During the late nineteenth century, sugar mills were concentrated in the hands of a small number of concerns—some of which also ran the biggest estates—such as

Tongaat and Natal Estates on the north coast, Reynolds and Crookes to the south of Durban, Huletts in Zululand. A tight hierarchy of property, wealth, and skills evolved which reflected the social divisions of British colonies in general and South Africa in particular. Sugar brought diverse people together in a single productive enterprise and ruthlessly divided them by colour and class.

The sugar barons were English-speaking, influenced both by the Indian empire and 'home'. The richest of them carved out the role of a gentry around landownership, clubs, polo, horses, and élite private schools. Generally supporters of Smuts's South African Party, they tilted to pro-imperialism when their interests were threatened and acquired the reputation of being amongst the most conservative English-speakers in the country. On the big estates, some technicians were Mauritians while supervisory and skilled mill-workers were often Indian. Once the importation of indentured Indians ceased in 1911, unskilled mill-workers were often Zulu, while many cane cutters were long-distance migrants from the Transkei or Mozambique. All tended to be housed separately; like the mines, a microcosm of the country's social divisions.

The sugar fields were notorious through the early decades of the twentieth century for their conditions of employment. Many young African people, even children, were taken on and rates of desertion were high. Youth and child labour was common on all the farms of South Africa but on the estates they were expected to perform at an almost industrial intensity and live in barrack housing without the minimum regulation of conditions that was enforced on the mines. The political power of the estate owners helped to fend off state intervention in their activities.

Wine, wheat, and sugar producers in the Cape and Natal benefited greatly from the Rand market but their activities were not initially shaped around it. In many other white-owned areas of the country, however, farmers depended more directly on the growth of internal markets for food and on mobilizing a labour supply from African rather than imported workers.

Treks by the Dutch-speaking Griqua (remnants of Khoisan

and slave communities) and by Boer communities and their servants penetrated the interior in the first half of the nineteenth century. Although they were called Boers, the Dutch word for farmer, it would be a mistake to think of the trekkers essentially as farmers. As in earlier phases of frontier expansion they were supported initially by hunting, dispersed pastoralism, and booty from war. During the first thirty years after the Great Trek, till the 1860s, ivory was the major export from the Transvaal. When settlers did secure control of large areas of land, many depended on taxing their African tenants. And by the early twentieth century, poorer Afrikaners worked as transport riders or left the land completely.

The frontier experience in the Cape and then on the highveld was identified by an early generation of historians as an explanation for the Afrikaner mentality, forged in isolation and conflict, as well as racial prejudice and segregation in the twentieth century. The argument has been countered by historians who point to the fact that even in the interior, trekkers were never completely isolated. They depended heavily on imported commodities such as arms and ammunition and drew merchants with them. Moreover, they developed trading, sexual, and military relationships with Africans. The origins of more rigid racial divisions, Legassick suggested, should be sought in the slave-owning Cape and in zones where agrarian capitalism and industry displaced the relatively loose relationships of the frontier.

These points are important, but there is room for a restated argument about the frontier's significance. The early Transvaal state, like some African states in the interior, was relatively weak and unable easily to control or tax its subjects. To some degree it replicated the precedents set in Mozambique, which might have become an alternative node of European expansion into the interior of southern Africa. The Portuguese thrust was weak and partially Africanized into the *prazos*—land concessions which became small chiefdoms trading in slaves and ivory. Some trekker groups, hostile to the British abolition of slavery, reconstituted servile forms of labour, including the capture and exchange of *inboekseling* (indentured) African children—a practice which the British authorities regarded as akin to slavery. But fragmented Boer states differed from the Portuguese *prazos* in that they retained to a greater extent their racial and cultural identity. Boer churches and governments in the interior were racially exclusive from the start.

Boer relationships with African people in the interior involved both interdependence and exploitation. In a hostile world, they accumulated partly by force. Similarly they slaughtered wild animals in order to survive in their new surroundings. These relationships lent themselves to a hard and sometimes violent masculinity as well as strong patriarchalism which were later available as cultural reference points. Compared to those who benefited from agricultural expansion and schooling in the more settled areas of the Cape, some frontier families, especially in the Transvaal, did live a rough life. And while isolation is a relative term, it is difficult to dismiss the conviction with which investigators into the poor white problem in the twentieth century dwelt on this social legacy in trying to understand the difficulties which dispossessed Afrikaners experienced in an urban and industrial world.

The settler impact was most powerful on the highveld areas of the Orange Free State and southern Transvaal. Inland Natal, the eastern Cape, and the eastern and northern Transvaal remained divided zones, where settler land was interspersed with large pockets of African settlement in a complex patchwork. In all these newly colonized areas occupation and control of the land remained an issue of contestation and political struggle in the early decades of the twentieth century. Cultivation on the farms was predominantly by African peasants and tenants. In the Transvaal it seemed briefly possible that they might retake the land during the South African War, when the devastation of Boer farms by British scorched-earth tactics gave tenants an opportunity to reassert their claims. But Boer and Briton united in repossessing the farms—an understanding which was at least as important for the future of white domination as the section of the peace treaty of Vereeniging (1902), which left open the question of the African vote in Britain's two new colonies.

The term 'rural', while it acquired more definite meaning in contrast to the growth of an urban industrial world in the early twentieth century, still encompassed very different social worlds. Hunting and extensive pastoralism coexisted with intensive maize farms, sometimes in the same district. But the ultimate logic of the South African pattern of white colonization was the subordination of African farm tenants. 'The relationships between landowners and their tenants, whether black or white, were by 1910 locked into a pattern which would enable the landlord to preside over the ever increasing commercialisation of agriculture' (Trapido, 58). African tenants found it was labour rather than crops or rent that was demanded from them on the farms as landowners brought more land under production controlled by themselves. Landless whites, or those with insufficient capital, were seen as less desirable tenants and shaken out of the farmlands more rapidly than Africans.

National markets were coalescing in the early twentieth century. The population of the urban areas increased from 22 per cent of the total (1.1 million) in 1904 to 31 per cent in 1936 (3 million). Given that townspeople had on average far greater per capita income, the urban markets were even more important than population figures suggest. By 1936 nearly two-thirds (65 per cent) of the white and Indian population lived in towns (Table 3). The highveld proved suitable for rain-fed, dryland grain production, especially of maize. Maize stored well, gave a high yield per acre, and did not require guarding against birds as did sorghum. It could be used for oil and fodder as well as food. Internal demand was fuelled both by the problems of the peasantry and the growth of the compounds.

White farmers, like black peasants, were dependent on *smouse* and trading stores, stock speculators, and wholesale merchants for their markets and credit well into the twentieth century. Marketing of grain was hardly regulated at this time. Both annual and seasonal gluts after the harvest produced periods of low prices. As in other agrarian systems, transport was a major constraint on the expansion of grain farming. Commodities with higher value for their bulk such as ivory, skins, and wool could be moved more profitably; sheep and cattle could walk themselves to market. In a tsetse-free zone, where all sections of society adapted quickly to the use of animal draught, South Africa had a great transport advantage over many other parts of the continent which were dependent on humans for porterage. But even then 'the sheer immobility of produce' made it difficult to reach new markets from grain-producing districts (Keegan, *Rural Transformations*, 98).

Wagons, commonly drawn by sixteen oxen, were adequate if slow for the transport of small quantities from field to farmstead and farm to mill. They were less efficient when large volumes, requiring tens of thousands of oxen, had to be moved long distances to the towns. War and cattle disease undermined the supply of animals. When there were enough oxen, the pressure on dirt roads and outspans was enormous. Imported American, Argentinian, or Canadian grain, rushed through the ports and by rail to the mining centres, could not only compete with local grain but served to depress prices. It was cheaper to transport grain 6,000 miles by ship and 1,000 by rail than a few hundred miles by wagon. During 1904/5 there was a glut of grain in some parts of the Orange Free State, but more maize was imported than exported.

Railways resolved these problems quite rapidly, although unevenly, facilitating the switch towards arable production. When Lord Lugard argued in his *Dual Mandate* (p. 462) that 'the development of the African continent is impossible without railways, and has awaited their advent', he expressed a view shared by many South African farmers, businessmen, and politicians. Railways were the sign of progress; heated debates were conducted in newspaper columns and parliament about their routes. By 1900 all the major ports were linked by rail to the Rand; over 4,000 miles had been constructed in South Africa. In the next ten years another 3,000 miles, much of it rural branch-line, was completed. The hub of the Rand provided links between railway systems lacking in other African colonies. Grain-producing areas of the highveld benefited particularly and farmers secured favourable rail rates. African reserve areas, by contrast, were largely bypassed.

As early as the 1880s, railways constituted the second largest head in the Cape government budget—over £1 million for the first time in 1890. Expenditure was exceeded only by repayments on the colony's public debt, more than half of which was incurred for railway construction. By the first decade of the twentieth century, railways were costing the Cape government a third of its annual budget, an average of nearly £3 million, not including interest on debts. Receipts from the railways were also the single largest item of government income in both the Cape and Natal. Taken as a whole, the railways of South Africa returned a good profit in the decade before Union, even if interest payments on loans are included. So successful was the improvement in transport that maize could be exported in significant quantities by 1907.

By the 1920s a state-subsidized system of grain elevators, silos, and storage at railheads helped to ease the cycle of glut and scarcity. Early pictures of the elevators show them surrounded by ox-wagons. These were gradually replaced by lorries. Afrikaner nationalists organized a wagon trek to Pretoria in 1938 to celebrate the centenary of the Trek and lay the stone of the Voortrekker monument. Like the springbok, wagons were loaded with heavy symbolism when their commercial significance began to decline.

Farmers received direct state assistance in numerous other ways. Generous loans were made both to English settlers and to Boers after the South African War. Restocking, fencing, boreholes, and seed were all part of the package. The Land Bank, established in 1907 in the Transvaal and expanded in 1912, has often been cited as a primary example of differential assistance to white agriculture. In fact, financing from other institutions offering credit and mortgages was quantitatively of greater importance. Further funds were available at various times through fencing, irrigation, and vermin legislation. The introduction of limited liability co-operatives in 1922 and increasingly systematic price subsidies in the 1930s transferred even greater resources to farmers. Especially after the First World War, governments were committed to food self-sufficiency based on white commercial agriculture.

State financing of research and agricultural schools assisted rapid diversification. Not only scab, but rinderpest and East Coast fever attracted considerable research funds. Veterinary scientists made their names in South Africa and their debates took on great political and social importance. The discovery that East Coast fever was carried by ticks, and was not directly contagious like rinderpest, paved the way for dipping of all cattle in the country. New scientific ideas—not always practicable—were applied across a whole range of agricultural problems and disseminated through the publications of the Agriculture Departments. The well-illustrated *Agricultural Journal* is a treasure trove of official thinking at that time. Blacks were not entirely excluded. In 1904 an experimental farm was established in the Transkei which trained African agricultural demonstrators, and they shared in the costs and benefits of dipping. But state services mainly served large farms and when new techniques were applied in African areas, official prescriptions tended to ignore local systems of tenure and knowledge as well as land shortage.

The state also entrenched legislation which expressed changing white attitudes to game. Wild animals had been a resource both for Africans and settlers in the nineteenth century. By its end, influential figures both in Britain and South Africa recognized that predatory hunting and clearing land of animals threatened a number of species. Some attempted to conserve animals to protect hunting as a socially exclusive pleasure pursuit for the colonial élite. But a more scientific conservationist ethic soon predominated. New methods of protection involved not simply enforcement of existing hunting laws, but the establishment of game reserves.

In 1926 a large area in the far eastern Transvaal, some of it reserved in the 1890s, was demarcated as the Kruger National Park. The first warden felt that Kruger himself 'had never in his life thought of wild animals except as biltong'. But the use of Kruger's name assisted the park, and wild animals, to become powerful new symbols of white nationalism. Africans who had formerly hunted in the area were excluded and became poachers. In the 1930s they lost their battle over rights of access as tourism (over 30,000 annually) and police posts provided the park with the resources for tighter control. Capitalist land use patterns entrenched a sharper division in the functions of land than had been the case in pre-colonial society.

The Fate of Tenants

Changing forms of tenancy must be considered against the backdrop of agricultural improvement. In parts of the country, land held for speculative purposes was rented out to tenants who paid rent in cash. Nearly 20 per cent of the farms in the Transvaal were owned by companies, rather than occupying farmers, in 1905. Sharecropping became a means by which landowners could respond to new internal markets with little investment, and without the difficulties of procuring and controlling workers. African tenants contracted to pay one half, later more, of their crop to the landlord for the right to cultivate and graze their cattle. They had to attempt to produce double their own subsistence needs. Sharecropping offered a viable option for families who had implements and preferred to escape the constraints of crowded communal reserves or the demands of chiefs.

It was the more resourceful, more incorporated, rather than the most abject black rural families that took this route. Some of those on the Vereeniging Estates, prize land-holding of early Transvaal industrialist Sammy Marks, produced hundreds of bags of maize a season where they needed less than twenty for their food supply. Kas Maine, most famous of black sharecroppers, was a highly skilled agriculturalist. Afrikaans-speaking and adept at finding good contracts, he was sufficiently confident and proud to move when he felt he had been sold short by a farmer. These Christian families were a black yeomanry in the forefront of the peasant revolution. Insecurity taught them how to get the maximum out of the land in a short period and they had to remain mobile. One route of migration took sharecroppers from the Sotho-speaking areas around lowland Lesotho to the north-eastern Free State and southern Transvaal. When such areas, well placed for transport to new markets, became more intensively capitalized, sharecroppers moved further north and west.

While the interests of tenants and landowners could briefly intersect in the sharecropping relationship, this could also be tense, particularly at the moment when the crop was divided in a 'ceremony' at the end of the harvest. Tenants made two piles, and landlords then chose one. Sharecropping ultimately bene-fited farmers in that they could accumulate through the sale of surplus and eventually dispense with such independent tenants. Those whites who survived rinderpest, the South African War, and East Coast fever, did so partly by off-loading the costs and risks of production on to African sharecroppers. One tenant's daughter recalled of her father many years later:

Naphthali was a hard worker. Indeed, he worked very hard in his fields. He produced a lot from the soil. Hundreds of bags, half of which he gave to Theuns [the farmer], who in turn would proceed to sell them and get a lot of money from the labour to which he had never contributed anything.   (Matsetela, 227)

The family had by then moved to Soweto, victims of the rise of the mealieboer—archetype of white dominance on the platte-land (countryside; literally flat, open land)—whose success often depended first on black tenants, then on black workers. 'South Africa's maize revolution', Bundy argued, 'was to a considerable extent predicated upon black peasant enterprise.'

Tenants' survival depended on their capacity to mobilize and control their own family's labour for more intensive agriculture. Here the legacy of African society proved important. Women and youths, as well as men, were expected to work. This gave black tenants a competitive edge over white families, where it was not easily accepted that women and children should work in the fields. Boer urbanization in the early twentieth century was so rapid not only because of disease, indebtedness, and private land tenure but also because they were reluctant to work as families for white masters. Farmers preferred black tenants who produced more on less land.

As farmers accumulated, they required labour rather than crops from their tenants. Some were able to retain 'servants' (or wage labourers) on their farms. But relatively few African families were prepared to accept this relationship while any alternative remained open. Labour tenancy was the most common compromise reached. Tenants worked or sent family members to work for part of the year in exchange for the right to stay on a farm, run animals, and grow crops. African men who wanted to become tenants usually needed to have wives and, as in the reserves, the wherewithal to pay bridewealth for them. Cattle remained important to farm tenants both as draught and marriage payments. As labour tenancy became widespread, many contracts between tenants and farmers revolved around the exchange of grazing for labour by the tenant's children. Some then tried to keep their wives working on their own plots for the family's subsistence. 'I must work for the baas', argued a Transvaal tenant, 'but not my wife. . . . I buy a woman to work for me' (Bradford, 37). As late as 1930 Africans on farms still held 1.5 million cattle, 14 per cent of the total in South Africa. (Those in reserves held a further 37 per cent.)

It was not least in regard to labour that farmers asserted their interests in the political sphere. Few farmers could compete with the mines for migrant labour from the reserves or Mozambique. Their concern found one focus in opposition to 'squatters'—African tenants who paid largely rent. Squatters were seen to be responsible for stock theft; rented farms were seen to bottle up labour. In the Transvaal, legislation limited the numbers of tenants on any particular farm to five. If it had been enforced, the tenant population would be more evenly dispersed through the farmlands. In the Cape, a different strand of legislation tried to enforce registration of 'private locations' on farms with large numbers of tenants. Inspectors were appointed and farmers had to pay fees for their tenants. In neither territory were such measures effective.

But in the early twentieth century, various interests coalesced to demand tighter controls on tenancy. Whites forced to leave the farms increasingly saw African sharecroppers and tenants as responsible. They found willing leaders in churchmen and politicians advocating tighter segregation. Powerful groups of farmers were now prioritizing labour procurement. They wanted a general change in the form of tenancy so that there were no bolt-holes for tenants who wished to avoid more onerous contracts. These provisions were written into the 1913 Natives Land Act. The Act aimed to prevent Africans from buying land in areas designated as white, and disallow residence on farms unless tenants provided a minimum of ninety days' labour annually to the landowner. Forms of tenancy which did not involve a transfer of labour to the farmer were thus to be outlawed.

The Land Act became a major issue for African politicians. Solomon Plaatje published a scathing indictment of its effects entitled *Native Life in South Africa* (1916) (Chapter 4). Perhaps the first major political polemic by an African author, it is still in print and a central text of South African history. Plaatje was especially influenced by the struggling landowners in the Barolong community of Thaba Nchu, Orange Free State, whose interests were threatened as well as their morality deeply offended. But he travelled widely and *Native Life* includes a harrowing description of the broader fate of sharecroppers who, given no option but to trek or become labour tenants, found themselves in thousands along the roads, their cattle dying. The African was becoming a 'pariah in the land of his birth' with nowhere to bury his dead. Plaatje blamed the Boers for the Act, more specifically the repressive Free State spirit epitomized by General Hertzog, then still in Botha's South African Party (Chapter 3).

It is true that the Afrikaner members of parliament supported the Act almost to a man, while many English-speakers did not. (They questioned its detail rather than its principle.) But Plaatje, in trying to secure British intervention, glossed over the forces behind the Act. He noted that not all Afrikaners supported it. Poorer Boers depended on their sharecroppers and paternalism was evident in 'the kindness of Boer women' to individual families. But he tended to overlook the role of accumulating English-speaking farmers and officials committed to segregation on the land and agricultural improvement on the basis of wage labour.

In order to get his point across, Plaatje romanticized life on the farms before the Act. Yet as one black leader had noted, 'barbarities' had long been practised 'and no one intervened' (Keegan, *Rural Transformations*, 148). Plaatje also exaggerated the immediate effects of the Act. For the most part, its provisions were not enforced in courts. The government accepted that the promise of extra land for reserves should be fulfilled before removals were sanctioned—a task hardly begun until the 1936 Native Trust and Land Act was passed. In the Cape, the Natives Land Act was declared *ultra vires* by a court in 1917 as it impinged on the capacity of Africans to qualify for the franchise by gaining a property qualification. Sharecroppers and rented farms could be found in rural districts, especially in the Transvaal, for at least another few decades. By the late 1920s it was estimated that nearly a quarter of a million Africans in Natal either hired ground from absentee white owners, or were tenants on crown land. Some also worked for wages, but not necessarily on the farm which they occupied.

Nevertheless, grain-producing Free State farmers did treat the Act as a charter to narrow options for their tenants. It signalled a changed trajectory for tenants, their mobility restricted by passes and permits, and increasingly vulnerable to demands for servile labour. In some districts labour tenancy terms became more onerous by the 1920s and 1930s. The social revolution imposed by landlords and the state set the scene for a further sustained increase in output on the white farms—by about four times between 1918, when the first reliable annual statistics were collected nationally, and the 1950s. Segregation on the land was therefore not about keeping Africans off white-owned farms, but about regulating the conditions under which they remained on them. Up to the 1950s, the number of black people on farms increased significantly, although not as quickly as the urban population.

By the 1920s white farmers in South Africa were a highly differentiated group. Despite state aid and overall increases in production, many farms were unprofitable. Yields were comparatively low, land values were high relative to income, and indebtedness widespread. Labour tenants, intent on salvaging some of their status as peasants, were often reluctant workers. Youths resistant to the authority of both their fathers and white farmers tried to find some means of escaping to town. Volatile agricultural prices induced farmers to rush into particular commodities and thus flood the market. By 1930 many farms were heavily mortgaged. Subdivision was common and the number of farming units increased. An anonymous poem, 'Die Arme Boer' (the poor Boer) captured their sense of helplessness.

> Our sheep have 'brandsiek' [scab]
> Our wheat has the rust,
> The cattle have redwater
> And the horses die of *droes* [glanders].
> The money is scarce
> And the coffee so dear,
> The foreign banks are our 'baas'
> And the interest eats like fire
>
> The locust and the drought
> Are heavy on our land,
> What's going to become of us
> I cannot comprehend.

(Groot Verseboek)

'Cheque book farmers', with other interests and other sources of income, could do well. The lawyers and agents secured quantities of land on a rising market by foreclosing on debts owed to them; some white and black landowners were barely literate and easy prey for those skilled in the complexities of land law and contract. The state subsidized a number of resettlement schemes for poor whites, but they hardly reversed the flow from the land. Poor whites, in turn, demanded protection from the state in labour markets.

Agricultural capitalism was born in early twentieth-century South Africa but was still in its brutal youth. The farms were well-springs of white reaction and racism. Paternalism allowed limited interactions—white children were nursed by black nannies and could play with black children. Surprisingly close social contacts were possible on western Transvaal farms in the

inter-war years when sharecropping survived, van Onselen
argues, but even these took place within tight constraints. If
Afrikaner politicians did not concentrate their efforts primarily
on racial issues, in the sense of a formulated national policy by
which to control Africans, they clearly expressed white rural
feelings about appropriate racial relationships which exerted a
powerful influence on national policy. These ideas were shaped
by the received scientific notions of Social Darwinism (Chapter
3) but not caused by them.

Few white farmers supported the extension of African
reserves since this implied giving up land and providing escape
routes for tenants whom they wanted to tie to their farms. They
could not compete with the mines in wages for migrant workers
from the reserves. Some were against the idea of African
reserves at all, but in many districts farmers were more ambi-
valent. They were perturbed about the juxtaposition of farms
and land occupied by Africans.

When they have a beer drink they go though your fences, their dogs
are worrying one's sheep continually and destroying your game:
whenever you are adjoining a location they have their rams, their bulls
and their horses, and they are continually breaking through your
fences and getting at your stock. (*Putting a Plough to the Ground*,
300)

Many farmers therefore came to support more stringent segregation of Africans not under their control.

The language of the farms could be harsh—it was the
language of insecure landowners, many of whom had only
freshly acquired property through conquest. 'Native rebellion'
remained a pervasive fear in recently colonized rural districts,
even when military power had been decisively demonstrated.
Poor whites, who saw African tenants and workers as unfair
competition, played on racial fears to win support and protection. Priests and politicians took little persuading that miscegenation was the ultimate consequence of economic
degradation. It was a world where terms like 'kaffir' were
everyday currency. Slaves in the Cape had sometimes been
called by months of the year—there are still large families with

the surnames February, April, and September. Whites distanced themselves and dehumanized their workers by calling them after coins, kitchen implements, or animals: Sixpence and Shilling; Saucepan or Bobbejaan (baboon). (Many workers also took Afrikaans or English Christian names.) Mature men were called 'jong' or 'boy'; women 'meid' or 'girl'.

Power relationships were expressed not only in language. Farmers tended to be armed, tenants unarmed. Violence may not have been an everyday occurrence but it was frequent enough—not least in the more intensive farming zones like the sugar fields. It would be misleading to see violence simply as the result of some frontier hangover. As in the case of the American South or Italian rural Fascism, the efforts being made to extract labour in the 1910s and 1920s tended to produce a particularly harsh system of control. On occasion, the state had to step in to contain settlers who exceeded the law in what they perceived as their own domain. The intermediaries and supervisors—mostly but not all white—in this process could be the most careless in their violence. Poor whites who joined the police or drifted to small towns could be quickest to defend their racially arrogated status.

The intensity of social division in the countryside had many roots. For whites, *baasskap* (domination) on the land was legitimized at the national level by the rise of exclusivist Afrikaner nationalism and segregationist ideology which undermined more liberal paternalist sentiment. The legacy of the frontier was reshaped by the new antagonisms between those undergoing dramatic social changes. Ultimately, as on the Rand, racial divisions did not preclude rapid economic growth in the countryside and in certain contexts coercive controls facilitated capitalist development.

3 War, Reconstruction, and the State from the 1890s to 1920s

War, Reconstruction, and the Logic of the Mines

John X. Merriman, long-serving and acerbic Cape politician, regarded Johannesburg, 'its Stock Exchange, and its prostitutes and prize fighters', with a combination of fascination, horror, and disdain. His failure to succeed either in diamonds or gold perhaps led him to appreciate and assert the more legalistic and genteel traditions of the Cape. The brash new city seemed to lack natural beauty; mine dumps were its mountains; the contours of race were harshly drawn. His wife, Agnes, wrote of the Exchange on a boom day: a 'scene of mad excitement— men taking their coats off and shrieking like maniacs—fortunes were made and lost in hours; St John Carr, an ex-clerk . . . . made £20,000 in a day' (Lewsen, xli. 277). Nor was it only those from the Cape who found that the 'struggle for wealth' was 'at no times an edifying spectacle' (van Onselen, introduction). But money spoke; Carr became the first mayor of Johannesburg's new city council in 1901. Mine owners who made even more money did not hesitate to use their influence.

By 1895 the fast-amalgamating Randlords knew that the future of the gold mines lay securely with the deep levels which required large and long-term investment. It took the cavalier ambition of Rhodes to translate this realization into the Jameson Raid which tried to use the growing *Uitlander* (foreign) population in the Transvaal to help bounce out Kruger's republican government in a coup. In 1895 Rhodes's colleague Dr Jameson—fresh from colonizing Rhodesia—was to ride into the Transvaal at the head of a small force which would be met by cheering supporters. The plan failed. It was not a very British coup, but had more of the mark of settler politics. True, Britain's military adventures in South Africa had not all been successes, but they were usually better organized if a great deal more costly.

Merriman, who was by no means unwilling to work with the titan Rhodes up to the Jameson Raid, then developed a clearer critique.

Those who compare him with Clive or Warren Hastings are those who take their history from the *Daily Telegraph* or *Tit Bits*. He is a pure product of the age, a capitalist politician . . . In Australian or English or, I conjecture, American politics he would have made no figure, as he cannot stand up to his equals in debate and has neither moral courage nor convictions, but he has the sort of curious power that Napoleon had of intrigue and of using men . . . for his purpose which is self-aggrandisement under one high-sounding name or another. (Lewsen, xliv. 254–5)

Merriman was surely underestimating Rhodes's idealism and wrong about politics elsewhere, but he was right to identify a new 'mixture of Imperial politics and Stock Exchange' (Lewsen, xliv. 255). Son of the Bishop of Grahamstown and educated in England he, like most English-speaking South Africans, valued the imperial connection. But he was alarmed that the political direction of the subcontinent was apparently being shaped not by order, bureaucracy, and the civilizing mission, but by massive share deals in city offices, nods and winks in gentlemen's clubs. In particular, the logic of the gold mines seemed to rule supreme.

The logic of gold mines was, their owners argued, that they operated within particular constraints shaped by the fixed price of gold and the low grade of ore. They had to draw in large quantities of machinery, supplies, and labour to a spot remote from transport links and they saw Kruger's South African Republic government to be less than sympathetic to their requirements. Explosive issues such as his policy of granting a monopoly concession for the supply of dynamite confirmed their belief. About 200,000 cases of dynamite were used annually between 1894 and 1899, between 10 and 20 per cent of working costs. The capacity of the industry to organize itself in the Chamber of Mines (founded 1889) and propagate its position in newspapers such as the *Star*, was important in establishing the logic of gold production in the public mind. Many Afrikaners did increasingly recognize that the mines were the Transvaal's golden egg and tried to come to terms with the giant in their midst. But to the mining industry, the South African Republic government represented an essentially rural agrarian community; they claimed a 'general inability of the Boers to understand capitalist industrialisation and progress'.

Kruger was also faced with the demand for *Uitlander* rights— votes for thousands of foreigners including the skilled workers required to establish the mines. They came from Australia, America, Eastern Europe, and especially Britain, where the decline of the Cornish tin-mines coincided with the rise of gold. Pro-imperial newspapers and political groups felt that rapid enfranchisement of immigrants to the Rand could swing the balance of power in the Republic to favour the mining industry. But even if Kruger had given way on *Uitlander* rights, this may not have been enough. Britain had long sought to retain an exclusive sphere of influence over the Boer republics and had annexed the Transvaal before (1877–81); now the Transvaal's new wealth seemed to threaten British interests in the region as a whole. Other European powers, such as Germany, were spreading their wings and extending their interests. Kruger had established a rail link with Portuguese-held Delagoa Bay in Mozambique. And if Britain did not need to control the gold-producing areas directly, its commitment to an international gold standard and gold backing for sterling made privileged access to this major new supply advantageous.

The South African War was essentially about the effects of gold. It was probably unnecessary in that some kind of political accommodation could have been reached between mine owners, the Republics, the colonies, and Britain, which would have facilitated the development of the mines. As long as Britain did not wish to impose political rights for blacks in South Africa, which it showed no signs of doing, many other issues were negotiable. The war was in part a failure of British diplomacy. It was difficult for the most important power in the world to negotiate with lesser states controlled by Boers or blacks. Even though the most aggressive phase of the Scramble for Africa was over, military mobilization to protect interests, make labour work, avenge slights, or maintain face was still an option for British policy-makers when the stakes were so high.

Afrikaners harboured an enormous sense of injustice about British intervention which helped to make them impervious to any criticism about their style of control in the Transvaal. Boer self-righteousness comes through powerfully in books like *A Century of Wrong*, in which Jan Smuts, youthful Attorney-General in the Transvaal after graduating at Cambridge, had a hand. It feeds on the version of nineteenth-century history increasingly propagated by nationalist intellectuals which asserted unquestioningly the depth and unity of the *volk* and perfidy of the British who seemed to favour Africans. Afrikaner history became a search, sanctioned by God, for independence and identity against the combined forces of Mammon and Ham. Such ideas about morality and justice were powerful spurs to political action in turn-of-the-century South Africa, not least because of the violence of the nineteenth. These moral issues subsequently recurred in political debate between Boer, Briton, and African: who got there first; who invaded whose land; who ignored whose rights; to whom did the wealth and resources of the country belong. There is nothing so dangerous as people who feel they have been deeply wronged, and are blinded by their own sense of injustice. Afrikaners fed on that sense and the scale of British intervention was partly responsible.

The issue for Britain was not so much whether it was capable of winning the war but whether it was committed to doing so. That commitment was displayed in the tactics used finally to suppress waning Boer military capability. Unable to compete in set-piece battles after their initial successes in 1899, Boer generals resorted to guerrilla warfare. British generals responded with a scorched-earth policy, burning farmhouses and collecting women and children into concentration camps where the death-rates from disease were very high. About 28,000 Boer civilians died, as did many thousands of blacks in similar conditions. Boer losses in war, at about 7,000, were light in comparison. (British forces lost three times this number.) But over one tenth of the Republics' Boer population lost their lives.

Despite persisting till the Republics surrendered, Britain did not have a clean slate on which to reconstruct them, nor did it wish to shoulder aside all Boer claims. White dominance over Africans on the land was reinstated at considerable cost. Moreover, Milner, High Commissioner in South Africa from 1898 to 1905 and the main architect of British policy, could not directly control the Cape and Natal. Their governments had been a critical source of support in the war but they were self-governing. Reconstruction in the former Boer republics involved extending the governmental system of the Cape rather than imposing a new one from Britain. Though it fell into a deep recession in 1904 after the removal of imperial troops, the Cape was still the biggest and most populous of the colonies, with the most sophisticated bureaucracy and parliamentary system. Cape officials were influential throughout South Africa and Rhodesia. And in the Cape, pragmatic Afrikaners in the Bond worked with explicitly South African-minded English-speaking politicians such as Schreiner (Prime Minister 1898–1900) and Merriman (Prime Minister 1908–10). This alliance—forged after Rhodes's demise—took the name South African Party, which was adopted by the white coalition which came to power after Union in 1910.

Nevertheless Britain's brief period of direct rule (to 1905) in the Transvaal was significant in shaping South Africa's future. Merriman scathingly labelled Milner's officials—young, unrepresentative, and from Oxford—a Kindergarten. But he underestimated the extent to which apparently untamed capitalist imperialism also held by a philosophy of order and planning. The infant bureaucracy anxiously set about creating the conditions for the mining industry to expand—reshaping transport and customs, abolishing concessions, initiating improved housing for workers, reforming municipal government and agricultural services, and policing Africans more assiduously. The mines also benefited from a favourable tax regime. Up to the early 1930s, the state usually took well under £2 million annually in revenue directly from the mines although the value of gold produced rose from £20 million in 1905 to £45 million in 1930 (Yudelman). Reconstruction bound the state and the mines together in many different ways, some officials moving freely between them.

Perhaps the major problem facing the industry was its labour supply. While the exact balance between white and black workers had not been settled at the time of the war, mine owners were convinced that they required a very large proportion of cheaper black workers. Key mining houses such as Wernher, Beit and Eckstein (the Corner House group), which controlled about 50 per cent of production, committed themselves to maximizing output by mining lower-grade ores which intensified the requirement for unskilled workers. Radical historians revising the understanding of South African history in the last twenty years did not simply invent the idea of a colonial obsession with labour; it springs out of the documents and archives of the time. 'The dignity of labour' was a catch-phrase of the 1890s and if politicians seemed preoccupied by war, peace, and Union, then labour recruitment and control was increasingly the meat of everyday 'native administration'.

While the war was still in progress, the Chamber re-established the Witwatersrand Native Labour Association (WNLA) to recruit workers. In 1901 Milner renegotiated an agreement with the Portuguese colonial government in Mozambique to allow recruiting there in exchange for direct payment in gold and preference for Delagoa Bay as a port. Southern Mozambique supplied 60 per cent of the total black labour force (about 50,000 annually) from 1903 to 1907 (Figure 1). Although the percentage gradually dropped to 35 per cent over the next couple of decades, Mozambican numbers increased to peak at 80,000. One of the ironies of the early twentieth-century Transvaal is that despite conquest, its economy faced increasingly east to Delagoa Bay, rather than south to the British sphere. Cape ports were not easily able to compete for the Transvaal trade because of Milner's agreement and their distance from the Rand. By 1909 their combined share of Transvaal trade had fallen to 13 per cent while Durban had 22 per cent and Lourenço Marques (now Maputo) 65. This greatly contributed to the Cape's recession; customs revenues declined by more than half between 1902 and 1908.

Despite the depressed state of the Cape and Natal, the mines could not initially win back labour supplies from their densely populated African reserves. Cape workers complained of the danger, high death-rates, and the ruthlessness of discipline under white overseers and 'Tshaka guards'—the Zulu-speaking mine police. Black workers in the Cape benefited from high wages in the ports, on the railways, and in British army employ to 1903. When these options closed, tens of thousands went as far as German South West Africa (now Namibia) to find similar work during the devastating German war against the Herero and Nama from 1904 to 1907.

In response to the perceived labour shortage in the mines, Milner set up the Transvaal Labour Commission, whose report was published in 1904. The majority report, reflecting the position of the industry, concluded that 129,000 workers were lacking and a further 196,000 would be required in the next five years. It saw both South African and imperial interests at one with rapid expansion of mining. A minority group of Commissioners, expressing the views of white labour and some commercial interests, suggested both that these figures were inflated and that the number of white workers could be increased instead. It presented an alternative vision of the future where growth would be less rapid, wealth would be more widely spread within the settler community, and less attention paid to the clamour of foreign shareholders. The minority report recognized that low wages were a major cause of the shortage of black labour.

Milner and the mining houses ignored clear evidence that a reduction of mine wages for Africans to 35 shillings a month had caused the labour shortage and that an increase in 1903 to 45 shillings attracted Mozambicans back. (A 'month' involved 30 daily tickets which would take more than a month to complete.) Instead they tried to hold down wages by extending recruitment to China. Many nineteenth-century British settler enterprises had drawn on the international market in Asian indentured labour after the abolition of slavery; Natal's sugar estates were only one. Wages in South Africa for unskilled labour were relatively high in international terms and between 1904 and 1906 over 60,000 Chinese workers came. Although they were expensive to import, they stayed longer than most Africans and therefore had the opportunity to become more efficient.

Together with Mozambicans, Chinese workers carried the mines through a period of rapidly expanding output to 1907. Unlike Indians in Natal, however, they did not become another minority in South Africa. Their contracts forbade this and the Transvaal's new responsible government (1907), intent on protecting whites, and the British Liberal government, uneasy about imperial overreach and 'Chinese slavery', were determined that they should go. Subsequently, as mine wages increased to about 60 shillings a month, Cape workers replaced them. Many peasant families in the Cape were 'passing through a period of stress' and few other options remained on the labour market. Between 1904 and 1910 their numbers on the Rand increased from 6,000 to 60,000, from 7 per cent to 29 per cent of the total mine labour force in the mines.

The labour shortage was effectively solved. Despite the evidence that the supply of migrant workers was linked to wage increases, the Chamber developed an argument to suggest that if Africans earned more, they would work less. It was based on the assumption that migrant workers with land had only a very limited desire for 'luxuries' or consumer items: 'the only pressing need of a savage are those of food and sex' so the *Labour Commission* opined, 'and the conditions of Native life in Africa are such that these are as a rule easily supplied' (p. 71). If wages were higher then consumer requirements would be met more quickly.

It is true that some African men did not have to work continuously at the turn of the century, but this argument ran counter to the mines' own experience. Moreover, in West African colonies British officials directly linked increased peasant production to the expansion of consumer demand. In fact poverty pushed many Africans on to the labour market while others tried simultaneously to expand agricultural production and wage income. But the Chamber argument resonated with white racial ideas and was extensively used in justification of the low wage regime in later years.

Recruitment of workers in the first twenty years of gold-mining had been a relatively haphazard process, a sub-industry in itself of contractors, agents, touts, and runners. By 1910 some 200,000 black workers had to be found each year. The Chamber of Mines was keen on a single recruitment agency in order to limit competition between different employers which had the effect of driving wages up. They also wished to diminish the numbers of middlemen involved as each wanted a cut. WNLA, the initial vehicle for this policy, succeeded in Mozambique but failed in South Africa where there was more competition. It was only by about 1920 that all the major mining houses recognized the Native Recruiting Corporation (NRC) as sole internal recruiter. In later years, the blue and white buildings of Kwa-Teba—the place of Taberer, first head of the NRC—dotted rural districts alongside the magistrates' offices and trading stores.

Colonial and Union governments attempted to control the worst features of recruiting at the same time as facilitating the flow of workers. Acts and regulations dealt with touting, desertion, recruiting licences, written contracts, pre-contract medicals, child labour, and large advances. This legislation helped to squeeze out smaller operators. Desertion rates, over 10 per cent in 1909, dropped to insignificant proportions by 1920. Controls were consolidated in the Native Labour Regulation Act of 1911, for many years the corner-stone of industrial legislation for black mine-workers. It established basic standards for compound accommodation, food, and medical services, but gave few rights to Africans as workers and retained criminal sanctions for breach of contract.

Social Policy and Urban Growth in the Reconstruction Era

'Native policy', though deeply influenced by the imperatives of labour supply, was far broader in its scope and aims. The

incorporative elements of Victorian liberalism were being jettisoned in British and colonial thinking, replaced by the loose
amalgam of ideas sometimes called Social Darwinism. Race
became an increasingly important category of social thought
and races were ranked in a hierarchy of civilization. Biological
ideas of supremacy justified European pre-eminence and there
were fears that this might be diluted or corrupted by intermingl-
ing with 'lesser' races. John Buchan's adventure story, *Prester
John*, is a highly revealing account of British attitudes at the
time. Later Governor-General of Canada, Buchan was a
middle-ranking official in the Reconstruction Transvaal. His
novel, published in 1910, has as hero a young Scotsman, Davie
Crawfurd, who goes to trade in the rural Transvaal and quells
an African rebellion led by the Revd John Laputa. The book
reflects a still pervasive fear of 'risings', fuelled by discontent
amongst tenants in the Transvaal, by the 1906 Bambatha
rebellion in Natal (Chapter 4), and by new racial anxieties
about the 'black peril'—whether male servants in the kitchen
or 'swamping' in the towns.

Buchan depicts the Transvaal along strict lines of racial
hierarchy. Davie is the model of efficiency and heroism.
Women hardly feature in the novel at all; colonialism is
portrayed as a male enterprise. Earlier settlers are cruel and
violent or simple, unable to understand the white man's burden
in Africa or the value of fairness and bureaucracy. The 'half-
caste' Portuguese character, who sides with the Africans and
deals illicitly in diamonds, is the quintessence of evil; 'miscegenation' and social degeneracy are explicitly linked. Africans are
represented as 'hordes', without individuality or rationality,
impervious to pain and responsive to rousing emotional
appeals. Laputa alone has a personality biologically reflected in
his 'aquiline' rather than 'squat' nose. A Christian with a
classical education, he was also a subtle manipulator of traditional magic, invoking the power of a legendary black king
Prester John. Laputa's ability to straddle both worlds made
him a creation of empire and a threat to it. He had to be
crushed, but the dilemma of dealing with him reflects British
uncertainty about the 'civilizing' mission.

Davie not only quells the rebellion but finds his fortune—a clear statement about who has rights to the wealth of a colony. He is sufficiently cognizant of his imperial duties to sell his diamonds to de Beers, 'for if I have placed them on the open market I should have upset the delicate equipoise of diamond values' (p. 200). The rest he takes home to Britain. The novel ends with the establishment of a 'great native training college . . . no factory for making missionaries and black teachers' but a 'technical workshop' (p. 202). Civilization increasingly meant different things for different 'races'.

What Buchan expresses in popular fiction comes through in a more considered way in the report of the South African Native Affairs Commission (SANAC, 1905). The assembled English-speaking experts aimed to arrive at rational and socially beneficial solutions to the 'native problem'. The Report tried to subsume the differing heritages of the Republics, the Cape, and Natal into one policy, to arbitrate competing interests as well as pay some attention to the evidence from African witnesses. SANAC affirmed that the Cape franchise should not be extended. Conferring on blacks political power 'in any aggressive sense, or weakening in any way the unchallenged supremacy and authority of the ruling race', was out of the question (para. 442). The Report assumed—despite evidence to the contrary in Cape African politics (Chapter 4)—that all 'Natives' would behave in essentially the same way and 'voting of the future may proceed upon race lines'. Racial mixing and squatting on the land was seen to be undesirable both for whites and for blacks, making it 'far more difficult to preserve the absolutely necessary political and social distinctions' (para. 192).

Chiefs, now under colonial control, were less frowned upon than they had been in the nineteenth century when they led rebellions. The black Christian élite were no longer seen as loyal allies, but a potential threat—'precocious' and 'troublesome'. Education could give 'an exaggerated sense of self-importance', while 'the stolid good sense of the more experienced but less lettered men seldom if ever finds expression in print' (para. 328). SANAC did not completely jettison the rhetoric of 'civilization'. It was one of the last major government reports which saw some future for educated Africans 'uplifting' themselves and their people within a common national context. 'Responsible' expressions of opinion through newspapers and independent churches were considered legitimate safety-valves. But SANAC proved to be a powerful source for the ideas of what was becoming known as segregation. The Cape, Natal, and the Republics had already imposed many elements of that policy; these were now being reworked to meet new social circumstances and pressures.

Many historians agree that the edifice of the modern South African state and racial domination was definitively erected during the period from 1901 to 1910 and that Milner's policies set the design. But Milner is often considered to have failed in one central aim.

On the political side, I attach the greatest importance of all to the increase of the British population . . . If, ten years hence, there are three men of British race to two of Dutch, the country will be safe and prosperous. If there are three of Dutch to two of British, we shall have perpetual difficulty . . . We not only want a majority of British, but we want a fair margin, because of the large proportion of 'cranks' that we British always generate, and who take a particular pleasure in going against their own people.   (Thompson, 7)

Milner arranged state-sponsored settlement schemes on the land to supplement the flow of immigrants. Women were given assisted passages both to replace black men in domestic service and, by providing marriage fodder for white male mineworkers, to help establish a settled English-speaking white working class.

While it is true that settlement schemes and immigration projects directly sponsored by the state were of limited success, the white population of the area to become South Africa nearly doubled between 1891 and 1904, from 621,000 to 1,117,000—the last period in which the rate of white population growth significantly exceeded that of the black. The growth rate averaged nearly 5 per cent per annum, compared with an average of less than 2 per cent per annum, including immigration, for whites between 1904 and 1936. Without immigration, the white population was unlikely to have topped 800,000 in 1904. Perhaps 350,000 immigrants and their progeny were added to the population in these thirteen years, roughly 70 per cent of them British and many of them men. South Africa attracted a significant proportion of the voluntary emigrants pouring out of Europe in an era of high population mobility.

The mining industry, which employed some 14,000 white workers by 1904, was only one attraction. Many soldiers stayed on after the war. Natal's largely English-speaking white population nearly doubled. English-speakers dominated commerce, professions, and municipal government in most of the rapidly growing towns of the interior, which only became Afrikaner bastions in later decades. An estimated 40,000 Eastern European Jews arrived between 1880 and 1914, about half moving to the Rand. They hawked, speculated in livestock, opened shops, hotels, and liquor outlets, and moved into the professions. Considerable numbers of other European immigrants arrived, some absorbed into Afrikaner society. They included the Dutch parents of one of the strongest Afrikaner nationalists of the twentieth century, Hendrik Verwoerd. The rapidity of immigration and movement within the country set the scene for cultural change and reaction.

Judged against the longer term of South African history this period saw a startling 'anglicization' if that term is taken to mean more immigration. Although Dutch-speakers remained more numerous, Milner's miscalculation was not so much about the potential for immigration as about the congruence between culture and class. His assumption that 'race' or culture determined political interest and behaviour was a very powerful one amongst imperial thinkers at the time and has flawed many analyses of South Africa since. Milner was wrong to think that English-speakers, barring a few cranks, would share his view of the world. Many of the working class and some in the commercial world backed the anti-imperial Responsibles in the Transvaal, later absorbed in the South African Party led by Smuts and Botha. Some were responsible for trade union and worker organizations that shook the mining industry to the core in the next few decades; some even made contact with blacks in socialist organizations. Conflicts between essentially English-speaking social groupings, the mine owners and white workers, became a critical nexus of early twentieth-century politics. Even if there had been a majority of English-speakers, they probably would not have united politically.

White immigrants landed up in the towns at the same time as poor whites and blacks were beginning to drain more rapidly from the land. There was a significant movement north from the other colonies. In 1891 well over 60 per cent of those classified as white still lived in the Cape, less than 20 per cent in the Transvaal. By 1904 the figures were 52 and 27 per cent respectively and by 1921, 42 and 36. Turn-of-the-century governments had to confront the problem of how to house this diverse new population. There were precedents. The mining towns which grew so rapidly in the late nineteenth and early twentieth centuries were a third layer of urban settlement following the ports and subsequent inland administrative, market, and transport centres such as Queenstown, Pietermaritzburg, Bloemfontein, and Pretoria.

Kimberley, Johannesburg, and the Rand towns were all sited primarily because of their proximity to mineral deposits. The same applied to the coal towns of northern Natal such as Newcastle. Like other mining enclaves, the Rand was boisterous and rough with a preponderantly male population demanding more than the usual quota of liquor, sexual services, and boarding-house accommodation. There were 153,428 more men classified white than women in the country in 1904 and 59 per cent of the white Transvaal population was male. The Reconstruction government's aim was to encourage a stable white working-class community which included family housing for whites on the mines and in new suburbs. Large brick and cement works, which displaced the small-scale operations of Afrikaners who had moved to town, reduced building costs, and tram transport to the new white suburbs was rapidly installed.

This was also a period when Cape Town's working-class suburbs expanded around the lower slopes of Devil's Peak.

The railway line down the eastern side of the Peninsula to Simonstown created new pockets of suburban settlement. Victorian colonial houses with balconies and delicate iron-work, now much valued as 'broekielace', gave way to more prosaic single-storey buildings. Suburbs and roads were given British names so that it was possible to live in Fulham Road, Brixton, Johannesburg. City-centre development followed in the British architectural mould. Office blocks, banks, public buildings, and shops of four to five storeys with ornate gables and cupolas lined the streets of central Johannesburg, Cape Town, and Durban. The British architect Herbert Baker was influential in developing a distinctive style of public architecture manifest in Rhodes's mansion at Groote Schuur, the majestic stone Union Buildings in Pretoria which housed the new government offices, and the University of Cape Town on a prime mountainside site.

Rapid migration by women both from Europe and the countryside reduced the preponderance of white men in the cities to negligible levels by 1921. To the great relief of those concerned about enforcing segregation, the incentive for white men to marry or cohabit across the colour line was reduced. In 1902, at a period of heightened racial anxiety, the Cape parliament outlawed the sale of sexual services by white women to black men (but not vice versa); the Transvaal had already done the same. The legislation was extended in 1927. Surprisingly, marriage between whites and others was not made illegal. Such marriages were rare and segregationists believed that public opprobrium would be an adequate safeguard.

Urban space and 'racial' mixing became fraught issues. Market forces and municipal regulation had laid the basis for partial segregation in most towns by the late nineteenth century. But poorer districts near the fast-growing city centres tended to reflect the very diverse origins of the country's working class. Where there were separate African locations, they were often centrally located and freehold property rights were usually allowed. Bubonic plague, which arrived on board ship from India in 1901, galvanized white communities to change this pattern. Cape Town was packed with highly mobile

people in the latter phases of the South African War and could
have been an ideal location for the disease to spread. Following
the Indian example, the Public Health Department laid down
stringent plague rules. It was known that rats spread the plague
but it was also associated with squalor, poverty, and, in the
colonial mind, with Africans.

Public health legislation provided the means to push Africans
out of town and the growing demands for urban segregation
could now draw on the 'sanitation syndrome', a powerful
language of disease and purity. In 1902 legislation provided for
central government funding of new locations in Cape Town and
Port Elizabeth. In 1903 Johannesburg followed suit; Klipspruit
was founded towards the south-west of the city near the sewage
works. Urban segregation was not fully enforced for many
decades (Chapter 5). Indeed, the continued presence of resident black servants in most white households might be construed to negate the apparent health benefits of segregation.
But blacks in this context were no doubt seen as sanitized by
their surroundings and inferior status.

Afrikaners Re-emergent

By 1905 Britain, bowing to Boer pressure, began the process of
decentralizing authority in the Transvaal and Orange Free
State. Settlers who paid taxes had everywhere shown themselves determined to have political control, even if Britain
maintained that it bore the costs of their defence. Moreover,
the Liberal Party which came to power in 1906 believed 'that
liberty, not force, was the cement of Empire' (Thompson, 23).
It had been less committed to the war and included a pro-Boer
group. In its determination and haste to transfer power, the
new British government granted the Transvaal and Orange
Free State local self-government barely five years after the end
of the war. As agreed at the Peace of Vereeniging, whites were
able to restrict the franchise to themselves. To African political
leaders, Britain seemed to be selling out the interests of blacks
to its bitter enemy, the Boers.

The two Boer generals, Louis Botha and Jan Smuts, who

emerged at the head of Transvaal politics, opted for conciliation between the English and Afrikaners. The fact that both had heroic war records and the authority of military leadership helped them to take a wounded Afrikaner population in a new political direction. Botha was a highveld Afrikaner with limited education and patriarchal demeanour, more charismatic and popular than the clinical and efficient Smuts. But both recognized the primacy of ensuring favourable conditions for the gold-mining industry as the foundation for a modern state and accepted that some kind of union of the South African colonies was desirable. It was achieved in 1910, after lengthy negotiation about its exact form. A racially exclusive, British-influenced parliamentary system was agreed, though Cape politicians managed to salvage and entrench a non-racial qualified franchise in their province. The only other clause entrenched in the South Africa Act was that there should be equality between the two predominant settler languages: English and Dutch, rather than Afrikaans.

The South African Party which took power after Union had English-speaking support but was dominated by Afrikaners. The main opposition Unionist Party, largely English and associated with mining, did not prove a parliamentary threat. In the first half of the twentieth century, Afrikaner nationalism increasingly became a major force in fleshing out the contours of the Union's body politic. The demographic calculus of white South Africa, which offered the possibility of Afrikaner ethnic power through the franchise, did provide a lodestone for exclusivist leaders. But Afrikaners were 'no chosen people'; unity was not natural or self-evident and they proved just as incapable of maintaining a single political front as English-speakers despite economic and cultural movements which tried to weld Afrikaner identity.

Afrikaners were of course not the only carriers of the language. They shared this, their history and even some of their ancestry with people of colour, especially in the Cape, who had long been part of colonial society. Although the possibility of incorporating coloured people into the ethnic camp as 'bruin Afrikaners' was occasionally mooted, it was never seriously pursued. Not only was colour of overriding importance in the early twentieth-century white ideology, but Afrikaner intellectuals and leaders perceived coloured people through the eyes of masters, as poor people who should be servile. The most educated group called coloured tended to be Moslem and those who did have the franchise were not usually sympathetic to Afrikaner parties. Racial boundaries in the poorer suburbs were often fluid but this alarmed rather than encouraged the Afrikaner élite.

Divisions within the Afrikaner population stemmed partly from the differing experiences of the Cape and the former Republics. Ironically, Botha and Smuts aligned themselves with a pragmatic white South Africanism while the Cape continued to produce radical intellectuals who gradually turned to republicanism and led the language movement to replace Dutch with Afrikaans. Divisions between *bittereinders*, who fought to the bitter end in the war, and *hensoppers* (who surrendered) also cut across other boundaries. Above all, the stress laid by Botha and Smuts on a new white South African identity, which might include all those who sought their future in the country, made many Afrikaners uneasy. Dutch Reformed ministers, who played a major role in social reconstruction after the war, opposed Smuts's secular attitude to education and his lack of commitment to the future of Dutch in schools. They started Christian National Dutch-medium schools.

J. B. M. Hertzog, like Smuts a former general and ambitious lawyer, took up the fight to extend Dutch in schools and enforce full bilingualism in the civil service. The leading politician in the Orange Free State, he was not explicitly Republican but advocated more tenuous links with empire. His insistence on language equality would greatly facilitate Afrikaner access to the expanding bodies of state. It was the clarion call for the long Afrikaner trek into the bureaucracy. Botha tried to contain Hertzog within the South African Party, but their disagreements were sufficient to split them asunder at the very moment that Afrikaners achieved control of the country. Hertzog formed a separate National Party in 1914.

Political unity was further tested when South Africa went to

war as part of the Empire in 1914 and invaded German South
West Africa (Namibia). Afrikaner opponents of the invasion
rebelled; they included Boer war generals and members of the
newly formed South African Defence Force. Their support was
largely from poorer whites, in rural areas such as the western
Transvaal, marginalized by the changes sweeping through the
agrarian world. Rebels included *bittereinders* in the South
African War, some of whom had been exiled. A prophet, van
Rensburg, emerged to articulate their anxieties in the folk
language of the frontier. Although the threat of a split in the
army made the rebellion potentially dangerous, it was controlled by Botha and Smuts at the head of Afrikaner troops.
They then led their forces against the Germans in Namibia and
German East Africa, conquering territory for the British. It
had been part of their aim to win control of Namibia; they were
given the Mandate at the Treaty of Versailles.

Hertzog did not rebel, but his party became more closely
associated with Afrikaner cultural movements and rural
demands throughout the country. Botha's death in 1919 left
Smuts and the South African Party very vulnerable. The 1920
election was indecisive: Hertzog's Nationalists became the
largest Party with 44 seats to the SAP's 41; the Unionists
retained 25 while the largely English-speaking white Labour
Party peaked at 21. Smuts, now being absorbed into the highest
councils of the British Empire, was pushed into an alliance with
the Unionists who had shed their most ardent pro-imperialists.
Although Smuts was able to retain some Afrikaner support,
Hertzog won a close election in 1924 in alliance with the white
Labour Party. Nationalists and Labour formed a Pact
government.

Nationalist politicians won support not only because they
espoused Afrikaner causes, but also because they took up the
issue of white poverty. The closing of the hunting frontier,
rinderpest, the South African War, indebtedness, and agrarian
change all contributed to increase poverty after the turn of the
century. Especially in the Cape, where the boundaries between
white and coloured could be fluid, poor whites were seen to be
losing their racial identity. Afrikaners were found to intermarry

or cohabit with English-speakers or, in non-racial zones of the
towns, with black people. In an era of intensified racial ideology, poverty was increasingly defined in racial terms as poor
whiteism, requiring particular attention. New social explanations of poverty and the role of the state placed the issue
high on the political agenda.

White poverty found its main expression in urbanization,
though the process often involved a move to small towns first.
Here those with rural skills such as transport riding could generate some income. In turn-of-the-century Johannesburg, Afrikaners ran small brick-making works and transport businesses,
but were again marginalized by new industries, trams, and
railways. Unskilled or supervisory jobs on the railways and
mines were an alternative but here they had to compete more
directly with blacks. Many saw great advantage in defining
themselves as white and seeking protection from the state.
English-speaking white workers, representatives of a craft-
based trade unionism, did not work to include the Afrikaner
poor in their organizations, who were thus more easily attracted
to the ethnic messages articulated by Afrikaner politicians.
Their vote gave them an influence denied to poor blacks. White
politicians saw both the potential of harnessing, and the
danger—illustrated by the rebellion—of ignoring this group.
Smuts was portrayed in cartoons sitting alongside Hoggenheimer, symbol of capitalist greed, or spoken of as too wily (*slim*)
and untrustworthy. He could not compete with Afrikaner exclusivists, despite his legislation effectively restricting apprentice-
ships to whites (1922) and intensifying urban segregation (1923).

Afrikaner churchmen and politicians were adept at turning
social deprivation to the national cause. But even the religious
field had to be fought for. Louis Leipoldt, medical man, writer,
and author of cookbooks, documented Afrikaner beliefs in
witchcraft, ghost stories, healing, and prophecy in his *Bushveld
Doctor*. Less-educated rural Afrikaners wove these ideas, some
derived from Africans, into their version of Protestant Christianity. In town, some were attracted to fundamentalist churches.
Johanna Brandt, daughter of a minister, organizer of resistance
in occupied Pretoria during the South African War, and co-

founder of the women's section of Hertzog's party, was one such unconventional religious leader; her philosophy included millennial beliefs. Orthodox Dutch Reformed ministers preached against such manifestations of popular consciousness. One of the victories of Afrikaner nationalism in these years was both to incorporate and partly conquer popular folk beliefs with a modernizing nationalist message. African ministers and politicians were less successful in this task.

Hertzog was able to ally with English-speaking workers and win power in 1924, not least because they were so bitter about Smuts's role over a period of intense industrial conflict from 1907 to 1922. South African white workers had to replay nineteenth-century European struggles for trade union recognition, shorter working days, and reasonable conditions. Death-rates from silicosis, miners' phthisis, and tubercular diseases were very high on the Rand. White miners were initially perhaps even more susceptible than black because they tended to stay for longer continuous periods on the mines. Research into Cornish miners who had worked in Johannesburg and died in Cornwall between 1900 and 1902 revealed an average age of death of 36.4 years old (Richardson and Burke, 151). Of the eighteen leaders on the 1907 strike committee, fourteen died of phthisis before the next major strike in 1913 (Yudelman, 93).

While working conditions were initially critical to the white miners' struggle, the issue which became central in the early decades of the century was more particular to South Africa: the protection of jobs on a racial basis. Although skilled workers from Europe had been required for the initial development of the mines, demand for them gradually declined. The fact that African workers also acquired some skills allowed a dilution of tasks. An increasing proportion of whites worked above ground or in supervisory rather than skilled roles. Mining companies knew that they could employ black miners for less and tried to limit the number of whites employed. In this context, white workers wanted to defend their access to certain tasks such as blasting. They also wished to control the intensity of work. The 1907 strike was triggered by a dispute over how many drills should be under one supervisor. Afrikaners were drawn on to the mines to replace strikers. Over the next decade, the proportion of South African-born white miners steadily increased—from 17 per cent in 1907 to 50 per cent in 1918. They tended to rely even more than immigrant workers on racially based agreements and legislation.

In 1907 the new Afrikaner government of the Transvaal brought out the troops against strikers. Free-born Englishmen, the former *Uitlanders*, proclaiming their civil rights, found no imperial support. Government intransigence and the imposition of martial law during the 1913 strike helped to transform it rapidly from a more limited action to a general withdrawal of white labour from the gold mines. After a mass meeting, the offices of the Johannesburg *Star*, then as now owned by mining interests, were set alight. The government deployed British troops from the imperial garrison left in the country after Union, killing over 100 strikers. Botha and Smuts were forced to negotiate but when labour leaders tried to push their advantage in 1914, Smuts made pre-emptive arrests. Facing a reorganized army and 70,000 troops, the miners stood down; Smuts illegally deported the leaders. The Riotous Assemblies Act, subsequently often invoked against blacks, was passed to control whites.

White workers did succeed in achieving some of their industrial aims, including Union recognition, an eight-hour day, and further protection of some categories of work in the 1911 Mines and Works Act. The principle of a job colour bar was not seriously in dispute. Though white workers cost on average about twelve times more than black, mine owners found advantages in maintaining racial divisions and using established lines of domination. It was the exact proportion of whites in the labour force that remained contested. In the period of high inflation after the First World War, companies feared that their lower-grade ore would become uneconomic to mine. Although their wages were under pressure, white miners did not come out on strike during the peak years of industrial action, locally and internationally, between 1918 and 1920. They did not support the black miners' strike of 1920. But after a concerted effort was made to reduce white mine employment, they struck again in 1922. Socialist ideas spread and a workers' government seemed momentarily possible but the strike, a near revolt, was suppressed with even greater ruthlessness than before.

Historians have argued that the white working-class movement was defeated in 1922. The subsequent Industrial Conciliation Act (1924) sought to incorporate trade unions, restrict their capacity to initiate industrial action, and lay down tight legal control over disputes. If this was a defeat, it was hardly a devastating one. The percentage of whites in the mine labour force dropped temporarily from about 11 prior to the strike to 8 in 1922, but by 1926 it was back to 10 per cent. During the great expansion of the 1930s, white employment kept pace with black so that by 1937 there were over 37,000 white miners, more than 11 per cent of the work-force. Real wages rose again from the mid-1920s and differentials between whites and blacks were maintained.

The idea of a defeat perhaps stems from reading too much into the political aims of these strikes. In both 1913 and 1922, a radical syndicalist strike leadership briefly emerged. But the primary demands of many white workers seem to have been security of employment and wages. Certainly there were socialists amongst them, such as Bill Andrews, who were initiators of a political tradition in South Africa that has survived to the present day. In some industries, where they were less threatened by black workers, trade unions were less concerned about statutory colour bars. But miners used their political strength to secure segregation and preferment in the labour market and colonial society—hence the slogan 'workers of the world unite and fight for a white South Africa' at the height of the Rand revolt.

If, as Yudelman argues, there was a symbiotic relationship between the mining industry and the state, then the Pact election victory brought greater convergence between these two interests and white workers. The colour bar was entrenched and broadened during Hertzog's period of government from 1924 to 1933, partly through further legislation and partly in the 'civilized labour policy'. Civilized in this case unambiguously meant white. The compromises made by white workers in the mining industry were relatively insignificant given the scale of protection elsewhere. Afrikaners, in particular, gained favoured access to employment in state-run enterprises such as the railways on a scale far greater than before and were paid at higher rates than blacks.

Mining provided the major basis for economic growth during the early decades of the twentieth century. Unlike Kimberley, the Rand did not become a single monopoly surrounded by a company town which ceased to grow. Its sheer size and range of demands stimulated developments in industry and agriculture. But mine owners' demands were for cheap food, cheap labour, and an open colonial economy. They were answerable to foreign shareholders. Industrialization was narrowly based and the logic of the gold mines pervaded economic and political thinking until the 1920s. The mining industry was not taxed to protect domestic manufacturing.

Liberal critics such as W. M. Macmillan in the 1920s argued that South Africa was effectively one country with one economy and that a freer labour market would increase national efficiency and development. Rising wages for blacks would hasten the growth of the internal market. Whites would no longer be threatened by undercutting if blacks were not so poor; all would benefit from a larger national cake. But few South African whites recognized the degree of economic integration that had been achieved. They saw blacks as different rather than poor and most supported racial protection. The nature of industrialization, based around exports of primary products, diminished the interest of the major industrial and agricultural producers in their domestic consumers. Black workers were unlikely to buy gold, however generous their wages.

South Africa was not exceptional at this time in the degree of state intervention that began to characterize policy, only in the degree of segregation. While industrialization seemed to create the potential for social fluidity, it ultimately resulted in hardened racial divisions. That is why the radical historians of the 1970s and 1980s have emphasized so strongly that capitalist growth was not a harbinger of liberal government and an inclusive political system. Economic growth interacted in intricate ways with the legacy of the frontier, changes in the countryside, and new racial thinking to produce segregation. No one segment of the white population achieved all its aims but most found some of their interests served under the segregationist umbrella. In the competition for shelter, immigrants became white and Afrikaner identity was reinforced rather than diluted. The legacy of the war and intensity of impoverishment helped to ensure this outcome. The compromises which characterized late nineteenth-century Cape parliamentary politics were undermined and the Transvaal's counter-conquest of the Cape was beginning.

4 Black Responses and Black Resistance

The Black Élite and African Nationalism

Solomon Plaatje, destined to be the first secretary of the South African Native National Congress (SANNC) in 1912, arrived in Kimberley in 1894. His Tswana-speaking forebears, some of whom had been Christians since the 1830s, acquired their Dutch surname when living with Griqua people. Plaatje was brought up on Lutheran missions near Kimberley and the town was an obvious place of employment for a promising product of their school. He joined the Kimberley Post Office, which in a late Victorian liberal gesture had staffed its telegraph department with black graduates of Lovedale, the most prestigious black school in the colony. In 1898 Plaatje moved to Mafikeng as the court interpreter. He played an important part in the South African War, supplying the British forces with intelligence about Boer combatants and African communities.

Living at a German mission station on the periphery of a British colonial town peopled by Africans from different backgrounds, Plaatje became familiar with a range of cultures and languages. But it was the culture of the imperial outposts, Kimberley and Mafikeng, which most coloured his experience. Amongst the 20,000 or so African inhabitants of Kimberley were a small minority of several hundred more-educated people, many of them English-speakers from leading Xhosa and Mfengu Christian families in the eastern Cape. They created a distinct community bound together by the churches. Some of the men held the franchise and were involved in the 1898 election contest between Henry Burton, a young liberal lawyer, and Cecil Rhodes for the Barkly West parliamentary seat. They organized a South Africans Improvement Society, holding fortnightly debates on subjects historical and moral.

Plaatje attended Shakespearian performances by a visiting British company at the Queen's theatre. A few of the black American Jubilee singers, who toured South Africa in 1895, stayed on in Kimberley and helped form a Philharmonic Society. An eclectic music culture included the new African church choral music as well as adaptations of traditional songs, British ballads, and American spirituals. African cricketers formed the Eccentrics and Duke of Wellington teams.

This African élite was partly forged in the colonial world and claimed a place in the colonial order. But their position was anomalous. Though segregation was not yet rigid many of their activities were restricted to their own community. Everywhere the barriers seemed to be moving up against them. Plaatje's perception that opportunities for mobility within colonial society were declining helped persuade him to leave the civil service in 1902 and start a newspaper in English and Tswana. As their capacity to influence policy declined, the élite looked for wider political constituencies. One turning-point was in 1902, when British and Boer signatories of the Treaty of Vereeniging agreed 'to secure the just predominance of the white races'. Africans sensed they would not be rewarded for loyalty in the war. J. T. Jabavu's *Imvo*, expressing his gradualism, was challenged as the leading black newspaper. Jabavu had allied himself with those Cape liberals, such as Merriman and Burton, who jettisoned Rhodes in 1896 and worked with the Afrikaner Bond. Rhodes responded by funding a new eastern Cape black newspaper *Izwi Labantu*. After his death, *Izwi* projected a more independent radical position, critical of big capital, segregation, and Jabavu's dependence on white politicians.

Together with Plaatje's paper, *Izwi* was associated with the foundation in 1902 of a Cape-based South African Native Congress (SANC), which aligned itself neither with the Bond nor with Jameson's Progressive Party, inheritor of Rhodes's mantle. A network of local organizations known as the *Iliso Lomzi* (eyes of the nation) or vigilance associations, proliferated alongside Congress. In 1903 a Transvaal Native Congress was launched. Walter Rubusana, an SANC member, was elected to the Cape Provincial Council in 1910 in the Thembu-land (Transkei) constituency where almost half the registered voters were black. He was the only African ever to gain a seat in the Cape. The antipathy between him and Jabavu was such that Jabavu opposed his candidacy in 1914 and Rubusana failed to hold the seat.

In the western Cape F. Z. S. Peregrino, a West African who had lived in Britain and the USA, launched the *South African Spectator*, broadly aligned with the SANC. The African Politi-cal Organization (APO), founded in 1902, was less certain of its direction. Dr A. Abdurahman, from a Moslem family and British educated, led the APO from 1904, edited its newspaper, and organized missions to England in 1906 and 1909 to claim rights for coloured people in the former Boer republics. By 1910 he was sharing political platforms with African leaders and calling for unity in opposition. But the APO was split on the issue of African membership and his constituency remained largely coloured and Cape based. The APO also maintained an uneasy relationship with the populist politicians of 'the stone', a large boulder on the slopes of Table Mountain which served as Sunday meeting-place. And they all distanced themselves from the riots which exploded in Cape Town in 1906 at the height of the depression. Poor and unemployed of all races, clustered around District Six, participated. Mountain vagrants rushed into town looking to loot.

African leaders also arranged frequent deputations to Eng-land—notably in 1909, to oppose the terms of Union and in 1914, following the promulgation of the Natives Land Act. It was not entirely clear that Britain had abandoned black interests to the settlers, nor was there much alternative. Chief Bambatha's brief rebellion in Natal in 1906, which was brutally suppressed, clearly demonstrated the hopelessness of violence. These appeals to the 'sense of common justice and love of freedom so innate in the British people' all failed, but the pro-imperial sentiments of the élite died hard.

John Dube was one of the most important early Congress diplomats. An American-educated minister who became the leading spokesman of the Natal *kholwa* (Christians), he laid particular stress on self-improvement through education. Influenced by the American model of Booker T. Washington's Tuskegee College, he founded a similar Ohlange Institute in Natal. Like SANAC, he emphasized industrial as much as academic education. But he placed less reliance on the goodwill of whites, more on the realization of black aspirations. Links with the USA were forged more widely by independent churches such as the AMEC. For those few who could raise the funds, university education at black American colleges was highly prized; it was not then obtainable in South Africa.

As the segregationist direction of white politics became clearer, Plaatje, Dube, and others were convinced that the time had come for them to be 'race leaders'. A growing sense of South Africanism amongst whites had its mirror image in an explicit attempt to create a more assertive African national identity. In 1912 various regional African organizations met in Bloemfontein in 'tophats and tails' to form the SANNC. Dube (first President), Plaatje (Secretary), and Seme, a Transvaal-based lawyer, initially shaped its policies. A nominated upper house of chiefs did not function effectively but was important as a statement about Congress's all-inclusive ideology. Some chiefs were involved; Seme married into the Zulu royal house and the Swazi royal family provided funds for their first newspaper *Abantu Batho* (Our People).

Although Congress leaders were redefining their role, they still tended to be suspicious of mass politics. Nevertheless, they were drawn into broader representations. At a local level, some *Iliso Lomzi* groups were becoming involved in tax protests and passive resistance. As the Cape franchise became progressively diluted, so its defence became less of a preoccupation. Land issues, in which national leaders had the skills to assist in representing popular demands, became more central. J. T. Gumede, later president of the ANC, was long involved as a lawyer in the case of Tlokoa people in Harrismith, Orange Free State, who were asserting claims to ancestral lands. The Natives Land Act galvanized Congress. Some of its leaders were personally affected as landowners or potential purchasers, but they also took up the general cause of African tenants. Plaatje was one of a number of politicians who travelled widely, speaking against the Act and investigating its implications. His experience gave him the material for *Native Life*.

Jabavu initially supported the Land Act. He was certainly constrained by his loyalty to white liberal politicians, shareholders in his newspaper company. They argued for the protective elements of the Act in a context where Afrikaner politicians, now in control of the Union, might alienate even more land from blacks. Jabavu and some rural communities echoed such views, prioritizing the entrenchment of some reserved land rather than the right to compete on the land market. A spokesman in the Transkei noted:

Supposing the whole of South Africa were today cut up into farms, and offered for sale to both whites and blacks, what native millionaire would secure land for these millions of natives? . . . South Africa would at that moment become absolutely 'A White Man's Country' and natives hurled headlong will-nilly into the mines. (Beinart, *Pondoland*, 123)

Congress politicians did not oppose African reserves and communal tenure, nor a degree of segregation on the land. They wanted to retain reserves plus the right to purchase and rent elsewhere. Some liberals and rural chiefs felt that as there was no possibility of winning both, it was better to settle for the promises entrenched in the Land Act, despite its unfairness.

In 1913, the year of the Land Act and the Rand Strike, another issue that was to become central to black politics— urban rights and passes—was highlighted by a major protest of African women in Bloemfontein. African women had not yet migrated in large numbers to the cities and most municipal authorities did not attempt to impose restrictions on them. But Bloemfontein was one of the few cities where the number of African women was nearly as high as men and the Orange Free State authorities alone demanded that women carry urban residential passes. Following the SANNC's foundation meeting in the city and an address by Charlotte Maxeke, its leading woman member, 5,000 signatures against passes were collected and a deputation sent to Cape Town. When arrests increased in 1913, women tore up their passes in the centre of town while police watched—thus starting a long tradition in South African protest politics. Imprisonment was met by passive resistance; the example of Gandhi's campaigns was invoked. Orange Free State women, dubbed by papers 'our local black suffragettes', with cautious Congress support, eventually won one of the few victories by black political activists in these years.

Unlike Afrikaner nationalists, early African nationalists did not become strongly anti-imperial. They retained a liberal belief in multiracial civilization and citizenship in South Africa. Aside from some white liberals and later socialists, they were the only political grouping at the time to articulate this goal. Their interpretation of non-racialism and their strategies for achieving it were often uncertain, as was their view about incorporating the uneducated masses. But they were not offering a black version of exclusive white South Africanism—whites as well as blacks were part of the nation. They opposed, at least in frequent rhetorical flourishes, the ethnic concerns beloved of Afrikaner politicians. Their politics was born in the optimism imbued by partial incorporation in an imperial world; their political edge came from the shattering of that optimism.

Far more so than their Afrikaner counterparts, the African élite was hampered by having to conquer divisions of language; they were having to create a new cultural identity rather than remould an old one. English seemed the most appropriate medium for their movement but was not widely spoken and was the language of the conqueror. Despite new opportunities for mobility, problems of travel as well as communication were immense. Widespread illiteracy made it very difficult for educated leaders to transmit their ideas and develop a national political discourse. African newspapers were important in the formation of a new identity but had a relatively small circulation: *Imvo* at its height perhaps 4,000; the others all less than 2,000.

Indian political leaders, even more so than coloured, worked within their own diverse communities, attempting to weld them together and challenging the state to protect sectional rights and interests. Nevertheless, the political position of the Indian élite in the early twentieth century was in many ways similar to that of Africans. The literature concentrates on Mohandas Gandhi, who lived in South Africa from 1893 to 1914. Trained in London as a lawyer, Gandhi was employed to represent a firm of Durban Indian traders in a major legal case. He arrived in South Africa wearing a suit and a turban, believing he could bridge the European and Indian worlds. He left, at least metaphorically speaking, in a *dhoti*.

In some respects, Gandhi's political development paralleled that of African leaders. He started learning his politics shortly after arrival when Natal settlers, flexing their political muscles on receipt of responsible government in 1892, were determined to undermine what few voting rights Indians had. Gandhi also claimed to have been thrown out of a first-class railway coach, an indignity which exactly expressed the ambiguous position of the black élite. Merchants in the Natal Indian Congress (1894) and the Transvaal British Indian Association led the defence of these rights. After the South African War it was their position as traders and property owners which initially concerned Gandhi.

The British had been the shopkeepers and merchants of South Africa in the nineteenth century and resented Indian competition. Indians were well established in Natal and the Transvaal, but Britain upheld the Boer ban on their entry into the Orange Free State. Indian traders were also prohibited from the Transkeian Territories. Attempts were made to register and control traders in the Transvaal, the most valuable new retail market, between 1906 and 1909 and this provoked passive resistance protests led by Gandhi. Like African leaders he recognized the centrality of the press in politics and took over the newspaper *Indian Opinion*.

Gandhi's *satyagraha*, soul force and passive resistance, drew on Western and Hindu ideas but was a method—already employed by African peasants—suited to the constituency which he wanted to mobilize: a relatively powerless group in a political context where settlers had a monopoly of coercion. 'Soul force' also offered ideas of community and identity in a fragmented Indian population. At this stage, however, Gandhi was still a supporter of imperial authority and assisted British forces in the South African War and the Bambatha rebellion. Like African leaders, he hoped to win moral authority and use this in bargaining for a better deal.

Gandhi's campaigns attracted attention and provided a cathartic focus for Indian politics. A new generation of 'colonial born' Indians, children of indentured workers, launched organizations which took up broader issues such as the £3 tax on ex-indentured workers designed to push them back into work or return to India. In 1913 a strike on the Natal coal-mines was followed by a march to the Transvaal and massive withdrawal of labour on the sugar fields—probably the largest strike there has been on the estates. Gandhi did not play a major role in mobilizing sugar-workers but their strike gave him a lever when he met Smuts and negotiated a withdrawal of the tax. Indian politicians and the Viceroy ensured that for once the Imperial government did not turn a blind eye to events in South Africa.

More so than educated African leaders, Gandhi was immersed in the racial language of the time and it clearly appealed to some members of his constituency of Indian merchants. 'If there is one thing which the Indian cherishes more than any other,' he said, 'it is the purity of type.' His political language made clear distinction between 'British Indians', 'coolies', and 'Kaffirs', and he did not try to mobilize Africans. Nevertheless Gandhi's political thinking did broaden dramatically in South Africa; his political skills guided Indian protest and provided a model for others. The techniques of resistance which he forged were to have a major impact in India. He did also have wide political contact with Jewish and Christian intellectuals and with African leaders such as Dube, whose Ohlange Institute was close to Gandhi's Phoenix rural settlement in Inanda, Natal. It was very difficult for any leader to organize across ethnic lines at the time in South Africa.

Chieftaincy, Ethnicity, and Rural Protest

The problems of nationalist and élite politicians were not simply those of transmitting their message. Though the ANC today is the major vehicle for African political expression, there is no simple continuity from Plaatje's time to Mandela's. Nationalist struggles produce their own mythologies and versions of history but African Nationalism was not the predominant response to colonization at the time. The history of black political opposition is certainly rich, but more diverse, less predictable, and less united than has been supposed. The fact of oppression did not necessarily determine the trajectory of responses.

One aspect of this diversity was the very different social roots and experiences of African, Indian, coloured as well as poor white subject communities. As important, any analysis of African political responses must start with an understanding that the people of pre-colonial chiefdoms intermarried, treated, and traded, absorbed or conquered one another, but were not politically or culturally united. Subsequently, colonization was piecemeal and responses to it localized. Colonial forces were frequently able to find African allies or levies, such as Mfengu people in the eastern Cape or Swazi in the Transvaal. Within chiefdoms there were often divisions as to how to respond to encroachments. Early colonial rule through 'loyal' intermediaries shaped local political conflict and left a deep legacy in many rural areas which their opponents did not find easy to forget. Political thinking and action grew out of real and self-conscious rural communities, where the great majority of African people still lived. In particular, the political processes surrounding the remnant chieftaincies remained important.

White rule and common experiences on the land and in towns began to define general political issues, but people from different rural areas were absorbed into the labour market in different ways. Whereas the urban world and workplace could provide the basis for new identity and action in the early twentieth century, these were also contexts for ethnic redefinition as communities competed for employment and space. The dominant colonial obsession with race and racial distinctions of all kinds sometimes fed into the ideas of the dominated. Ethnicity has a bad name amongst opponents of segregation and apartheid and understandably so, as the South African state systematically used divide and rule strategies founded on ethnic categories. But it is important to recognize the salience of cultural as well as class divisions amongst the dominated.

Local identities and associations could be unifying social forces for the multitude of pre-colonial societies and immigrant groups that made up South Africa's population. Sometimes they were critical in defending the interests of the weak, enlarging their political horizons and enabling them to establish leverage in a new context. Indian and coloured people, Zulu and Mfengu, as well as white workers were defining themselves as such as well as being defined in the early twentieth century. Coloured people in Cape Town instituted a popular carnival in the late nineteenth century; it became an annual event in which they temporarily claimed the city centre. Such identities were not necessarily exclusive and they were often fluid. People could conceive of themselves as clan member, Zulu, and African; as coloured, Malay, and South African.

The politics of Gandhi, Dube, Plaatje, and Abdurahman were of limited relevance to the great majority of Africans who remained on the land. Rural political struggles tended to be defensive, though they were often also innovative. They were geared to maintaining access to resources such as land, forests, and grazing, which were critical to the survival of peasant families. New impositions and taxes or tighter controls over the way people managed their land and cattle were often the spur to mobilization. This could take many different forms from polite petitioning to rural riot. Age-old peasant strategies of delay, demands for consultation, refusal to listen, silent boycott, and attempts to restrict the state's knowledge were frequently deployed.

The fact that chieftaincy remained an important focus of politics did not mean that all chiefs received support. The institution itself had many layers, from paramounts of large, recently conquered chiefdoms to local headmen of royal descent. Claims to office were often disputed, the more so because the state recognized, paid, and extended limited powers to many members of chiefly lineages as government headmen. Disputes over genealogy and succession were often intertwined with broader political issues. Chiefs who attracted popular following were likely to be those who resisted colonial intrusions, but 'loyals' might have strong support in particular locations where there was a tradition of co-operation or Christian influence. Chieftaincy could be a focus of resistance but also of ethnic expression.

Bambatha's rebellion in Natal in 1906 was the most dramatic incident of rural protest in the first decade of the century—as much for the intensity of white reaction as for the degree of black mobilization. Conquest and annexation was only completed in the 1890s. In 1903 a Commission was set up to carve coastal land out of Zulu territory for the expansion of settler sugar farming. Natal's colonial government was dominated by white farmers determined to take advantage of the rise of urban markets. Tenants, especially those on the best-placed farms near the railway, bore the brunt of the resulting social pressures. When the post-war recession began to bite in 1904, the Natal government decided to ease its own revenue problems and labour shortages by levying a poll tax on all those who did not already pay hut tax. 'If Natal liked to revert to medieval methods of taxation,' a British Colonial Office official commented, 'I do not see that it is any business of ours' (Marks, 142).

There was a new focus as well as a new cause for dissent. Dinuzulu, the Zulu king, returned from exile in St Helena in 1897 when Zululand passed from British to Natal rule. His Usuthu royal house became associated with a revival of 'national feeling and the desire to remain one people under English rule' (Marks, 98). The term Zulu itself, more strictly applicable to those who had been part of the Zulu kingdom rather than those in Natal, began to be used more widely by officials and Africans to refer to both. Whether he wished it or not, Dinuzulu's name was invoked as a symbol of resistance.

It also became associated with other rumours—that Africans should kill white goats, pigs, and fowl, and destroy tools of

European manufacture. Pigs and lard were thought to attract lightning and people were told that if they deposited their lard on hillsides, they would be saved and lightning would strike those who attempted to collect the £1 poll tax. Whites feared that the killing of animals was a warning to them, but this is unlikely. Episodes of mass animal slaughter had a long history in South Africa. The best known of these, the Xhosa cattle-killing of 1857, was perhaps an extension of the sacrifices which were so central in African religions—a search for purity and rebirth through mass communication with ancestors. Pig-killings were frequent until the 1920s following prophecies aimed at cleansing society by purging an introduced animal. Such millennial or purificatory ideas were a persistent feature of rural politics in the early twentieth century, but they were were not universal nor did they preclude more instrumental political behaviour at the same time.

Many Zulu chiefs refused to co-operate in paying the tax, provoking dispersed confrontations and arrests. Bambatha, a deposed chief in Umvoti district, was a farm tenant already subject to court action over rent demands. In an encounter with the police, his people used the royal cry of Usuthu. Shula Marks, historian of the uprising, sees it as a 'reluctant rebellion' and largely restorationist. An African witness to the subsequent inquiry explained that Bambatha 'went to extremes simply because he was tied hand and foot by the network of troubles in which he found himself . . . like a beast which on being stabbed rushes about in despair'. But if the rebellion was reluctant, its suppression was not: twenty-four whites died and perhaps 4,000 Africans. After his capture, Bambatha's head was cut off. Dinuzulu was exiled again, this time to the Transvaal. The limits of armed resistance were demonstrated but the reputation of the royal house, uncorrupted by having to work within the system, was enhanced.

The issues surrounding the Bambatha rebellion were echoed in other parts of South Africa. In the Cape, the state's attempts to extend the Council system, based on the Glen Grey Act of 1894, became a major issue. An additional ten-shilling levy on all hut-tax payers guaranteed the councils' unpopularity. Many traditionalists also feared that appointed councils would be 'puppet governments' dominated by those 'who had sold themselves to government'. Some of the educated élite argued that they were the basis of a segregated system of local government, with only advisory capacity, which further threatened common rights. Although the councils were generally implemented, it was around their extension that some of the most important early political alliances formed between dissident Christians, chiefs, and people.

For people in the countryside, new laws such as those governing access to game or forests could criminalize what had been everyday activity. The introduction of cattle-dipping to combat East Coast fever, a tick-borne disease, was equally fraught. At issue were different perceptions of disease and how it should be dealt with. Restrictions on the movement of cattle struck at the heart of rural life, hampering transhumance, sales, and cattle transfers for marriage. Dipping truly made rural Africans subjects of the state by extending state control over one of their most prized assets. Protests were essentially about the extent of control and fines levied for breaches of the regulations. In three districts of East Griqualand between 1914 and 1917, men took to the hills with rusty rifles retained from anti-colonial wars and blew up dipping tanks with dynamite abducted from road construction parties. Trading stores were looted and telegraph wires cut. These were local riots that fizzled out quickly rather than rebellions. But disputes about how to respond to intervention continued to feed political tensions within African communities throughout the country. The violence which has characterized Msinga district, northern Natal—so that the area has become a byword in South Africa for revenge killings—had roots in nineteenth-century conflicts, overlaid by disputes over land and state intervention in the twentieth.

African people who lived on farms faced some different impositions from those experienced in the reserves. Isolated and unprotected, their direct action, such as ham-stringing cattle, cutting fences, and going slow at work, tended to be dispersed and individual. Mobility was often the best defensive strategy, though difficult where large communities tried to maintain their social cohesion. The African tenants of Harrismith district, Orange Free State, whom Gumede helped to represent, found that their land was prime maize territory. They claimed it had been sold from under their feet by an unscrupulous Afrikaner official in the nineteenth century. When legal cases and a deputation to Britain failed, some saw their future in playing the segregationist game. They identified themselves as a tribe with a chief to claim reserved land; unsuccessful in this strategy many ended up 'everlastingly moving from one place to another . . . a nation sorrowing for our country' (*Putting a Plough to the Ground*, 247).

Redefining ethnic identity on the farmlands was not simply an instrumental way of trying to acquire land. People identifying themselves as Ndzundza Ndebele in the southern Transvaal have been best known in the twentieth century for their elaborate 'traditional' patterns of dress and house decoration—highly attractive to photographers. Yet they suffered a particularly brutal experience of dispossession. A small chiefdom of perhaps 10,000 people in the 1870s, based around a strongly fortified village, they sided with the British and Swazi in the conquest of the Pedi in 1879. In the 1880s they came into conflict with the newly restored republican Transvaal government: the capital was burnt down; their chief imprisoned; their land largely turned into farms; and many people indentured to Boers. The South African War provided some of the Ndzundza, scattered on farms throughout the Transvaal, with an opportunity to escape and regroup. Their traditionalism grew out of their quest for identity and attempts to reconstitute families split by conquest. Most remained as farm tenants, but after some decades succeeded in registering themselves as a recognized 'tribe' and competed successfully for a reserve. Their decorative traditions, a reworking of pre-colonial motifs, were partly an expression of individual artistic skill, partly a collective assertion.

At Bulhoek in the eastern Cape, resistance was framed by fierce religious rather than ethnic commitment. Enoch Mgijima, from a Mfengu Methodist family, had formed his own church of Israelites in 1912. Mgijima, guided by visions and prophesying the end of the world, established a religious community in 1919 who saw themselves as chosen and awaited the coming of the Lord. Settled on land to which they were not legally entitled, and refusing to pay taxes, the Israelites soon came into conflict with the authorities. They asked, unsuccessfully, to be left alone 'for the purpose of praying and fearing God's wrath which is coming upon the whole world' (Edgar). In 1921 a police contingent was sent to disperse the 3,000-strong community. After protracted negotiations, white-robed Israelites ran towards the police and were mown down by gunfire leaving nearly 200 dead.

Popular Struggles in the 1920s

Rural responses and political movements appear fragmented and localized, difficult to incorporate into regional or national struggles, but it should not be suggested that peasants were simply backward-looking, ultra religious, and unable to make broader political linkages. In order to discern more general trends it is important to turn again to the large towns. The Rand was the biggest centre of African urban population; by 1920 nearly 100,000 blacks were employed in non-mining activities and a further 200,000 on the mines. Though many of these were migrant workers, housed in compounds and barracks, urban slumyards and locations were growing rapidly. East Rand mine-workers, faced with declining real wages as prices inflated after the First World War, boycotted mine stores in 1918. Participants were largely migrants from Mozambique, then still the most numerous and well-established segment of the work-force and most dependent on wage income.

Soon afterwards, white power workers plunged the city into darkness for five nights and were awarded a large wage increase. Their action was followed by African municipal employees working in the sanitary services who asked for a more modest rise. Johannesburg, sited for its gold, had no natural channel for effluent and the municipality, slow to develop underground sewage systems, operated nightsoil collections. By 1918 some 6,000 Africans were employed as 'bucket boys', mostly Bhaca migrants from the Transkei and southern Natal. A distinct urban presence, they were probably originators of the gumboot dance where teams of men stamp and slap their boots in complex rhythms. This kind of specialization by particular groups of workers—other examples include Zulu washermen and rickshaw pullers—was not unusual nor did it preclude organization. It could provide the kind of solidarity which men at work required to launch united action in the era before trade unions.

The 'bucket boys' were dealt with harshly and their punishment sparked renewed urban protest. The Transvaal leadership of the ANC was drawn into a more radical working-class politics and in 1919 organized a campaign to boycott and destroy passes. In 1920 black mine-workers staged a major stoppage following the arrest of two miners. Led by Pedi and Shangaan workers, the strike had wide support—a figure of 71,000, or one third of the total is often quoted—organized along the networks of compound solidarity and migrant associations. Again it was self-organized migrant workers who participated in the strike, but there were limits to the possibility of sustaining it. While the action was unsuccessful, it nevertheless encouraged mine-owners in their determination to ease the job colour bar which in turn helped precipitate the 1922 white Rand Revolt.

In addition to a more explicit worker consciousness, ideas of black self-assertion suffused urban communities. Black American influences, already widespread in independent churches and in music, were extended by advocates of Garveyism. Marcus Garvey's radical black consciousness and back-to-Africa movement that had found widespread support in US cities did start branches in South Africa. But it was more significant in adding muscle to the language of black unity and protest. 'Amelika' became a symbol of freedom.

ANC leaders found it difficult to steer a path, in a segregationist era, between liberalism, rural traditionalism, and urban radicalism. Regional organizations tended to go their own way. Transvaal leaders were drawn briefly into workers' issues, the eastern Cape remained more concerned with older questions of the vote and land, while western Cape leaders espoused Garveyite ideas. A breakaway independent Cape ANC tried to organize rural farm-workers. Dube in Natal was equivocal about segregation policy and, ousted from the presidency in 1917, cemented his links with the Zulu king. The movement could not establish a role as intermediary with the state; officials preferred to deal with rural chiefs and headmen or members of the new Councils. Although the national leadership swung in a radical direction in 1927 under Gumede, it soon reverted to a more conservative position and did not become a mass movement. White liberals and the mining industry worked hard to moderate the black leadership through the Joint Councils movement where white and blacks met together to discuss social issues.

The ANC was partly supplanted in the 1920s by the Industrial and Commercial Workers' Union of South Africa (ICU) and its various offshoots which attracted those who sought a more radical political vehicle. An analysis of the rise and fall of the ICU helps to clarify some of the ideas and strategies necessary to create a mass movement at the time, but also the problems of doing so. The movement was launched in 1919 in the Cape Town docks, drawing on the heritage of less explicitly racial trade unionism in the Cape. Ports, docks, and railheads have often been the crossroads for people, ideas, and political organization in colonial Africa.

The ICU rapidly became a general rather than a craft or industrial union, highly adaptable to the demands of disparate groups of workers, tenants, and peasants throughout South Africa. Clements Kadalie, a mission-educated migrant worker from Malawi 2,000 miles to the north, became leader. While it drew some support from the same communities as the ANC, the ICU's reach was greater and links with Congress soon faltered. Early successes included a major strike of both African and coloured workers in Port Elizabeth in 1920. As so often in this period of Smuts's premiership, the episode ended in tragedy; police fired upon a crowd, killing twenty-four.

From the mid-1920s the ICU took up the cause of rural

tenants and spread rapidly through the countryside. Membership perhaps briefly exceeded 100,000 by the late 1920s—far
outstripping the ANC—and the movement reached to Zimbabwe and Malawi. Its leaders could talk the language of trade
unionism, workers' rights, and wages; they also stressed black
unity and nationalism, black commercial opportunity and
Christianity. Members of the Communist Party, founded in
1921, briefly became involved in the mid-1920s when they
ceased to prioritize white workers. But Kadalie, anxious about
his control and uneasy about communist ideas, expelled them
in 1926. Kadalie was charismatic and ambitious, a rousing if
sometimes bombastic speaker, who did not easily work in a
collective or subordinate position.

ICU influence in the rural areas was strongest in the regions
undergoing rapid transition towards capitalist agriculture such
as the eastern Transvaal. It also attracted a following in Umvoti
district, Natal, former home of Bambatha, where African
labour tenants were being evicted or squeezed for more work.
Local ICU leaders married Zulu nationalism with claims for
the rights of tenants to land. Despite the highly dispersed rural
work-force, wage claims were advanced by work stoppages.
Violent incidents studded the conflict which exploded when
gravestones were desecrated in Greytown's white cemetery and
the ICU offices were razed to the ground in response.

The ICU's mushroom growth was not sustained. It fragmented into regional groups in the face of state repression and
amidst accusations of corruption against the leadership. Kadalie
launched an Independent ICU in East London and in 1930 the
city was rocked by a major strike. When Kadalie was arrested
(and tried to call off the strike), local organizers sustained the
action for nearly six months, drawing in not only dock and
railway workers, but domestic workers and women beer brewers in the locations. They mobilized in support of the right to
brew, a right severely curtailed by the municipal council. In
this phase of radicalism, Independent ICU leaders espoused a
powerful anti-white rhetoric, invoking separatist Christianity
and, in a striking image, a black Jesus.

None of the ICU successor groups was able to cement a

lasting organizational framework. The depression, unemployment, failure to deliver on promises, ideological differences, and personal squabbles rendered the movement moribund by the early 1930s. Some historians have argued that populism and lack of an industrial strategy were its downfall. But it was the one black movement which was able simultaneously to develop some national organization and to secure, on occasion, mass local support amongst disparate and divided communities. Industrial unionism was in its infancy amongst black workers and was not an alternative as a means of attracting a mass following. The ICU's flexibility enabled it to bridge town and countryside, although it was sometimes captured by its diverse rural constituencies and could become a catalyst for protests which were not essentially union struggles.

The ICU was not the only movement which attempted to fuse rural idioms and nationalist politics. In Herschel district, bordering Lesotho and the Orange Free State, state attempts to enforce councils radicalized the peasantry. In 1922 local women inspired by events on the Rand boycotted trading stores. When the magistrate tried to register their land in 1925, they boycotted mission schools because the teachers were seen to be sympathetic to the government. Many joined African churches and some independent schools were started. Protestors organized themselves into a religious and political front named the *Amafelandawonye* (people who die together in one place) and called for local self-rule under a popular chief.

The *Amafela* were sufficiently organized to sustain a movement over some years, develop their own political ideas, and call in help from the ANC in Cape Town. Wellington Buthelezi, a product of Lovedale school, was another of their champions. He made his living as a itinerant populist politician, evangelist, and vendor of patent medicines in the Cape and Natal. His Garveyite ideas, celebrating black pride, self-help, and the American model, resonated well with militant rural anti-colonialism; he helped to set up independent schools and churches. Elsewhere, his movement was associated with millennial and purificatory messages, including pig-slaughter. In some versions, non-believers would find their homes burnt by bombs dropped from aeroplanes flown by American blacks come to liberate South Africa. Buthelezi identified strongly with the widespread rural sense that help would come from 'Amelika' and was far more attuned than ANC leaders to the separatist impulses in rural politics. The idea of liberation by aeroplane imaginatively inverted control of that new instrument of power which Smuts had used to quell protest.

Christianity was one of the binding forces of 1920s' radicalism and Africanist thinking. It was still not the majority black religion, but its language reached far beyond the old mission communities. Some of the early independent churches had fragmented further by the 1920s. They were joined by a new religious force—fundamentalist Apostolic and Zionist churches. Most of these had their roots in the USA but adapted rapidly to the South African context incorporating African symbolism and practices. Many split again and a bewildering array of denominations emerged; Sundkler listed nearly 1,000 African churches by 1945.

The attractions of Christianity were many and complex. As a religion of sacrifice, blood, saints, spirits, purification, and redemption it had much in common with pre-colonial African beliefs. The biblical world, evoking a pre-industrial and patriarchal society clearly resonated with African ideas. For early converts missions had often been a refuge, now conversion was a route to literacy and education. Christianity provided universal belief and networks as well as a more individualist moral alternative to the bonds of rural communality. In the 1920s political messages of social as well as religious redemption were often drawn from the Bible. Increasingly, Christianity was moulded by African people into forms they found useful. Women, in particular, were the backbone of many churches.

By this time women were the majority in most rural districts because so many men were migrants. By contrast, they were a minority in town. Last off the land, they found it most difficult to secure niches in the urban labour market. Some did move as wives, while others came to escape conflicts and restrictions at home, or as migrant workers themselves. Women in town had to earn money either for themselves or because the wages for

African men were so low. Domestic service increasingly opened up to them; those nearer the white suburbs took in laundry. But many women earned their keep on the peripheries of the urban economy, renting out rooms, selling sexual services, or more especially, brewing home-made maize and sorghum beer for sale to the large number of men. Beer was central to African rural life: a means of using grain; an important part of the adult diet; a lubricator of ceremonies and celebrations. It was also a medium of payment for labour after communal work parties. African women carried their rural skills into the urban areas, much as Afrikaner brick-makers and transport riders had done, and adapted their practices to sell beer for cash, sometimes making it stronger and more quickly.

Manufactured alcohol, especially spirits which were thought to be destructive of industrial discipline and moral fibre, was banned to all but a few exempted middle-class Africans. Only weak maize beer, incorporated into the compound diet for nutritional reasons, was allowed on the mines. Durban municipality tried to raise money from monopolizing production and sale in beerhalls; elsewhere domestic brewing for consumption was allowed, but brewing for sale was widely restricted. Urban women were thus deprived of potential income and police raids, searches, and conviction for petty criminal offences became everyday experiences. The right to brew and the politics of liquor were key issues, a trigger of riots in Natal in 1929 and important in the 1930 East London strike.

The majority of workers in the cities and mines were still male migrants who retained a strong attachment to their rural homes. Migrant workers did take part in strikes, in the ICU, even in Congress politics. But this type of politicization was not their central experience and many were involved in other kinds of associations. Youths and young men predominated in some spheres of employment, such as domestic service in Natal and the Transvaal. Those from the same rural districts sometimes congregated in towns or compounds. At home, many were involved in dance, stick-fighting, and courting groups which met regularly. These were transposed to town where they took on a new form.

Amalaita groups in Natal and the Transvaal were one of the most striking examples. The name came into use soon after the turn of the century in Durban to describe unruly African youth gangs. It was probably derived from English, perhaps from the idea that violence was like lighting a fire. An African newspaper suggested that youthful miscreants would ask for money to light their way, in the same way as African doctors called for their fees. The *amalaita* were not one group or organization, but a name given to a range of street gangs and youth associations. Accounts tell of them marching four abreast through the streets of Durban, colourfully dressed and playing mouth organs, ready to beat unprotected lone youths.

The *amalaita* were Zulu-speakers in Natal, but in Johannesburg and Pretoria Pedi youths from the eastern Transvaal formed similar associations. Some were simply dance and play-fighting groups for domestics on their off-days. Some developed a more elaborate hierarchy of *Morena* (chief), captains, and sergeants. Up to 100 strong, gangs wore knickerbocker trousers and red cloth badges (van Onselen, ii. 57–9). 'The servile "boy" of the day became the aggressive "Sergeant" of the night.' It was the alleged rape of a white woman by such a gang that gave rise to a 'black peril' panic on the Rand in 1912.

In Natal competitive dances, called *Ngoma*, and pitched stick battles expressed a 'tightly-bounded sense of rural identity', a popular culture 'infused with military symbols and rituals drawn from a pre-colonial past'. *Amalaita* gangs were anti-authoritarian and powerfully masculine but not easily available for broader political enterprises. They could, however, be mobilized. In Durban around 1929/30 the *amalaita* were absorbed into ICU activities and the beerhall riots. Regimental anthems were sung at Union meetings and cries of Usuthu, the Zulu royal praises, accompanied demands for the right of women to brew beer. Migrant culture differed from that of the more established urban Christian communities. For example football, which was eventually to replace stick-fighting, made some impact on the Rand and in Durban but had limited following amongst migrant youth.

Criminal gangs, distinct from the looser *amalaita* youth

associations, spread in prisons and compounds in the early twentieth century. They boasted complex hierarchies of officials, drawing both on Zulu regimental terms and those of colonial armies. Major mine and prison gangs, such as the Ninevites and the Isitshozi, also played some part in regulating homosexuality within the compounds. In the 1910s and 1920s, 200,000 African men employed in gold-mining lived in vast single-sex compounds for months at a time. It was difficult for them to form relationships with urban women, expensive and dangerous for them to buy sexual services. Homosexuality on the mines was a response to the need for affection, but it became locked into the hierarchies of the compound. Well-established older men would be in a position to offer newly recruited youths favours in return for physical comforts. Youths in this position (*amankotshane*) would be looked on as wives. These relationships sometimes became susceptible to control by gangs.

Male associations were a particular feature of the South African social landscape; in the absence of trade unions, these were the predominant forms of migrant worker self-organization. They drew on rural influences but were adapted in the mine and urban contexts. Patterns of discipline and ethnic housing in the mines tended to reinforce their development. Control was exercised by white compound managers and supervisors through African *indunas* and *isibonda* (room representatives). Fanakalo (probably from *enza fanakalo*—do it like this), a restricted Zulu-based hybrid language, provided one general means of communication. Wildcat strikes or protests could result if too autocratic an approach was adopted; these could transcend ethnic boundaries with workers negotiating between themselves and officials. But solidarities could also take on a more explosive and ethnic character in compound 'faction fights' which were most likely when established workers felt threatened by large groups of new arrivals.

African political and social responses included many oppositional features, but the South African state was not without allies. Rural headmen and teachers took on major responsibility for maintaining order. African levies fought in nineteenth-century wars; there were black members of anti-stock theft units and, over a long period of time, a significant number of black policemen. The mines were seldom short of 'boss boys' and compound police. A black undercover constable reported in detail the proceedings of the meetings of the International Workers of Africa, the first socialist organization on the Rand to incorporate blacks. Similarly, records of ICU meetings in East London between 1928 and 1932 survive in the archives because they were reported by both white and black policemen. (Kadalie tried unsuccessfully to convert them.) Such 'loyalists' provided state officials with a constant if uneven stream of material which has also been, ironically, an important source of information for historians of protest. They were of some significance in providing a ballast to the state as it implemented segregationist measures.

Perhaps more important were the attempts made to reach accommodation with chiefs. The Native Affairs Department (NAD), which sought to enlarge its own powers by separating the administration of Africans, supported this strategy and secured the passing of the Native Administration Act in 1927. Chiefs had been given some recognition in the Cape and Natal before Union. This Act extended state support for chieftaincy and prepared the way for recognition of chiefs' courts throughout the reserved areas. It was an important step in consolidating the system of administration around a conservative rural hierarchy. Segregationist politicians sought to 'retribalize' African society in order to defuse national political organization.

Not all chiefs supported the government's aims. However, many rural political movements had been developing ideas of popular chieftaincy. Men like John Dube, former president of the ANC, became increasingly involved in the politics of the Zulu chieftaincy in the 1920s. A first version of *Inkatha*, the Zulu cultural movement, was launched. Dube was concerned by the radicalism of the ICU and thought the Zulu king Solomon ka Dinuzulu might provide an alternative political focus. Solomon himself struggled for recognition. Some Zulu workers and farm tenants had shown themselves in various popular movements to be sympathetic to ethnic appeals associated with the royal house. Segregationist ideologues and officials tried to feed off and entrench these varied rural political impulses. They seem to have met with some success. The uncertainty of the African élite, which was under great social and economic pressure, and the failure of the ICU helped undermine national movements by the early 1930s. Radical nationalist rhetoric so characteristic of the 1920s was not abandoned, but could find fewer organizational homes or charismatic leaders to take it forward.

Historians have increasingly emphasized that Africans were not passive victims of colonization, oppression, and segregation, but were involved in a wide range of inventive political responses and innovative forms of action. The protests of African women in such diverse locations as Herschel, East London, Durban, and Potchefstroom are especially striking. At the same time, the limits of nationalist and working-class organization have been recognized. Africans could not mount any co-ordinated political action which might challenge the state. In many senses, the rural areas rather than the cities were the primary locus of political conflict in the 1920s. There were signs, albeit faint, in the ICU and similar organizations that a revolutionary or nationalist movement linking urban activists to the rural masses might have been possible as in China or India. But this was not to be. State control was more far-reaching in South Africa. And the incomplete transformation of African societies, together with the thrust of state policy, opened areas of compromise in the reserves where opportunities for African advance sometimes seemed more tangible. Some popular movements were actually separatist in character. The accommodations reached ultimately helped to defuse conflict in the inter-war years at the height of segregation.

The origins of the homelands can certainly be detected in this period. But other powerful influences were forged which influenced black politics in South Africa over many years: a non-racial and non-violent political ideology which took up the legacy of the Victorian Cape and developed the idea of Africans as Africans in a white-dominated state.

5 The Settler State in Depression and War, 1930–1948

The Settler State and Afrikaner Politics

The great depression of the early 1930s signalled a sharp break in South African history. Hertzog's National Party, victorious in the late 1920s, succumbed to the economic whirlwind. As a result, Afrikaners lost their relatively united political front between 1934 and 1948. Smuts and the South African Party were brought into a national government which presided over a period of rapid economic expansion. From 1939 to 1948, Smuts again ruled as Prime Minister. Despite Afrikaner demographic preponderance, white party affiliations remained fluid. The broad accommodations that had been reached by different white interest groups under the umbrella of segregation did not preclude bitter divisions. White dominance was assured but its pattern by no means predictable.

Hertzog's first five years in office were highly successful from the point of view of the specific groups he represented. Afrikaans rather than Dutch was installed as an equal language in 1925 and bilingualism introduced into the civil service—measures which favoured the employment of Afrikaans-speakers. The Bible was now available in Afrikaans. Hertzog was an important architect of a more independent status for the British self-governing Dominions following the agreements at the Imperial Conference of 1926. A compromise was struck on the troubled issue of the national flag. Based on bold blue, white, and orange stripes, last used in the Dutch East India Company period, the agreed design was even more syncretic than the British flag: it included at its centre miniature Transvaal and Orange Free State flags and a Union Jack. A recently composed Afrikaans national anthem 'Die Stem' (voice) was adopted formally in 1934, to be played alongside 'God Save the King'. The new medium of radio facilitated its popularization.

Hertzog could also feel satisfied at the success of his policy of job protection for poor whites. To the cost of both African and coloured workers, the South African Railways became the single largest employer of Afrikaners. The figure climbed to 77,000 by 1942, perhaps one in eleven adult male Afrikaners (O'Meara, 90). At small country stations throughout the land, processions of wheel-tappers rang the victory of protected employment on the wheels of countless trucks and engines. Though the state had less direct influence on industry, white employment in mining recovered and most manufacturing and commercial enterprises employed a far higher proportion of whites than did the mines. Hertzog was also able to finalize the plans for national electricity (ESCOM) and iron and steel (ISCOR) corporations, as well as increase protection for infant consumer-oriented industries. The entrenchment and renaming of the Kruger National Park provided a strong set of symbols for both English and Afrikaners. An Afrikaner-based, but relatively broad South African settler nationalism seemed to be flourishing.

Although Hertzog was not able to move as fast as he would have liked on legislation regulating African rights, he success-fully made race domination into a major issue in the 1929 election. The scale of his victory allowed him to drop his sometimes uneasy alliance with the English-speaking Labour Party. In 1930 he agreed to the extension of the franchise to all white men, without qualification, and to white, but not black women. Up to this time, gender had been a more rigid category of exclusion from the vote (if not from other legal rights) than race. The women's suffrage movement in South Africa was led mainly by English-speaking women from leading families, such as Lady Rose-Innes, and professionals. It was weaker than in Britain and abandoned its commitment to the Cape's qualified colour-blind franchise in the mid-1920s. 'Sex loyalty', Walker comments, 'stopped at the heavily guarded boundaries of white privilege' (p. 314). Hertzog's cabinet saw white women's enfranchisement not least as a means of further diluting the influence of black voters and increasing the predominance of Afrikaners.

The National Party looked well set to ride out the depression. Its failure to do so resulted partly from its severity, but partly from the government's inability to manage the crisis, even in the interests of Hertzog's own narrow base of support. This is the more surprising because South Africa had decisive advantages in the depression in that gold production prospered. After Wall Street crashed in 1929, prices in general deflated. South African gold producers found that their costs declined. With gold at a relatively fixed price, their profits increased. Demand for the metal nevertheless remained high because of financial instability.

In order to reflate its economy, Britain abandoned the gold standard in September 1931 and sterling was devalued. Hertzog, however, stayed on the gold standard for over a year. He was initially attracted by the prospect of cheap imports, which would lower both the costs of production and of consumption. He also construed his refusal to follow the British lead as an assertion of economic independence and nationalism. However, the highly valued South African pound made life very difficult for agricultural exporters in already depressed markets. Hertzog's cabinet therefore resolved to tax the profitable mining industry in order to support agriculture till these markets recovered, but his immediate political calculus was wrong.

Wool producers, most dependent on international markets, were hit hard and early. Australia had also abandoned the gold standard and deflated its currency, making it even more difficult for South African wool to compete. The wool clip increased, but its value plummeted and pastures came under enormous pressure as farmers tried to maintain their income by increasing sheep numbers to unprecedented heights. By 1935 drought and depression resulted in the loss of nearly 15 million sheep. The price of maize, the major agricultural commodity on the internal market, declined by more than half from 1929 to 1933.

Hertzog was eventually persuaded to abandon the gold standard only in December 1932 in the face of strong opposition both from Afrikaner politicians and the mining industry. His popularity had suffered and, insufficiently confident to call an election, he was driven into Smuts's arms in 1933. With the economic tide turning, their 'Fusion' coalition won the great majority of seats when elections were held. In 1934 the SAP and National parties amalgamated to become the United South African Nationalist Party (UP). Hertzog stayed on as Prime Minister and Minister of External Affairs while Smuts became his deputy and Minister of Justice.

Despite their rhetoric, Smuts and Hertzog had a good deal in common. Smuts agreed to safeguard a 'sound rural population' and a white labour policy, as well as to respect the constitutional devolution Hertzog had achieved. Hertzog had already expressed a desire to halt further demands for constitutional change. 'After what has been achieved at the Imperial Conferences in 1926 and 1930,' he argued, 'there no longer exists today a single reason why, in the constitutional and political fields, Dutch- and English-speaking South Africans cannot feel and act in the spirit of a consolidated South African nation' (O'Meara, 40). Smuts was a super-bureaucrat as much as a politician, far more effective in office than in opposition. While he and Hertzog differed on the details of segregation, Smuts was prepared to compromise in order to stay in power.

South Africa's economic recovery in the 1930s was fuelled by gold. Following the demise of the gold standard, the metal's price doubled within a decade. Lower-grade ores could be exploited on a scale previously impossible. Although gold production only increased 33 per cent from 333,316 kg. in 1931 to 448,128 kg. in 1941, the tonnage of rock processed leapt from 29 to 63 million and total income from gold increased 2.5 times to £120 m. in 1941. Employment reflected the tonnage figures: the African work-force, at about 200,000 in 1929, peaked at over 383,000 in 1941 and the number of white miners rose from 22,000 to 41,424. South Africa was again beneficiary of a windfall gain blown by forces unleashed in the international economy.

The mining industry had not been a major direct source of state revenue prior to the depression. But economic thinking was changing in the post-depression world, especially in Franklin D. Roosevelt's 'New Deal' USA. Hertzog and the Fusion government broke with precedent and imposed an excess profits tax on gold. State revenue from the industry increased from about £1.6 m. annually between 1925 and 1930 to over £12 m. in 1933 and £22 m. in 1940—from 6 per cent of total revenue to about one third. With resources on this scale, the government could conceive of projects that had not been possible since the days of reconstruction after the South African War.

White farmers, who had been a major casualty of the depression, were the greatest beneficiaries. Considerable sums were transferred through Land Bank loans and, for example, the £2.5 m. distributed under the 1932 Soil Erosion Act for dams, boreholes, and contour works. But support came to farmers not primarily from direct grants or loans but via a complex system of price protection. The process of stabilizing and protecting prices, begun with wine and tobacco in the 1920s, spread to almost every agricultural commodity in the 1930s. Following the trend in Britain, Control Boards were established to manage the markets. In 1937 the system as a whole was regulated by a Marketing Act under which Boards would work with white farmer co-operatives as sole purchasers of a number of commodities. By 1950 over 90 per cent of white farmers belonged to at least one co-operative. Afrikaner financial institutions benefited greatly from the co-operative accounts which they held. De Kiewiet argued in a memorable if not accurate aphorism that South Africa 'came . . . to be farmed from the two capitals, Pretoria and Cape Town' (p. 253).

Manufacturing industry, also deeply affected by the depression, received less overall support but grew more rapidly than the agricultural sector. Agricultural development was in itself one stimulus as dips, fertilizers, windmills, machinery, and fences were required for more intensive production. Internal urban and mining markets were more important. During the First World War, a number of local consumer-oriented and engineering industries had been able to take advantage of the protection arising out of disruption to international shipping.

The fact that the major concentration of population and industry was on the Rand, well away from the ports, provided some further protection from overseas commodities. Hertzog was prepared to back this advantage with tariffs though they may not have had a great effect in themselves.

Industries such as clothing, textiles, and food-processing all expanded rapidly, so that their work-forces grew even more quickly than in mining. Employment in metal and engineering trebled to over 50,000 between 1932 and 1940. Some white women had already been absorbed into secretarial and factory work and many more, mostly Afrikaners, now joined them in the industrial work-force. Unlike African women, they tended to come off the land first while their families tried to hang on to a rural livelihood. They were also paid less than men and considered dextrous in using machines.

In the light of these advances for whites, the reasons for the headway made by D. F. Malan's *Gesuiwerde* (purified) National Party, founded in 1934 in protest over Fusion, are not self-evident. Three times in this century, in 1913, 1934, and (following a small 1969 breakaway) in 1982, a sizeable group of Afrikaner exclusivists have split away from Afrikaner leaders attempting to cement a broader ruling alliance. Each phase involved a battle for the hearts, minds, and pockets of Afrikaners. But despite the cyclical pattern and some intriguing similarities, it cannot simply be assumed that there was always a bedrock of uncompromising ethnic opinion seeking a political outlet. Each split requires a different kind of explanation.

Ironically, the constituencies to which Malan's party appealed—farmers, civil servants, teachers, workers, and poor whites—benefited from the economic boom after Fusion. Economists and ideologues for the gold mines certainly thought so and objected strongly to the level of taxation and state intervention. Malan, first editor of *Die Burger* and formerly in Hertzog's cabinet, had his base in the well-financed Cape provincial organization. He could attract disillusioned communities in the wool districts, savaged by the depression, drought, and dead sheep. Those wealthier Afrikaners in the western Cape who had supported *Die Burger* and Stellenbosch University helped to build an Afrikaner intellectual class. Keeromstraat in Cape Town—centre of the party offices and literary production—was also at the heart of the movement. Its arteries now included not only the far-flung rural districts but sprawling white suburbs.

The speed with which Afrikaners came from countryside to town, dispossessed by their own brethren as much as the depression, should not be underestimated. The 'civil religion' offered by Dutch Reformed Churches gave moral and social security to highly mobile and disoriented people—a means of recreating communities. Afrikaans magazines such as *Die Huisgenoot* spoke across the divide of town and country. Profusely illustrated, it became probably the most popular publication in the 1920s. The Burger Boekhandel publishers alone produced 1,100 Afrikaans books which sold 3.25 million copies over the period 1917 to 1940 (Hofmeyr, 112–13). Publications dwelt on women's role as bearers of their cultural tradition and language. Afrikaner women were newly empowered by more extensive literacy and the franchise. An inquiry into poor whiteism in the early 1930s, funded by the Carnegie Corporation in the USA, laid great stress on the deleterious effects of isolation and impoverishment on rural white women and children. The authors of the Carnegie report, largely Afrikaner academics, felt that these women no longer had the knowledge and support to fulfil their role as mothers. They argued strongly for education and social welfare in order that women might play their role as *volksmoeders* of a new and modern Afrikaner nation.

Hertzog initially won the northern provinces for Fusion. For some northern Afrikaner intellectuals, however, the compromises he had made were too much to bear. The Afrikaner Broederbond, formed in 1919 by a small group of largely urban exclusivists in the Transvaal, expanded significantly, incorporating white-collar workers and professionals. More so than the Freemasons, widespread amongst English-speakers, the Broederbond was a secret organization restricted to carefully chosen white Protestant men. Its influence behind the scenes of Afri-

kanerdom was only fully revealed later. A major foundation of
Malan's Transvaal support, it became a font of Christian
national, republican, and sometimes pro-Fascist tendencies.

The Broederbond concentrated on winning influence in educational institutions, the bureaucracy, and white trade unions.
It sought specifically to unite Afrikaners across class barriers
and opposed political alliances with non-Afrikaner organizations. The railway union was the first to espouse this position.
The Bond worked closely with Afrikaner cultural organizations
and it was responsible for a major cultural coup—the 1938 ox-
wagon trek from the Cape to Pretoria to celebrate the centenary of the Great Trek and lay the foundation stone of the
Voortrekker monument.

The imagery and language conjured by Malan's *Gesuiwerdes*
drew on a century of treks, conflict, and warfare. His movement
sought purification and cleansing from old enemies such as
mining capital, the Empire, and Smuts. To some degree, it
gained religious sanction in the Dutch Reformed Churches.
The language of Christianity was far more important to ex-
predikant Malan than to the religiously agnostic Hertzog. The
meaning of *volk* was given additional content and system by a
younger generation of ideologues, some of whom had trained
in German universities and developed the idea of *Nasionalisme
as Lewensbeskouing* (a total outlook on life). These new ethnic
nationalists confronted the poor white problem energetically.
They were not critical of capitalism, but of foreign capital.
Indeed, *Volkskapitalisme* and economic organizations designed
to enlarge the Afrikaner stake in the economy were central
projects. And to an even greater extent than Hertzog, they
argued for racial protection against the rising black tide as
much as cultural protection from the tentacles of empire.

The political loyalties of Afrikaans-speakers nevertheless
remained divided. Many stayed in the United Party. Some
Afrikaner women on the Rand were successfully organized into
trade unions, notably the Garment Workers. Its radical leaders
such as Hester Cornelius and Solly Sachs advocated socialist
ideas and tried to encourage activities which might provide its

members with an alternative social focus. Malan's nationalists gained steadily but were not yet close to electoral victory when the Second World War broke out. By a narrow majority, parliament decided in 1939 to enter the war on the allied side. Aware of the deep opposition amongst Afrikaners to fighting a war with Britain and against Germany, Hertzog first advocated neutrality, then resigned.

Segregation and Urbanization

In addition to protecting whites in the labour market, establishing controls on African political organizations, and restoring chieftaincy, Hertzog had begun to address the broader position of the African reserves and African political rights. He appointed a Native Economic Commission (NEC, 1930–2) whose report proved critical in formulating policy. The Commission's terms of reference explicitly linked the poor white problem to black urbanization and the deterioration of the reserves. Its report distilled much of the segregationist thought of the 1920s and, like SANAC in 1905, projected a far-reaching programme for the future. Incorporating the ideas of liberal segregationists in the 1920s, it sought to find a 'middle way between tying him [the native] down and trying to make of him a black European, between *repressionist* and *assimilationist* schools' (Dubow, 36).

The report was organized around a cluster of concepts evoked in the idea of 'tribe'. Africans, so the report argued, had a different mentality from Europeans, shaped not only historically but racially. They were essentially rural and their way of life emphasized continuity, subsistence, and security. The colonial peace inhibited Africans' supposed natural propensity to violence and was thus leading to a large increase in population. Africans were also perceived to suffer from a 'cattle complex', recently defined by anthropologists, which led to hoarding of cattle for religious purposes and the payment of bridewealth. Uncommercial use of cattle caused overstocking, soil erosion, and 'desert' conditions. The Commissioners felt that environmental decay and population increase were the cause of rapid urbanization which threatened to swamp the white population.

The Commission's conception of Africans not only explained the problems of the reserves but led them to a solution which was compatible with white interests. Most Africans should stay in the reserves, but these had to be developed and made ecologically safe to facilitate increased agricultural production. Development and social modernization should come from within the 'tribal' system under the chiefs. The NEC also expressed widely-held white suspicions of educated Africans, arguing that those in town were 'exiles' who had abandoned their true role of uplifting their people in the rural areas.

The report worked with the idea of racially-based cultures which should now become more congruent with separate territorial zones. Its solutions sat easily with the system of large-scale African male labour migrancy although it was not an ardent proponent of the system. The NEC minimized the effects of dispossession and lack of land for Africans and failed to recognize that it aimed to concentrate future African population growth in what were already the most densely inhabited rural districts of the country. Other observers of the reserves noted their poverty and the spread of diseases such as tuberculosis from the cities and mines. Malnutrition was also noted. Although wage income and the rural trading network appear to have solved the problem of severe famine, economic incorporation tended to restrict the range of foods available—not least milk for children.

The new segregationist thinking materialized in the Native Trust and Land Act and the Native Representation Act, passed in 1936 after ten years of tortuous negotiation within the white body politic. The crux of the legislation was that some additional land and development funds would be made available for the reserves, but Africans in the Cape would finally be removed from the common voters' roll. African political rights were envisaged in a segregated context. A new Native Trust was empowered to purchase and administer farm land with funds from the central legislature and thus make good the unfulfilled promises of the 1913 Land Act. The Act also further tightened provisions governing tenancy on farms. As a concession, Africans in the Cape were allowed to elect three white MPs on a separate roll. A Native Representative Council was established at the apex of the now widely implemented African local council system but proved to be little more than an advisory 'toy telephone' body.

The loss of the Cape vote was of limited significance by the 1930s. Enfranchisement of white women had further diluted it and the number of African voters had declined absolutely to little over 10,000 (1.2 per cent of the national total). But the issue remained important in white politics as a reminder of an alternative political route and the old Cape liberal tradition. Political groupings which differed little about the broad parameters of segregation nevertheless haggled long about the detail and language of 'native policy'. Conservative Natal English-speaking MPs such as G. Heaton Nicholls, adamantly opposed to an African franchise, helped to achieve a compromise. He was a powerful protagonist of African communalism—of going 'back to the native kraal, to the native family, to the tribe, to the tribal council'—in order to counter African demands for representation and the threat of communism (Dubow, 145). Positively formulated in this way, segregation was conceived to have ideological and moral justification and would protect Africans against further expropriation of land, the corruption of urban life, and alien ideologies. Proponents argued that it was similar to indirect rule and trusteeship which characterized British colonialism in Africa.

In addition to parliament, the South African bureaucracy was of great significance in shaping the policy, the legislative details, and everyday administration of segregation. As in many other countries, both the size and functions of the bureaucracy increased dramatically after the depression. The way that government revenues were expended in assisting white farmers was critical in sharpening divisions between farmlands and reserves. State aid to African farming, though it did increase through the programme of agricultural demonstrators, was organized separately through branches of the NAD and Transkeian Council. The scope for African employment above menial positions, except in Native Affairs and the Police, diminished as the Afrikanerization of officialdom proceeded. The NAD gained authority and became more centralized. Officials governed by proclamation and government notices which could not easily be challenged in court—one of the last refuges for constitutional opposition. Municipalities also expanded their own separate Native Affairs sections to administer urban segregation. (Education, although segregated, still remained under the same provincial inspectorates.) Other state institutions, such as Provincial Councils, the Post Office, forestry, and railways, developed their own practices which often intensified segregationist tendencies.

The 1920s and 1930s can be seen as a high point of segregation. Formal ideologies and policies were underpinned by widespread everyday racial prejudice in the language and behaviour of whites and sometimes others. Political accommodation in the rural areas, together with the difficulties of organization, stalled black national opposition. But state policy was by no means uncontested. There were alternative visions within the black and white population. Moreover, at the very moment that segregation seemed entrenched, Smuts's UP Cabinet (1939 to 1948) began to relax some of its elements. Rapid expansion in mining and industry, which may have defused opposition in the 1930s, drew more African workers to the cities. Economic demands and social fluidity during the Second World War further undermined controls over African urbanization.

Urbanization has been a continuous process in the twentieth century, but an uneven one. Censuses suggest that African urbanization was relatively slow between 1911 and 1921. Black population growth as a whole was probably retarded by the influenza epidemic in 1918 which killed up to 5 per cent of people in some districts. It increased sharply between 1921 and 1936, but by this latter date, still only 17 per cent of Africans, including migrant workers, were counted in urban areas. The most dramatic surge occurred between 1936 and

1946 when masculine predominance in the urban African population also declined noticeably. By 1946 the percentage of women in the African urban population of Johannesburg rose to 36 (139,900 out of 387,175) while about half the Africans in Port Elizabeth, Bloemfontein, and East London were now women. (The African population of Durban and Rand mining centres remained mainly male.) Up to the 1936 census the major movement to town seems to have been from the farms, but in the next decade, from the reserves. In some reserve districts, numbers remained almost stable between 1936 and 1946.

The 1923 Urban Areas Act, passed during Smuts's first premiership, gave municipalities greater powers to control movement to town with passes, segregate housing, and police African urban communities. The Act and its many subsequent amendments proved difficult to implement. Municipalities might have wanted segregation, but the Act specified that alternative housing should be built for those removed and neither ratepayers nor government proved enthusiastic about funding. City slum landlords could make money from African tenants and city traders had an interest in maintaining lucrative custom. Some employers, especially in smaller businesses without compounds, were uneasy about restrictions on the housing.

The result was that by the early 1930s legislative intent was not matched by social reality; many African people in the cities still lived outside the peri-urban locations. Domestic servants were dispersed through the white suburbs in backyard servants' quarters or *kayas*. Migrant workers lived in barracks and compounds some of which, such as Crown mines and the Municipal compound in Johannesburg, were centrally located. Slumyards abounded precisely because they diminished the cost and trouble of getting to work and provided economic opportunities for those servicing the large black working population. If women were going to make a success of brewing, they had more chance of doing so in Doornfontein's Rooiyard than in far-flung locations. By the late 1920s there were perhaps 40,000 Africans living in central Johannesburg slumyards. The population of older locations nearer to the city centre, like Alexandra and Sophiatown, where home ownership was allowed, also increased rapidly.

New peri-urban locations were initially less popular. Orlando, established in the early 1930s south-west of Johannesburg next to Klipspruit, was the node around which Soweto (acronym for South Western Townships) grew. It set the style for soulless municipal locations and its houses could not be filled despite the crush of the slumyards. But by 1940 Johannesburg's slum-clearance campaigns were under way and the flood of migrants to town had little alternative; Orlando's 5,000 properties housed 35,000 people. By the end of the Second World War, illegal squatter settlements on the urban peripheries were also absorbing large numbers of people.

African Urban and Rural Life

Black urban life in this pre-apartheid period inspired evocative novels and autobiographies. Modikwe Dikobe, one of the first black working-class novelists in South Africa, based his *Marabi Dance* on the Molefe yard, Doornfontein, in which he had lived: 'muddy as a cattle kraal' with a 'nauseating' stench of latrines and beer. In its passages, 'excrement and urine' mixed freely with 'mud and water'; in its buildings, cockroaches and rats abounded. Whole families and their tenants lived in single rooms. Peter Abrahams's *Mine Boy* and Alan Paton's *Cry, The Beloved Country* also etched images of urban squalor.

Hellmann's *Rooiyard*, one of the first systematic exercises in urban anthropology, documented the economic base of a slum in great detail. She demonstrated the importance of women's contribution to urban survival through brewing to supplement wages. As an informant explained to her, Africans 'eat from beer'. African families were not nuclear in the rural areas and the nuclear family was only one form of reconstituted family life in the cities. Many women fended for themselves and brought up children as single mothers. Powerful women who provided both financial and emotional strength in these transient communities feature strongly in writings on the slums. But brewers also lived in an enforced state of criminality.

While the details of urban poverty are clear, interpretations of its causes and implications differed. Like many white liberals and rural blacks, Paton did not support segregation but despaired of the slums—'the garbage heap of the proud city'. The power of his heart-rending novel derives not least from the contrast he drew between the romanticized decaying beauty of the countryside in rural Natal, where people could live a simple moral life, and the city which corrupted those who came within its grasp.

Dikobe, unlike Paton, does not see the slums from a distance; he sees the vibrancy and permanency of city life. In Paton's novel, liquor, the life-blood of the slumyards, breeds crime, vice, and violence. In contrast, Dikobe can celebrate the Marabi culture of music and dance that grew around the yards and shebeens (an Irish word which slid easily into urban black argot). Dikobe's heroine, in so far as he has one, is a young woman, finding her feet in town and impatient with traditions such as arranged marriages. While Paton, Hellmann, and others see urban Africans caught between two worlds—a city life which they cannot have and a rural life which they do not want—Dikobe projects a specifically African urban culture. For Hellmann, the piano in the slumyard is an example of Westernization and conspicuous consumption, a consumer item which people could not understand. For Dikobe, the piano was a cultural instrument for Africans and a means to an income for the Marabi jazz pianist in his novel.

All these works suggest a rather introspective and defensive African inner-city culture, symbolized by the necessity to post guards continuously to warn of police liquor raids. Dikobe's book is not explicitly political. Unlike Abrahams, he offers no romantic socialist view of white and black workers united, rising up to throw off the shackles of oppression. His characters interact individually with whites, some good and some bad. He describes a world of conflict. The young, turning away both from rural custom and churches, challenge the old. Christianity, witchcraft beliefs, and materialism vie with one another in the minds of his protagonists. Newly urbanized people are uncertain as to how far they should share in a consumer society where some blacks, as well as most whites, identify manufactured commodities as 'the things of the white man'. Yet Dikobe's world is a powerful statement about the vitality of inner-city black communities in a segregationist state which was trying to destroy them.

The Second World War stimulated internal industrial growth in an economy which was already diversifying rapidly. Even though the gold mines contracted somewhat after their peak of 1941, overall demand for labour grew dramatically. Of over 300,000 men mobilized for the armed forces, 186,000 were white. This was a significant proportion of the white labour force and it had to be replaced, especially in industry. When manufacturing and construction employment doubled to 330,000 between 1932 and 1939, 33 per cent of the increase was white (Hobart Houghton, in *Oxford History*). Of the further 125,000 people absorbed during the war, only 15 per cent were white. Rising real wages in manufacturing industry attracted more black people to the towns.

In the early years of the war, manufacturing overtook mining both in its share of the country's GDP and in employment. The concerns of manufacturers about new markets and a more settled labour force impinged on state policy. Smuts's government was unique in the history of the Union in that it was more English- than Afrikaans-speaking. It was certainly conservative and in broad terms committed to some form of segregation. But it was more pragmatic and more closely linked to manufacturing, commerce, and the professions than its predecessors. Jan Hofmeyr, who acquired considerable power as Smuts's deputy, was particularly open to the relatively well-organized white liberals in the South African Institute of Race Relations and in parliament.

South African politicians and bureaucrats were by no means immune to international trends in their pursuit of more systematic planning in the post-depression era. Government commissions, long important in shaping policy, were now supplemented by a Social and Economic Planning Council which explored many aspects of society. Deep concern was expressed about African poverty, crime, delinquency, and the effects of migrant labour. Hofmeyr pursued the cause of African education and moved considerable new central funds in this direction. In 1942 pass-law enforcement was relaxed temporarily in order to meet the demand for workers. The government was so worried about industrial unrest that it held down prices for key foodstuffs.

In 1944 a Commission on National Health advocated a health system on a non-racial basis which would have had enormous implications for state spending and social welfare. By 1946 the Minister of Native Affairs, no liberal, was publicly articulating the desire of manufacturing industry for a more settled labour force. This willingness to recognize some of the implications of mass urbanization was reiterated in the Fagan Commission report of 1948. Smuts did not seriously envisage extending African political rights, but state responses implied the possibility of new directions.

African national protest was muted in the early 1930s. The ANC was small and the ICU had dissolved as an organization. The Communist Party, which in 1928 had committed itself to a 'Native Republic' as the first stage of the revolution, was severely weakened by internal purges. But Hertzog's Land and Franchise Bills stimulated new attempts at organization. D. D. T. Jabavu, son of J. T., co-ordinated with the ANC to establish an All Africa Convention (AAC) in 1935. While the AAC failed in its immediate goals it prodded black ANC and Communist leaders such as J. B. Marks into calling their own national conference in 1937. Cape politicians meanwhile developed the AAC into a Non-European Unity Front.

Another important area of political advance was in union organization. Communists such as Gana Makabeni, and other socialists such as Max Gordon, revived unions in the service and small-industry sector when the economy picked up after the depression. Communists and unionists were particularly successful in organizing Indian workers in Natal from the late 1930s, attracting committed leaders like Dr Y. Dadoo. Organizers found that they had recourse to the Wage Board set up in 1925 to set minimum wages in certain sectors. It was the small African Clothing Workers, the Broom and Brush Union, and the Native Laundry Workers which were the foundations of a renewed movement. Rival co-ordinating committees were established. Most unions were organized on a racial basis, but there were a few co-ordinated strikes by black and white sections. Although the Communists committed themselves to the war effort after the end of the Nazi–Soviet Pact and were therefore hesitant to support strikes, they had particular success in launching unions amongst migrant workers in large industries such as the African Mineworkers Union under J. B. Marks.

By the end of the war, the Council of Non-European Trade Unions claimed 119 affiliates with 150,000 members. Although Africans had no statutory rights for collective bargaining and were liable to prosecution, the number of hours lost in strikes between 1940 and 1945 increased from 6,000 to 90,000 annually. Real wages for blacks in manufacturing increased during these years. Durban dock-workers staged sustained actions and the crest of the new wave of unionism was reached after the war in 1946 when inflationary pressures intensified and 70,000 African mine-workers struck for higher wages. It was the largest and longest strike by workers in this key industry. Although the solidity of the strike depended partly on the networks of migrant workers in the compounds, the Union was able to initiate and co-ordinate activities across a wide area in a way which had never before been possible. Smuts, his attention less diverted by war, resorted to his time-honoured tactic of calling in the army to break the strike.

Although the cutting edge of black politics had moved to the large cities and unions appeared to be a powerful vehicle at the vanguard of a black working class, they suffered severe set-backs after 1946. The wartime shortage of workers ended. Unions came under strong pressure from the state and the Communist Party decided to shift its priorities away from mass labour organization. At the same time, migrant workers remained fragmented and the Mineworkers Union had not struck sufficiently deep roots to survive state repression. The

Trades and Labour Council, largely the voice of organized white workers, had maintained some support for new African unionism in the war but now shifted away. The mine-workers' strike turned out to be the end of a phase of militant unionism, rather than the beginning.

Wartime political activity had many other facets. In 1943/4, the Communists directly addressed the issue of controls over black urbanization by organizing mass anti-pass protests. In 1944 one of the first major bus boycotts was launched in Alexandra township in the north of Johannesburg. The costs of transport from locations had been an issue since the beginning of urban segregation. In the 1920s and early 1930s African bus-owners dominated the urban routes and competition between them had driven costs down. But the state introduced a licensing system in 1930 which was gradually enforced to the advantage of white entrepreneurs. When they put fares up in the war, Africans responded with boycotts and many walked to work. Black transport entrepreneurs supported the protests and this alliance brought some gains in 1944.

Squatter movements also flourished. In the rural areas, the word 'squatter' was applied to tenants on farms or state land, including those initially within the law, who gave little labour to their landlord. In town, the word was applied to those who illegally took possession of land on the urban peripheries. Perhaps 90,000 people settled in squatter camps on the outskirts of Johannesburg by the late 1940s, 20–25 per cent of the city's African population. James Mpanza, a Zulu-speaking politician on the Orlando Advisory Board, led backyard subtenants in the location on to fresh ground nearby in 1944. His *Sofasonke* (we die together) movement, which included many recent immigrants from the rural areas, was perhaps named after the *Amafelandawonye*. He was able to secure recognition from the municipality and finance for a new settlement.

A spate of related movements were not always so successful. But as one leader commented: 'The Government was like a man who has a cornfield which is invaded by birds . . . He chases the birds from one part of the field and they alight in another part of the field . . . We squatters are the birds'

(Stadler, *JSAS*). In 1947 municipal attempts to establish control over trading in these areas precipitated a riot. In 1948 squatters moved to new land controlled by the council and attempted a rent boycott through the *Asinamali* (we have no money) movement. Ultimately provision of new settlements and tighter legislation undermined the squatter leaders' authority, though *Sofasonke* survived as a party in Soweto politics.

Mpanza was a charismatic populist who started his own church. Called *magebula* (slicer of land) he was a 'Messiah-cum-Chief-cum-Gangster Boss' who governed his settlement with little attention to the state. He controlled entry, issued residence permits and trading licences for a fee, administered justice, and punished misdemeanours with fines and beatings. Beer-brewing was permitted. He went about on horseback, hailed as chief; his speeches, dense with biblical allusions, included comparisons of himself to Christ. Urban squatter movements of the 1940s in many ways resembled rural movements of the 1920s, such as the *Amafela* and the ICU. Leaders intertwined both political and religious, both traditionalist and newly forged ideologies and symbols. They were particularly successful in mobilizing a female following.

The ANC, reviving in the late 1930s, received new organizational impetus under the Presidency of Dr Xuma from 1940. Although it developed some contacts with the unions and bus boycotts, its leadership was still uneasy with mass politics and the powerful language of deliverance 'amidst the hessian sacks' and corrugated iron of impoverished shack settlements. However, the 1946 strike and the squatters' movements galvanized younger men, recently moved into ANC politics on the Rand, into forming a radical group within the Congress Youth League. They included Nelson Mandela and Oliver Tambo, former students at Fort Hare. They were deeply aware of the progress of international events: the promises of the war for democracy, the moves towards Indian independence, and the surge of nationalist protest in other colonized countries like Ghana and Nigeria. By the late 1940s a plan of mass protest was being formulated.

While the urban areas were increasingly at the cutting edge

of radical politics, the rural districts were not quiescent. The Native Affairs Department, looking to work through chiefs and headmen, intervened more systematically to appoint co-operative men, sometimes precipitating conflict or storing it up for the future. In Pondoland, Transkei, where the state had reached a working relationship with the paramountcy, the government intervened in a succession dispute in 1937 and appointed Botha Sigcau, a pro-government chief, against popular feelings. Conflict over the role of chiefs remained central in rural politics and became bound up with rural protests against state intervention into African patterns of cattle-keeping and landholding.

Concern about environmental degradation in the reserves, expressed for example by the NEC, permeated official thinking. The government also felt that the success of segregation policy depended on ecological recovery. Evidence suggests that the number of cattle and sheep in reserves increased sharply in the 1920s after East Coast fever. As population grew, so did the herds: each rural homestead aimed to acquire enough cattle for milk and draught. While rising stock numbers enabled many peasant families to maintain production, they also took their toll on the land, as revealed especially in the depression and droughts of the early 1930s. By this time, officials had identified African districts which they felt required urgent attention. Programmes were instituted to fill dongas, build contour banks, and promote contour ploughing. Officials argued for a reduction in livestock numbers and (following the Drought Commission) proposed fenced paddocks where stock could be rotated through the year to increase carrying capacity and save the veld. They believed that this in turn would necessitate the removal of scattered African homesteads into villages.

These proposals were developed into a comprehensive 'Betterment' proclamation (1939) which included villagization, fencing, the separation of arable land from grazing, and provision for livestock culls. Betterment schemes changed through the years—and affected highveld communities in different ways from those on the coast—but it is not an exaggeration to say that officials planned to move millions of people. Any new

Trust land purchased for African occupation under the 1936 Act was to be planned before it could be settled. Betterment constituted one of the most far-reaching interventions into rural life since annexation, the introduction of taxes, and dipping.

When the state began to implement these policies, rural people claimed that contour banks traversed their fields, diminished their plots, and were washed away during storms. They complained that they were not consulted and that interventions, sometimes technically inadequate, were insensitive to rural social life. Little compensation was paid when people were moved into villages—the government assumed that the labour and materials which went into African hut construction were free. More than anything else, the threat of stock reduction persuaded many reserve dwellers to resist the whole range of agricultural policies. Cattle were still a key resource in the rural economy and any measure which threatened a family's capacity to build up an adequate herd for draught, milk, meat, and bridewealth would dig deep into the remaining, and waning, independence of the homesteads. Despite official arguments that stock reduction would benefit the population as a whole, individual interests were too deeply affected for it to be acceptable. Spokesmen argued that the solution was more land, not less cattle.

In the Transvaal, protests against Betterment became linked with battles by farm tenants to resist labour demands on the farms where the 1913 Land Act had not been universally enforced. In Lydenburg, eastern Transvaal, where the ICU had been active, tenants successfully countered farmers' attempts to use the 1936 Native Trust and Land Act to impose six months' unpaid labour on them. In 1939 Alpheus Maliba of the Communist Party started the Zoutpansberg Cultural Association which took on these issues. But implementation of Betterment was largely delayed till after the war and it was in the later 1940s that a wave of largely uncoordinated protests rippled through the countryside from Middledrift in the Ciskei, Mount Ayliff in the Transkei, to Witzieshoek, north of Lesotho. Rural resistance significantly delayed the Betterment and culling programme.

The Demise of Smuts

Had it not been for the war, the compromises which Hertzog and Smuts hammered out under the Fusion agreement might have lasted. Afrikaner exclusivist thinking, the tight equation of ethnicity with nation, may have been softened by the survival of a more broadly-based white party. But Hertzog's resignation from the UP sent him into the political wilderness. Many Afrikaners swung into extra-parliamentary politics, including various paramilitary groups which were either pro-Fascist or opposed the war effort. The restaged trek provided the symbolic springboard for the largest of these—the Ossewabrandwag (OB) or ox-wagon guard. Started in the rural Orange Free State, the OB spread through the country to draw support from Afrikaners across party lines. When its membership peaked at 130,000 in the Transvaal, about 60,000 were on the Rand; railway-workers were one strong source of support.

OB members wore uniforms, developed a militia, and incorporated *skietvereenigings* (shooting associations) in an echo of the commando military tradition. Smuts's commitment to the war touched the raw nerve of Afrikaner anti-imperialism and the OB organized terror groups and sabotage, including bombing, of the war effort. OB members directed a great deal of energy into the Afrikaner cultural revival: resurrecting the old trek game *jukskei*, organizing *braaivleis* (barbecue) evenings, celebrating the trek and Afrikaner motherhood. Again, such activities drew dislocated urban communities together and provided new scope for male solidarity. While the OB paralleled European Fascist movements, its form was distinctly local.

In 1943 Smuts, at the head of the UP, was able to win a wartime 'Khaki' election. Subsequently strikes, squatter movements, urban crime, and rural protests frightened many whites who felt that the government was being too liberal in its approach. The flow of Africans to the towns stimulated fears of 'swamping' which Hertzog had so assiduously fed in earlier years. Whites in Natal became obsessed with protecting urban space by restricting Indian trade and property ownership. When Smuts took on the issue of Indian representation and rights, he found even his plans for limited concessions along the lines of the Native Representation Act seemed too generous for many whites. A segment of the white population did emerge from this war for democracy believing that black aspirations had to be taken into account. But most responded to the wartime challenges from blacks by moving ideologically in the other direction. Economic stringency after the war reinforced this reaction.

Whereas Afrikaner paramilitary groupings were initially uncertain about their party loyalties, they moved towards Malan after the war. The United Party lost support in the 1948 election in the peri-urban areas, especially on the Rand: here the threat from the black working class was perceived to be especially acute. Whites coming back from the war found jobs which they considered their sphere to be occupied by blacks. It was here also that Afrikaners had been winning trade union support.

Even more important was the swing in the rural areas of the Transvaal and Orange Free State towards Malan's Cape-based Nationalists. In part this was because of the undiluted nationalist message which they offered. Despite the generosity of the United Party in the 1930s and rising agricultural prices from the mid-1940s, farmers began to doubt the United Party's commitment to their interests. Farmers felt that too much favour was being shown to urban consumers during and after the war when Smuts tried to hold down commodity prices in order to defuse urban militancy. Labour supplies were also a central issue. Mechanization of some parts of the agricultural cycle increased the land under cultivation, but farming remained highly labour-intensive. Legislation such as the Native Service Contract Act of 1932 gave farmers some legal powers to limit African mobility but they felt this was insufficient. At the same time, farmers could not compete with urban wages. The UP was neither able to solve the farm labour shortage nor to impose stringent controls on black urbanization.

Those who felt threatened found solace in the Nationalist 1948 election slogan of apartheid (apartness). Though this had not yet been closely defined, it was well known that Malan stood for more rigid segregation and white protection. But Smuts's defeat was not inevitable. Afrikaans-speakers made up about 60 per cent of the white electorate; an estimated 40 per cent of them voted for the UP and its allies. Indeed, the Nationalist victory was probably dependent on a protest vote of perhaps 20 per cent of English-speakers. Even so the United and Labour parties won 53 per cent of the votes in 1948 while the Nationalists received only 39 per cent. (Figures include estimates for uncontested seats.) Malan's victory was possible because Smuts had allowed rural and some peri-urban constituencies, where the Nationalists won a number of narrow victories, to retain their disproportionate weighting in the electoral system. By contrast, the UP won some large majorities in urban and English-speaking constituencies.

Perhaps the Nationalists would have won power soon afterwards, playing to white fears and Afrikaner cultural fervency. Smuts was old, preoccupied with international affairs, and uncertain in his policies. In contrast to the efficient Nationalists, the UP was a loose and inadequately funded coalition with few tightly organized branches. But Afrikaner unity had been difficult to achieve in the past and, without the victory of 1948 and the power which this brought, may have proved to be so again. Only in 1958 did the Nationalists win a majority of the vote and even then, if uncontested seats are included, the UP and its allies may have gained more votes.

Despite many biographies, Smuts remains an elusive figure. Except for interludes in the South African War and in opposition (1924–33), he was close to the heart of power continuously from 1898 to 1948 and a central architect of the new state. But on the one hand, he was extruded from the Afrikaner nationalist galaxy and on the other was too compromised a figure to be taken up later by white liberal or African movements. He often seemed to speak with a forked tongue and appeared more interested in efficient administration than political direction. Despite his sense of legality, he could resort to dramatic displays of armed might and air power to quell internal opposition with literal overkill.

Yet some of his legacies may be valuable: a personal sim-

plicity and asceticism; a love of nature and environmental
concern; and efficiency in government if not in party organization. His very capacity for political compromise permitted a
period of relative openness during the Second World War when
the country's more liberal whites and welfare planners briefly
had greater influence than at any other time till 1990. Even
African political leaders felt they could make some impact. His
defeat meant that his centrist and armed forces constituency
eroded rapidly.

State power in South Africa came to be dominated by a
group of whites who used the term nation narrowly to mean an
ethnically defined segment of about 12 per cent of the population. Their ruthless determination to entrench themselves over
the next four decades left a bitter legacy of suffering and social
division.

PART II

Afrikaner Power and the Rise of Mass Opposition, 1948–1992

6 Apartheid, 1948–1961

The Nationalist Mission

Striking documentary film footage records the ageing but wiry Jan Smuts descending the steps of the Union buildings in Pretoria in 1948 to take his leave following his election defeat. His place on the hill of power, in the building designed by Baker on a koppie overlooking the valley of Pretoria, was taken by D. F. Malan—for over thirty years a 'solid, conservative' nationalist. This was a moment when white politics mattered deeply. For fifty years South Africa had been ruled by men who cut their political teeth at the turn of the century in the politics of the South African War and the compromises of Union. In retrospect, they appear relatively pragmatic. But the age of the generals was over and that of the ideologues and technocrats had begun. These were men who came of age in the inter-war depression years—a time of extremes.

In very many areas, Malan's now *Herenigde* (Reunited) National Party (HNP) built its policy on the foundations of the segregationist legacy laid by Rhodes and Milner, Kruger and Shepstone, Hertzog, Smuts, and Creswell. But the Nationalist government contained new elements. It aimed to reverse the relaxation of authority by Smuts and to meet new challenges with a tighter set of racial policies. Moreover, although Malan was committed to the parliamentary process based on a white franchise, the Nationalists were increasingly prepared to stretch the system to its limits. If Smuts had been too prone to compromise, the new rulers of South Africa pursued their aims with conviction and self-righteousness. There is a book to be written about unimplemented legislation in the country but the Nationalists were, at least initially, more determined and more confident of state power than most of their predecessors.

Apartheid became so dominant a feature of life over the next forty years that it must be intrinsic to a description and understanding of this period. It gave South African society a distinctive profile and a long shadow. Although segregationist attitudes in earlier decades may have been more stringent than in many other colonies, or in the USA, they were not vastly different. Apartheid was a more intense system and increasingly jarred in an era of decolonization and majority rule. The South African government was by no means the only authoritarian regime in the world, but it rejected an all-embracing nationalism and enshrined racial distinctions—anathema in the post-holocaust and post-colonial world—at the heart of its legislative programme, and political projects. Despite many articulate exiles, it took more than two decades for international criticism to make an impact; when it did, apartheid was the issue.

Yet it is wrong to conceive of South Africa in this period simply in terms of apartheid. At its height in the 1960s, Verwoerd so closely defined his goals and so systematically attempted to engineer them that they were often mistaken for reality. Angry black autobiographers and anguished white academics highlighted racial prejudice, poverty, the formidable legislative programme, and the contorted social results of apartheid. But important changes were taking place which, though influenced by state policy, should not simply be subsumed in a discussion of apartheid. One was population growth; another was African urbanization. Apartheid was in part designed to control urbanization and its ultimate failure to do so has played a central role in the demise of the policy. The related erosion of old communities and ways of life on the land was traumatic, even if it was hardly new or unique to South Africa. With ever greater finality, the bulk of the population was sucked into modes of living which demanded new forms of consumption. As blacks lost their rural ballast, so the social and class divisions both within their communities and the society as a whole were further recast.

Although the classic colonial commodities of gold, minerals, raw materials, and crops continued to dominate exports, the country was becoming a medium-sized industrial power, like Australia, Korea, Mexico, or Brazil, with a great range of domestic manufactures. It was served, sometimes savaged, by an elaborate and ever more diverse bureaucracy. Ox-wagons had given South Africa an enormous advantage in communications over the rest of Africa at the turn of the century. Now road, rail, telecommunication, and air networks—though they were not universally accessible—continued to distinguish it on the continent. The Nationalists liked to think of the country in these terms: a conservative but modern industrial, capitalist, western-oriented nation. It was not quite that. Yet some of the features of the social and economic landscape delineated in the apartheid era might remain even when the system finally goes. At issue for many historians and social scientists considering this period has been the link between industrialization, modernization, and the repressive racial order (Chapters 7 and 8).

This chapter focuses on the more immediate impact of the Nationalist government. A powerful strand in the writing about Afrikaners emphasizes their preoccupation with their own nationhood and identity, rather than their policy towards blacks.

If there was any dominant ideology it was one that stressed the values of *volkseenheid* (unity), which transcended class or regional (the North–South antagonism) differences, and *volksverbondenheid*, the notion that the realization of the full human potential comes not from individual self-assertion but through identification with and service of the *volk*. (Adam and Giliomee, 116)

Malan and his successors were indeed deeply committed to unity, anti-imperialism, and anti-communism. But the rhetoric of cultural solidarity sat easily with racial exclusivity and the use of ethnic power for economic gain.

Nationalist politicians did not have a complete blueprint when they arrived in office in 1948. The way in which their legislative programme unfolded over the decades was influenced by contending interests in the party, by contingencies, crises, and the pattern of opposition. From the outset, the meaning of apartheid was disputed. Some intellectuals held by the chimera of total separation, including economic separation, dispensing as far as possible with black labour. More pragmatic views, not in themselves uncontested, always dominated. Farmers, for a start, could not conceive of managing without black workers. But the purists were influential in maintaining ideological goals and justifications. These tensions were often creative—contributing to a complex political ideology which could both be a creed for followers and remain attuned to the changing interests of support groups and opponents.

Succeeding Prime Ministers also modified policy. D. F. Malan, the architect of revived Afrikanerdom, was rooted in the Cape movement. He is usually characterized as a man concerned most with Afrikaner identity and culture. Nevertheless, his commitment to segregating coloured people in the Cape and other early racial legislation set the parameters for apartheid and resulted in acute political tension in his period of office. He was also pressed by more extreme interests in the party to appoint Verwoerd as Minister of Native Affairs in 1950. Malan was succeeded on his death by J. G. Strydom (1954–8), the 'lion of the north', an adept politician and skilled populist speaker, representing powerful Transvaal factions including white workers and farmers. He was less cautious in articulating the ideology of race and republic.

Apartheid in its broader conception has increasingly become associated with H. F. Verwoerd. As Minister of Native Affairs from 1950 and Prime Minister from 1958 to 1966, he dominated policy towards Africans. Partly educated in Germany, Verwoerd had been a professor of Psychology at the University of Stellenbosch before he moved north in 1937 as editor of *Die Transvaler*. Fiercely ambitious and inexhaustible, he became a republican and Broederbonder, but retained the sociological approach and language honed in his academic years. His concern for logical explanation, systematic theory, and social engineering—'a single constructive plan'—was the hallmark of his approach. He was one of those ideologues who had shifted away from the language of *baasskap* to mould apparently more justifiable notions of separate cultures, nations, and 'homelands'. 'Natives' became Bantu, a word derived from Xhosa/ Zulu for 'people'; apartheid became 'separate development'.

Whatever apartheid came to mean, party statements and documents over many years agreed on the irreducible aims of the 'maintenance and protection' of Afrikanerdom, white power, and the white race. Even if biological racism was not explicitly part of Nationalist rhetoric, its crude assumptions suffused everyday white language. Nationalist politicians were far more ready to exploit white fears of what was called 'miscegenation'. The killing blow in a political argument was, put delicately: would you let your daughter marry a black man? A staunch Afrikaner republican admitted 'that he was better able to raise money for the party by mentioning the fact that white women were dancing with black men in Cape Town, than by stressing the republican issue' (Moodie, *Afrikanerdom*, 250). Hostility to 'miscegenation' addressed the formal concerns about racial electoral power which might be diluted by the long-term arithmetic of mixing. It played on deeply set notions of purity, especially that of white women, and Social Darwinist fears that mixing would result in racial decline.

Such concerns quickly materialized in legislation: the Mixed Marriages Act (1949) and the Immorality Act (1950) which prohibited marriage and extramarital sex across racial bound- aries. It was not unusual for white men, including Afrikaner men in the rural areas, to have sex with black women. These relationships often expressed patriarchal domination over ser- vants and other subordinated women rather than mutual affec- tion. Legal controls in this sphere partly reflected a desire for social discipline of whites who strayed from the fold. But black women could also suffer harshly and unfairly from conviction. Court cases attracted wide publicity, especially from English- language newspapers which ridiculed snooping policemen who sought evidence for conviction by feeling beds (for warmth) in early-morning house raids. Relationships across colour lines were a central theme for critical novelists because they encap- sulated in a personal narrative some of the country's most dramatic social tensions.

In 1950 the Population Registration Act provided for compulsory racial classification on a national register. Documents would be issued to all stating their racial group; a Race Classification Board would adjudicate disputed cases. This insistence on ascription by race which increasingly determined public and private rights, as well as highly intrusive state regulation, seemed to epitomize the archaic imperatives of Afrikanerdom.

Legislation and Reaction

The HNP's apartheid edifice can be conceived as resting on seven pillars: starker definition of races; exclusive white participation and control in central political institutions (and repression of those who challenged this); separate institutions or territories for blacks; spatial segregation in town and countryside; control of African movement to cities; tighter division in the labour market; and segregation of amenities and facilities of all kinds from universities to park benches. Politicians insisted that there were only two alternatives: integration and the submersion of whites; or the increasingly elaborate system of apartheid.

In the early stages of their legislative journey, the Nationalists had very real concerns about their capacity to maintain power. They rapidly Afrikanerized the state both to provide jobs and to ensure a pliant bureaucracy. Key English-speakers in spheres such as the army, military intelligence, the South African Railways and Harbours, broadcasting, African administration, and the economic bureaucracy were sidelined or retired. An explicit attempt was made to fill Native Affairs posts with Broederbond members or party supporters. Afrikaners were gradually appointed to top posts in the rapidly expanding civil service; few English-speakers saw this as a career. The ethos of public service became more closely identified with the Nationalist project.

Neither was their parliamentary position, resting initially on a minority of the white vote, secure; in 1953 the vote for the opposition parties, at about 54 per cent, remained stable. A variety of manœuvres were designed to entrench control, including new white seats in Namibia and, in an echo of Krugerite politics, delays on citizenship for immigrants. Most important, the Nationalists removed coloured voters—at about 50,000, more than the total of African voters in 1936—from the common roll.

Coloured people, perhaps the most likely potential allies had whites offered them full political rights, were amongst the primary victims of the early apartheid years. In poorer Cape suburbs, 'racial' barriers remained relatively porous; coloured people occupied common residential areas along the Peninsula's Main Road. Nationalists had agitated for their segregation since the 1930s. Classification under the Population Registration Act caused enormous confusion and misery, with many uncertain cases and split families. There was no possible geographic 'homeland' for coloured people and it was difficult to develop a discourse of separate nationhood for the Cape's working class. Nevertheless, the Nationalists were so obsessed with making 'race' and nation congruent that they explicitly set out to intensify coloured self-awareness: 'one can only hope to succeed if one develops that sense of national awareness and that sense of pride in himself and his people'. They hoped to win support by giving preference to coloured people over Africans in the employment markets of the western Cape.

The policy of separation was driven especially hard down the long and tortuous route to disenfranchisement. Malan argued that South African parliamentary sovereignty was no longer restricted by the entrenched status of the Cape franchise clause in the 'Imperial' South Africa Act. In 1951 the Separate Representation of Voters Act passed through parliament: coloured people were to have four elected white representatives. With typical insensitivity, given the severe problems of alcoholism amongst the Cape working class, the Minister of Interior, Dönges, likened this to four full bottles of wine rather than fifty-five empties.

The Act sparked a wave of protest amongst both whites and blacks which alongside the Defiance Campaign was perhaps the most widespread in the early apartheid years. Mass white opposition may seem surprising in that the UP had proposed only to protect, not extend, the existing vote and did not allow coloured people to become full party members. But the UP clearly had some electoral self-interest in defending the franchise. Moreover, many of its supporters were ex-servicemen who had fought the war for democracy against Fascism. Even if their version of democracy for blacks was etiolated, they saw the 'rule of law' and constitutionalism as part of a distinctly British and civilized heritage. Many Nationalists had openly supported Fascism or had not fought in the war. They were now going beyond 'constitutional political conduct and solemn promises made to coloured people at the time of Union'—the compromises which salved the consciences of English-speaking white South Africans.

White anger found its outlet in the War Veterans' Torch Commando which organized motorcades, rallies, and dramatic torchlight processions in 1951. The symbolism of the movement was peculiar in that it evoked the commando and Fascist torchlight parades rather than dominion parliamentarianism. Perhaps this was one last attempt to capture icons which might appeal to the mass of Afrikaans-speaking South African whites. The Torch Commando agreed to put its efforts into the re-election of the UP in 1953 and when that failed the movement dissipated. The white opposition was soon to fragment. The UP, uncertain and compromised in its policy, lost support first to the right. In 1959 its liberal wing broke away as the Progressive Party. In 1953 a more radical Liberal Party had been formed while some of the white left allied with the Congress movement. The white Labour Party faded away along with its English-speaking working-class constituency.

Black protests were more splintered. A Communist Party and Congress-linked Franchise Action Committee (FRAC) did organize large rallies in Cape Town, as well as a strike, but the Torch Commando refused to co-ordinate activities with it. FRAC aimed not to defend the constitution, but to extend the franchise and the Congress alliance soon shifted its concern towards the Defiance Campaign. The Cape-based Unity movement (NEUM), with a strong following amongst both coloured and African teachers, pursued a strategy of total boycott rather than confrontation and were also unable to find sufficient common ground for an alliance with FRAC. Their influential local paper, the *Torch*, maintained a scathing commentary on South Africa's 'herrenvolk' rulers.

The main organization of coloured voters, acting with the UP and white liberal lawyers, challenged the Act in court and succeeded in having it invalidated by a relatively liberal Appellate Division. An unprecedented and bitter constitutional crisis was only resolved when Strydom succeeded in passing the Act with a two-thirds majority in 1956 after packing the Senate with nominated supporters. New judges were appointed to the Appellate Division. In the 1960s the government pushed coloured representation further towards the African pattern by removing the four white seats and creating a separate Coloured Council with some control over local government. The euphemistically named Prohibition of Improper Political Interference Act of 1967 outlawed most political activity across racial lines.

A parallel issue peaked in the Nationalist drive finally to segregate the railways in the early 1950s. Effective separation on mainline passenger trains was long entrenched, but station platforms and suburban trains in the Cape were not so tightly controlled. Increased usage of first-class carriages by black people at a time when some suburbs were being Afrikanerized irked Nationalists who decided to bring Cape Town into line. The language of racial inferiority and exclusion was used as unselfconsciously in this debate as it was on the franchise question. One politician argued that mixing on the railways might make South Africa like another Brazil. Brief encounters at railway station cafés were unlikely to have produced many 'mixed' marriages, but the sentiment expressed the stark alternatives in Nationalist thinking. Blacks were excluded from the main concourses of the new Johannesburg and Cape Town stations; ticket offices, platforms, subways, and bridges as well as carriages were racially reserved.

Railway segregation was significant beyond the station gates. Challenges to these rules in court, co-ordinated by the ANC, produced another anti-apartheid legal victory. In 1953 the Appellate Division asserted the principle (not enforced before) that while separation of facilities was legal, this should not result in substantial inequality. The government restored its freedom of action with the Reservation of Separate Amenities Act (1953) which allowed separate and unequal public amenities. The resulting 'petty apartheid' came to symbolize the Nationalist project in South Africa: the highly noticeable reservation of swimming pools, buses, park benches, beaches, post office counters, and many other facilities for whites. Signs saying 'whites only/*blankes alleen*' multiplied, a favoured target of opposition cartoonists and foreign photographers. Intriguingly, while some shops such as liquor outlets were segregated, many remained unregulated and served a mixed clientele.

Spatial division of urban residential areas was central to Nationalist aims. Africans had been effectively removed from many city centres, but some suburban freehold areas such as Sophiatown in Johannesburg remained under black occupation. Coloured and Indian communities were dispersed widely through city-centre zones. To the metaphors of disease and racial purity were added the languages of slum clearance, urban planning, and strategic control of internal enemies. Post-war planning was nearly as ambitious in the urban as in the rural areas (Chapter 5). As in Europe, where modernist visions and Second World War bombs ravaged inner cities, the poor were to be rehoused in purpose-built accommodation on city outskirts. There they were seen to be more easily controlled and would impact less on sanitized business centres remodelled for the car.

Durban had been wracked by conflict over Indian property ownership in the 1940s; its growing Indian population found that properties were available near the centre as whites moved to the suburbs. White protests led to the Pegging Act (1943) which restricted Indian purchase and Asiatic Land Tenure Act (1946) which envisaged strict racial zoning for urban expansion, using rivers and ridges as buffers. Cape Town's planners recommended the wholesale demolition of the centrally located District Six, by then a largely coloured area, to be replaced by roads, commercial zones, and new housing.

All these plans prefigured the policies pushed through under the Group Areas Act (1950) and the Prevention of Illegal Squatting Act (1951) which allowed racial zones to be defined and people to be moved between them. Once the Group Areas Board was established its enormous powers to expropriate property and enter the real-estate market provided a new momentum to urban segregation. Building firms and developers, some with inside knowledge, could purchase expropriated houses cheaply, improve them, and sell them off as whitewashed cottages to whites. Elsewhere, land was cleared and sold for new housing and office developments. Escalating from the mid-1950s, Group Areas impacted most on coloured and Indian people—an estimated 600,000 were removed over three decades as Cape Town and Durban were pulled apart and reassembled to conform to the new pattern. District Six lost around 60,000 people and many Victorian buildings were also destroyed. By the 1970s it was a city-centre wasteland dotted with a few churches and mosques and fringed by new highways; its reoccupation remains a politically charged issue.

Some of the most dramatic early removals, such as the destruction of Johannesburg's Sophiatown, also affected African people. Black freehold tenure had been established there for decades and it was not subject to the same array of regulations as the municipal locations. A wide cross-section of people lived there including black politicians and writers, such as Dr Xuma and Can Themba. It was the stamping-ground of Trevor Huddleston, the Anglican minister who became a central figure in the British anti-apartheid movement and initiated the musical career of Hugh Masekela. Sophiatown was a crucible of new black urban music, far more influenced by American jazz, which replaced Marabi. Like District Six in Cape Town, it was also a world of shebeens and gangs.

Sophiatown's racy, hard-drinking urban style, which attracted many of the young writers and intellectuals of the 1950s, was captured in *Drum* magazine. A weekly, financed and edited by whites, *Drum* nevertheless managed to find 'the black hand upon it'. It became a focus for a black journalistic revival and 'for readers who thought and spoke in jazz and exclamation marks' (Sampson, *Drum*). Sophiatown epitomized the urban African culture anathema to apartheid. It was displaced by the new brick bungalows of the white suburb Triomf. In the longer term, most black people came to live on the outer peripheries of cities, separated from white areas by industrial zones, open spaces, or highways. As in so much of apartheid practice, justified in that it would reduce 'friction' to the benefit of all, whites were beneficiaries; in the first two decades of Group Areas, only 2 per cent of those moved were white. Moving people about became a major preoccupation of apartheid planners.

Successive pieces of legislation impacted on an ever wider circle of people. Dr Xuma, who had helped place the ANC on a more stable organizational basis but remained cautious in his approach, was voted out of the presidency in 1949. The Congress Youth League pushed through a Programme of Action which aimed to generate a mass movement through confrontational protests, boycotts, and passive resistance. Communist activists, their party banned in 1950, put their weight behind mass action through the Congress movement. The Communist Party was especially important in cementing ties between the ANC, the Natal Indian Congress, and white radicals in the Congress of Democrats—partly as a response to the Durban riots of 1949, when Indian traders were attacked by Africans.

The Congress movement, although organized in racial groups, emerged as the most effective national non-racial leadership in the early 1950s, deeply conscious of the need for greater unity, a wider support base, and for the identification of popular issues. Its new strategy found focus in the Defiance Campaign of 1952 where unjust laws were to be breached by groups inviting arrest. The idea of filling the gaols was hardly successful in that little over 8,000 people were arrested. But the Campaign enhanced solidarity amongst committed supporters and gave Congress a sharper public profile. It echoed Gandhi's strategies of controlled confrontation by symbolic challenges to entrenched hierarchies and restricted spaces—including white railway carriages. Congress membership, probably less than

5,000 when Xuma left, soared to about 100,000 and the regional committees did succeed in working better together.

For the first time, the ANC seemed capable of becoming a mass movement. Its ideologues reflected the central concerns of anti-colonial struggles about freedom and succeeded in instilling the idea with meanings appropriate to its different constituencies. In 1955 an Assembly of the People met in Johannesburg to agree on a Freedom Charter. This committed the Congress movement to a non-racial democracy, equal opportunities for all people, and some redistribution of wealth. The programme remained at the heart of Congress campaigning for many years.

Apartheid, Labour Control, and the Homelands

In addition to the spatial division of the urban population by racial category, apartheid planners saw it as essential to protect white workers from competition, to control African movements to town and also their position in the labour market. The government greatly impeded radical worker organization through the Suppression of Communism Act (1950). Segregated procedures were formally set up for disputes involving Africans, and strikes by African workers were banned.

In many spheres of manufacturing white workers, who did not have as tight racial protection as in the mining industry, found their monopolies of skill eroded in the post-war period. In a series of splits and reamalgamations, at a time when anti-communist rhetoric was especially strong, white unions broke away from the less racially exclusive Trades and Labour Council and moved increasingly towards a policy of racial definition of jobs. Legislation in 1956 and 1959 reserved a far wider range of jobs for whites only. In some areas, blacks could be barred from skilled work in the clothing industry or prevented from becoming traffic cops. Black workers were not allowed to have authority over whites. Unions with white and coloured workers were required to have separate branches and a white executive. There is no doubt that together with the availability of state employment, job reservation cut white unemployment and poor whiteism sharply. Elements in the new Trade Union Congress of South Africa (TUCSA) did attempt to keep some contact with black workers. But the Congress movement set up its own South Africa Congress of Trade Unions (SACTU).

Some academics in the 1970s saw the maintenance of the migrant labour system as a centre-piece of apartheid. Migrant labour, they argued, had proved cheap for the mining industry because employers did not have to pay a wage which would support a whole urban family. Now the government hoped to extend its benefits to the growing manufacturing sector. In order to do so effectively, Wolpe suggested, the Nationalists wished to restore the crumbling economies of the African reserves, but this was insufficient in itself. Tight 'influx' controls were designed to check urban growth and inhibit the development of a black urban working class. Some industry would be moved away from the cities. Labour-hungry commercial farmers would benefit as workers would be bottled up in the rural areas. An extension of migrancy would also help protect white workers.

Mine owners certainly remained committed to migrancy. Their labour supplies were threatened as the economy grew after the 1930s depression and competition with industry and agriculture became more intense. In response, the Chamber of Mines adopted its previously favoured strategy of extending the range of recruiting activities rather than increasing wages. From 1932, when 'tropical' recruitment was again permitted, WNLA developed its activities in Zambia, Malawi, Angola, Tanzania, Zimbabwe, and Botswana, all lower-wage areas than South Africa. William Gemmill, the Chamber's labour 'czar', pursued a long-term strategy of investment in road and air networks, rest camps, and medical facilities in these territories.

By 1960 the mines employed about 75,000 'tropical' workers as well as roughly 80,000 from southern Mozambique and 50,000 from Lesotho and Swaziland so that well over 60 per cent of the black labour force were 'foreign' (Figure 2). The Chamber's South African black work-force, though declining slightly, was also employed on a migrant basis from African reserves and continued to live in giant single-sex compounds.

The mines were clearly committed in their policy documents to maintaining the 'traditional' role of South African reserves.

The test for the government, however, was the manufacturing sector where total employment had overtaken mining in the 1940s. By the 1950s African employment alone in industry exceeded that in mining (Chapter 7). The state faced a dilemma. Unlike the mines, the bulk of industrial establishments, many of them small enterprises, were not geared to receive migrant workers. Some manufacturers were convinced that they needed a more skilled and stable work-force with lower job turnover. Yet the areas in which industries expanded—the Rand, Durban, Cape Town, and Port Elizabeth—were precisely those which the government hoped to protect. Moreover, the proportion of women and of black families in these cities was rising.

In examining the government's response to these problems, scholars have diverged somewhat from the argument that apartheid simply involved an extension of the migrant-labour system and industrial decentralization. They have detected a more compromised policy involving an attempt to divide urban African 'insiders' from rural migrant 'outsiders'. Section 10 of the 1952 Urban Areas Act (one of a number regulating African movements and rights), which specified who was permitted to live and work freely in towns, became a critical instrument of this policy.

In order to qualify, Africans had to show either that they were born in town; or that they had worked continuously for one employer for ten years; or that they had lived in town for fifteen years. Spouses, unmarried daughters, and sons under 18 could also qualify. All others were obliged to register as work-seekers within seventy-two hours of coming to town. If employment could not be found they would be 'endorsed out'. For the first time a systematic attempt was made to incorporate women on a national basis in the web of legislation controlling African movements. State-regulated labour bureaux were established in the rural areas and smaller towns to oversee the flow of workers.

While these laws made it difficult for new families to establish themselves legally in town, they did not remove rights for those who had come before or even during the war. Those who qualified could benefit from preferential access to housing, services, and employment. Thus apartheid in its earlier years was certainly intended to keep many black people as migrants. But it was also an attempt at 'labour differentiation' and control of further African urbanization rather than a wholesale drive to extend migrancy.

It is also important to stress that these laws were only very partially successful. They required a huge bureaucratic and police effort. Xuma protested that 'flying squads, pick-up vans, troop-carriers, and mounted police are all abroad irritating and exasperating Africans by indiscriminately demanding passes . . . handling them in an insulting and humiliating way' (Posel, 123). Resentment at the 'dompas' was powerfully expressed in a march of 20,000 women, organized by the Congress-linked Federation of South African Women, on the Union Buildings in Pretoria in 1956. Nevertheless, by the early 1960s nearly 600 labour bureaux were created. Four million men and 3.6 million women had been issued with new pass books. Convictions under the influx control laws increased from 164,324 in 1952 to a staggering 384,497 in 1962—a total of three million in ten years—with hundreds of thousands of foreigners deported. Raids were stepped up in politically sensitive areas or after riots and protests.

Even these measures had only a limited effect on the rate of growth of the African urban population. Between 1936 and 1946, the annual average increase was 3.4 per cent. Between 1946 and 1951 the rate averaged 6.6 per cent per annum, though this figure is probably exaggerated because the definition of 'urban areas' in the latter census was extended. From 1951 to 1960 the rate of increase fell slightly to 4.5 per cent annually; that of African women fell from 8.5 to 5.4 per cent. But the pace of growth was still far faster than the heights reached under previous governments which were less restrictive in their approach. Influx control was no more than a partial holding operation. The number of Africans in urban areas increased from 2.3 million to 3.4 million in the 1950s, from 27.2

to 31.8 per cent of the total African population. Many people braved arrest and continued to come to town 'illegally'.

The government hoped that it would achieve relatively full employment amongst those Africans permitted to live as families in town. They would therefore simultaneously meet the demand of industry for a more settled labour force and address the acute problems of urban poverty, housing shortages, crime, and delinquency which had been so marked in the 1940s. Rather than providing services in the cities, population and unemployment would be externalized to the reserves where, in theory, 'separate development' would absorb them. This hope was not realized: high unemployment persisted; urban gangs such as the Russians, the *tsotsi* phenomenon, and delinquency flourished. The ANC's expansion also partly reflected that of the burgeoning city population.

Moreover, while some industrialists associated themselves with the view that migrant labour inhibited productivity and that low wages constrained the growth of an internal market, many firms drew on rural migrants whom they saw as cheaper. The large market for domestic servants was increasingly supplied by African women from the rural areas. Migrant workers themselves continued to shape the labour market—for example in the way that networks from particular districts tried to ensure that they were replaced by men or women from home. State regulation of the labour market proved only partly successful.

Another piece in the complex jigsaw of social engineering—closely related to employment—was the Bantu Education Act (1953). Education-funding and administration was removed from missions and provincial authorities and taken under central control within Bantu Administration under the iron hand of Dr W. Eiselen, Verwoerd's Secretary of Native Affairs. Education at the 5,000 or so mission schools produced, in Nationalist eyes, an academic training with too much emphasis on English and 'dangerous liberal ideas'. It was seen as the foundation of an African élite which claimed recognition in a common society. Now African vernacular languages, which would cement ethnic awareness in African children, would be more extensively used as the medium of instruction up to

Standard 6 (the eighth year of schooling). In higher classes, Afrikaans as well as English was to be used. Bantu Education also confirmed pre-apartheid tendencies towards more technical education and greater central control over syllabuses. By 1958 it was so large an enterprise that it became a separate department of state. Condemned as 'education for barbarism', it hit at the most articulate section of the African population. Critics saw it as a measure for retribalization which would produce a cheap but not entirely illiterate labour force. The large gap in expenditure on black and white children persisted and confirmed the worst suspicions.

Yet a striking feature of the system was the increase in educational provision for blacks in these years from about 800,000 school places in 1953 to 1,800,000 in 1963; numbers expanded even more rapidly afterwards. Even though there was gross underfunding and very many still did not get beyond the first four years of schooling, the proportion of students at secondary level gradually rose. School attendance was not yet compulsory or free, but many black families chose to stay in the system and make of it what they could. Teachers were often underqualified, but some schools were able to dilute the central directives—for example by not teaching in Afrikaans. The consequences of Bantu Education and more widespread literacy were to be far less predictable than either its planners or its opponents expected.

As far as possible Bantu Education was to take place in homelands as territorial separation became increasingly central to policy. 'We have the choice of giving the whites their own territory and the Bantu theirs,' Malan argued, 'or of giving everybody one state and seeing the Bantu govern.' In 1951 the Bantu Authorities Act prepared the way for a new system of local and regional government in the reserves which remodelled the old councils and elevated chiefs. During Malan's premiership, the Tomlinson Commission examined ways of developing the homelands economically within the parameters of apartheid.

Tomlinson's report (1956) strongly supported the Betterment policy in order to combat soil erosion and underpin agricultural expansion, but advocated 'economic units' of land for a limited number of African farmers who would become a 'farmer class'. This implied moving large numbers of people off the land. As apartheid policy precluded their absorption in established cities, they would be housed in urban zones within the home-lands. Decentralized industries would then be encouraged on the borders of the homelands. Fragmented reserve lands would gradually be consolidated through the purchase of land under the Trust. Thus while Tomlinson retained the old concerns of the NEC about agricultural development and retribalization, the proposals for consolidation, industrialization, and urbani-zation in the homelands went beyond earlier thinking. The report was less concerned with underpinning migrancy than with creating 'viable' homelands and preventing movement to cities.

Verwoerd accepted only limited parts of the strategy. He rejected concentration of landholding because it would under-mine the chiefs on whom the Bantustan strategy depended and precipitate even more rapid urbanization. Direct investment by white-owned firms into the homelands was precluded so that Africans could develop separately 'at their own pace'. Not only would this protect communal resources and local African entrepreneurs, but it answered critics who feared that home-land industries might undercut those employing white workers in established industrial areas.

By the late 1950s, with three election victories under their belt, the government's hold on power was more certain and parliamentary opposition neutralized. Ideologues in the Broe-derbond who advocated more thorough separation were in the ascendant. Verwoerd himself was deeply perturbed by the forces of African nationalism on the continent and resolved to push through the homeland policy as a means of internal decolonization. Dropping the distinction between 'tribal' and 'detribalized' Africans, Nationalists stressed 'the fundamental ethnic unity of Africans in the urban and rural areas'. Despite the rapid growth of urban townships these were now conceived as outposts of the homelands, the latter being the base of new nations.

Whatever the language of the government, their strategy clearly aimed to defuse the growing challenge of national and urban political movements. Whites from very diverse back- grounds were to be one group with one territory, while blacks with similar recent histories were to become a series of separate minority nations. There was to be no English homeland in Grahamstown and Durban; no Jewish in Sea Point. But there were to be Xhosa homelands in the Ciskei and Transkei, a Zulu homeland in Natal, Tswana in the fragmented zones which became Bophuthatswana, Pedi in Lebowa, Shangaan in Gazankulu, and others in more minuscule pockets of land (see Map 2).

The partial survival of old chiefdoms with land in communal tenure and distinct languages did of course provide some basis to the proposed balkanization. And in attempting to restore African chieftaincy as a means of decentralizing power to a conservative rural élite, officials were trying to rebuild rather than reinvent the institution. Through the 1950s, government anthropologists and black information officers scoured the reserves collecting genealogies and attempting to establish the legitimate incumbents of new Tribal Authorities. As Harold Macmillan was talking about the winds of change in parliament in Cape Town in 1960, other winds were blowing through African reserves. Bowler-hatted, dark-suited ministers were helicoptered in to wax eloquent in deliberately archaic language about the virtues of progress through tradition.

Whatever other interests it had in the restoration of chief- taincy, the state took the symbolic side quite seriously and sought some consistency on this question. 'Dear Mr' or 'Dear Sir' had already been abolished by the Native Affairs Depart- ment in letters to Africans before the Nationalists came to power to be replaced by 'Greetings!'. Chiefs were addressed by their African praise names. Leopard skins, neo-traditionalist insignia, made frequent appearances at the installation of chiefs. The Minister of Bantu Education instructed his officials 'not to greet Bantu people by shaking hands'. Part of the reason was to protect officials 'against tendencies towards social equal- ity' but part was also due to a belief that Africans did not traditionally shake hands—an issue which had confused whites since the nineteenth century. (Bishop Colenso was instructed not to shake hands with the Zulu.)

The state's obsession with African chieftaincy fitted quite neatly with the peculiar mix of ideology which characterized Afrikaner views of themselves: a celebration of the *volk* married with a determined sense that this could prosper along with technical advance in an industrial state. Segregationists in previous decades, and particularly those involved in the NEC of 1930–2, had done much of the ideological work necessary to square developmentalist ideas with traditional forms in relation to African societies. Now the government was taking these insights and prescriptions to their logical conclusion. While most British colonial states began broadening the range of African representation at the centre instead of narrowing it, and sought to court and contain the new urban élite, the South African state seemed to be moving in the opposite direction, even though its African urban classes were proportionately larger than in British colonies. Governor Arden Clarke was handing over to Nkrumah in Ghana at the moment that Verwoerd was beginning to discover Kaiser Matanzima in the Transkei.

The central state was not totally isolated in its mission. As in the 1920s, some chiefs and ambitious local politicians pushed the government hard to deliver on its fulsome rhetoric about the virtues of African self-rule. There was considerable promise for them in places like the Transkei or Kwazulu. They saw homelands as a means of coming to terms with white power, of getting whites off their backs, and of participating in the scramble for expanding political and economic resources on the South African periphery (Chapter 8).

In the late 1950s the Bantustan strategy, which the government increasingly used to justify restrictions elsewhere, became central to opposition as well as government politics. In Sekhu-khuneland, later the eastern Transvaal homeland of Lebowa, rural resistance to rehabilitation and Bantu Authorities found support from the ANC-influenced migrant workers' movement *Sebatakgomo*. In Zeerust, western Transvaal, women led a sustained protest against passes. In both areas, support was mobilized in favour of popular claimants to the chieftaincy against those seen to collaborate with the government. Though some rural people were renouncing chieftaincy, many still saw the institution as having the potential to represent them and stave off unwanted interventions. Women again took a central role in the protests that swept through rural Natal in 1959 and 1960.

Probably the most sustained protest took place in eastern Pondoland in 1960. Pondoland, with close to half a million people, was divided into eastern and western zones. Chief Poto, who inherited the western paramountcy as a youth in 1918, learned how to cope with the political brinkmanship which the role demanded. He was in favour of elements of tradition but a strong Christian. He supported enhanced powers for chiefs, but opposed balkanization of the country. Although he agreed to Betterment in his area, he managed to retain popular support through the troubled 1950s.

In contrast, Botha Sigcau's chieftaincy in eastern Pondoland had been disputed since his installation in 1938. In the 1950s he sided with the authorities in their homeland policy. Disputes escalated about popular access to forests for firewood, about Betterment, plantations, and coastal grazing lands. As power was devolved to the unpopular paramount, so his opponents argued that he had 'sold the people to the government'. His councillors were burnt out and a few killed. The government sent in the police and army, gunning down people at a mass meeting in Lusikisiki. Rebel leader Solomon Madikizela was a peasant and Methodist evangelist for whom legitimate chieftaincy and a measure of local independence remained central aims. But rebels did link up with Congress in Durban and were driven to a position where they began to ask for arms. There seemed again to be the potential for an anti-colonial struggle linking nationalists and peasants, town and countryside.

Sharpeville and the Republic

Rural rebellions alerted African Nationalist politicians such as Govan Mbeki, who later wrote *The Peasants' Revolt*, to the potential of this neglected constituency. The new President of the ANC, Albert Luthuli, was himself rurally based. But the largely urban leadership did not always find it easy to harness localized and sometimes particularist impulses in these movements. The late 1950s had in any case been a difficult period for the ANC. Attempts to extend its political strategies through boycotts and worker stayaways were hampered by bannings and imprisonment. SACTU remained relatively small. Its more successful strikes, such as at the Amato textile factory on the East Rand where it was particularly strong, were insufficient to provide the Congress-linked federation with a powerful national presence. The lengthy trial staged by the government, in which many Congress politicians were accused of treason, sucked in the energies of its leaders and lawyers despite their acquittals. Luthuli's balanced leadership and moral authority could not secure unity. Just as a broad political front incorporating urban women and rural rebels seemed attainable between 1958 and 1960, the Pan Africanist Congress (PAC), impatient with white and left-wing influences in the Congress alliance, broke away, dividing opposition and tearing at popular loyalties.

Espousing a militant Africanism the PAC, formed early in 1959 under Sobukwe, attempted to inject new urgency into campaigning and upstage the ANC in mass mobilizations. In March 1960 the PAC put its weight behind an anti-pass campaign; one centre of activity was Sharpeville, the African location of Vereeniging, south of Johannesburg. A crowd converged on the police station and despite the security of their Saracen armoured cars, nervous policemen opened fire, killing sixty-nine and wounding many more. Sharpeville sent a shudder through white and black communities alike. As the former responded with self-justification, the latter were galvanized into further action. Africans in Cape Town launched a march which seemed momentarily to threaten parliament. The government declared a state of emergency and sent the police and army into dissident locations and rural districts. Following mass arrests, the ANC and PAC were banned.

Nelson Mandela's dramatic life delineates the phases of black nationalist politics in these years. Born in Thembuland, Transkei, in 1918 his traditionalist father, a minor chief, died when he was young. He was brought up first by his Christian mother and then adopted into the Thembu chief's homestead where he attended school. 'I have the most pleasant recollections and dreams about the Transkei of my childhood, where I hunted, played sticks, stole mealies on the cob and where I learnt to court' (Meer, 7). Mandela later romanticized the African past as democratic and free with 'no rich or poor and no exploitation of man by man'.

Great emphasis was placed on schooling by the Transkeian Christian élite and Mandela's abilities led him to Fort Hare, the major educational institution for blacks. Like others of his generation he was politicized while studying there and expelled. In 1941 he moved to Johannesburg determined to train as a lawyer; living in Alexandra township, he was caught up simultaneously in a multiracial political world and in the radicalization of the ANC. In 1948 he became the secretary-general of the Youth League and a key organizer for the next decade. His legal practice with Oliver Tambo became a centre for Congress political networks. Banned on and off through the 1950s, and an accused in the Treason Trial, Mandela was at the heart of the transformation of the ANC from a nationalist protest movement to a national liberation movement after Sharpeville in 1960. 'Of all that group of young men,' Tambo argued, 'Mandela and his close friend and co-leader Walter Sisulu were perhaps the fastest to get to grips with the harsh realities of the African struggle against the most powerful adversary in Africa' (*No Easy Walk to Freedom*, p. xi).

While mass action was not immediately abandoned by the ANC and PAC, both developed underground structures, espoused the idea of armed struggle, and sent representatives abroad. The ANC argued that it had exhausted the potential for non-violent protest; the state itself was illegitimate and rested on violence. Events in rural Natal and Pondoland as well as some urban locations in 1960 suggested that the people were ready to fight. Fuel for armed struggle seemed to be there if only a spark could be found to light it and Umkhonto we Sizwe (Spear of the Nation, later MK) was established to do so. Anti-colonial movements from Algeria (which Mandela visited in 1961) to Cuba had shown what was possible and politics in Zimbabwe and Mozambique were beginning to move in the same direction.

Government control was sufficient to stifle any early success. By 1961 Verwoerd was reaching the height of his confidence. Internal opposition was neutralized and he wished to redefine the international position. Through the 1950s South Africa's relationship with Britain had been renegotiated across a range of issues such as control of shipping and the Simonstown naval base. In 1957 the Union Jack and 'God Save the Queen' were finally abolished from official ceremonies. In 1960 a new decimalized currency of rands and cents replaced British sterling. Britain rejected renewed South African efforts to annex the High Commission territories (Botswana, Lesotho, and Swaziland) but tried to deflect early attempts at isolating South Africa internationally. British interests in the country were very extensive. Nevertheless one of the aims behind the Federation of Rhodesia and Nyasaland, created in 1953, was to establish a relatively strong and independent colonial nexus north of South Africa—again an echo of late nineteenth-century politics.

By the late 1950s the Nationalists conceived themselves to be sufficiently secure to go their own way. In 1960 Verwoerd held a referendum on the long-promised republic, which he won narrowly. International attention was sharply focused on the country at the time; Luthuli was awarded the Nobel Peace prize. Powerful criticism from newly independent Commonwealth countries, shocked by the Sharpeville shootings, led to the formation of the Republic in 1961 outside the Commonwealth. Verwoerd remained Prime Minister and a largely ceremonial, non-executive presidency was established.

National Party victory in 1948 marked the beginning of an elected autocracy. The Westminster system had struck with a vengeance in South Africa. Though Nationalists took the institution of parliament seriously, checks and balances in the judiciary, the opposition, and civil service had been brusquely pushed aside as the government united the *volk* and forced through apartheid. Many historians have been seduced by the power of the Afrikaners' own myths—their preoccupation with apparently archaic ethnic concerns about *volk* and the obsessive ideology of race. Yet the Nationalists had also succeeded in taking rapid command of a complex bureaucracy, further developing a technocratic state and providing economically for their followers. Though they had provoked a potentially powerful opposition nationalism which defined South African citizenship in a non-racial and inclusive manner, they had also controlled it.

7 Economy and Society in the 1960s and 1970s

Apartheid and Economic Growth

Many opponents of apartheid in the 1950s and 1960s argued that it was not only morally unjust but economically inefficient. Yet the first two decades of Nationalist rule were distinctive as a period of rapid economic growth—in particular of new manufacturing industries. From the late 1960s, a new generation of radical historians and social scientists attempted to reassess the relationship between apartheid and economic growth. Elements of this debate have been discussed in preceding chapters, but it is worth summarizing here. It was a development of the high apartheid years and although analyses are more fluid now, a good deal of recent academic literature addresses it.

English-speaking liberals tended to see apartheid as a peculiarly Afrikaner policy. Some, taking Nationalist ideas about their past at face value, felt it was a hangover from the frontier and the Boer republics; 'the present Government's policies are acting out the same sick, violent drama as those of their ancestors' (Desmond, 22). Some gave more emphasis to the recent political role of special-interest groups like farmers or white workers. But they tended to dissociate apartheid from the major capitalist enterprises in the country. Even if segregation had its roots in the British colonial era, as in Natal, and even if migrant labour was initially a product of British-owned mining, nevertheless Afrikaners had made it their own and developed it to a point far beyond earlier practice.

The idea that apartheid was economically irrational was lent cogency by an increasing shortage of skilled labour in the 1960s. Labour migrancy was not only seen as socially destructive of rural and urban communities but as inefficient—leading to high turnover and low productivity. Black poverty limited the growth of internal markets. Drawing on a whiggish understanding of British history, some suggested that ultimately growth would undermine or 'explode' apartheid and result in a more open society along the lines of the established industrial democracies.

To radical scholars in the early 1970s, these ideas seemed unconvincing. They argued that except for a brief hiccup around the political crisis of 1960, growth rates were impressive on an international scale. The fact that few blacks had benefited did not seem to set the process back. At the very least apartheid and economic growth did not seem contradictory. Drawing on Barrington Moore and other social theorists of modernization, Trapido pointed out that democratic systems were by no means the only outcomes of industrialization. Extensive state intervention and 'Prussian', even totalitarian, regimes often characterized late industrializers.

Some developed the argument further in suggesting that apartheid suited not only the mining industry but also manufacturers by producing cheap migrant labour. Thus segregation and apartheid could be construed as the product of a particular type of capitalist development rather than a system at odds with capitalism. White workers and poor whites certainly played their part in its development but were not the main agents of the many regulations governing black workers and communities. It was perhaps on this point—the imperatives of capitalism, especially manufacturing industry—that the radical interpretation differed most with liberal positions.

The debate took many forms, intensified by its relevance to opposition political strategies such as sanctions. Those supporting boycotts and disinvestment emphasized that economic growth was unlikely in itself to bring change. They questioned the motives of those who argued for continued trade, investment, or 'constructive engagement' in the hope that growth would explode apartheid. This seemed an excuse for business as usual: foreign firms making fat profits from cheap black labour. Some radical academics, strongly influenced by socialist currents in European and American universities in the late

1960s and early 1970s, suggested—sometimes implicitly rather than explicitly—that capitalism as much as apartheid was the problem. Blacks were an oppressed working class, rather than just the subject of racial laws.

We will return to this debate at the end of this section and again at the end of Chapter 9. In examining patterns of economic and political change, the mid-1970s should be kept in mind as a turning-point. The oil crisis of 1973, the collapse of the Portuguese colonial Empire in 1974, the rise of black worker militancy, and the Soweto students' revolt of 1976 all combined to slow growth and jolt the government into reconsideration of its direction—especially after P. W. Botha succeeded J. B. Vorster as Prime Minister in 1978. A cycle of insurrection, reform, and repression began.

Manufacturing, commerce, and finance were the most rapidly expanding sectors of the South African economy at this time. The value of manufacturing output outstripped mining in the 1940s. In the thirty-year period from 1946 to 1975, growth averaged over 7 per cent annually. Manufacturing employment grew more quickly than any other sector, at 4 per cent annually from 855,000 in 1951 to 1.6 million in 1976 (Nattrass). Profits, size of firm, and productivity all increased. South African manufacturers produced very largely for the internal market, substituting locally made goods for imports in very diverse spheres.

Although food and clothing, the two best established industries at the end of the Second World War, more than doubled in size by the 1970s, they had become far less significant. The textile industry, still in its infancy with less than 10,000 workers in 1948, employed 50,000 workers by 1962 and 90,000 by the mid-1970s. Loans from the state's Industrial Development Corporation (1940) and foreign investment fuelled this expansion; small-scale entrepreneurs, some of them Jewish immigrants, became major industrialists with thousands of employees. Britain's biggest textile company, the Lancashire Cotton Corporation, established a plant in Natal with local tycoon Philip Frame.

Heavier industries such as metal products, machinery, and

chemicals also expanded rapidly. South Africa produced an increasing amount of its steel and mining equipment, tools, explosives, fertilizers, and chemicals, as well as consumer durables such as washing-machines, stoves, and cars. Production was protected where necessary by tariffs or, as in the case of the motor industry, the requirement that a proportion of parts should be locally manufactured. Demand for vehicles increased rapidly in the post-war years and by 1960 South Africa produced 87,000 cars annually, more than most developing countries, including Brazil, and all the South East Asian countries together. With less than 20 per cent of parts and components locally made, the eastern Cape car factories were initially assembly plants rather than manufacturers, and more people worked in garages (32,000) than in plants. But in the 1960s production doubled to 195,000 vehicles annually and a 66 per cent local content programme was introduced.

South Africa was very much part of the post-Second World War globalization of multinational investment. Its efficient communications and financial sector, the lively Johannesburg stock exchange, a well-educated local white management and professional class, as well as relatively cheap labour, all made it attractive. There was a momentary withdrawal when slower growth in the late 1950s was followed by political crisis in 1960. But the government acted decisively to block the export of foreign exchange, increase interest rates, raise protectionist barriers, and crush opposition. Foreign investors responded by rewarding the reimposition of political authority rather than penalizing the intensification of repression; rates of profit were especially high in the 1960s.

Britain remained the largest source of investment and trade but German involvement increased dramatically in the late 1960s as did French, especially through military and related contracts. Japan became the second most important market for South African goods as early as 1964 though it was not until the 1970s that Japanese products made an impact. American influence was evident especially in high-profile consumer products. Coca Cola signs were emblazoned on city-centre buildings and corner cafés. While the proportion of capital generated from overseas had declined since the early days of mining, foreign capital poured into manufacturing and commerce as never before.

The mining industry itself, powerhouse of early growth, was constrained by the restitution of a fixed price of gold against the dollar ($35 per ounce) after the war. The industry contracted a little in the 1940s, but by 1955 the previous employment peak (1941) had been surpassed and by 1970 production doubled to over one million kilograms. Recently discovered gold in the Orange Free State and West Rand underpinned this expansion, with uranium a profitable by-product. In 1968 events outside South Africa's control presented another one of those windfalls which, de Kiewiet noted, have been so important in shaping the country's history. As in the 1930s, the gold price was freed. By 1973 international demand drove the price to over $150 per ounce and, in the years of the oil crisis and a weakening dollar, to a brief peak of $800 in 1980.

Profits in gold-mining increased dramatically; so did state revenue from gold—from under R1 billion in 1970 to over R10 billion in 1980. As manufacturing growth faltered in the late 1970s, mining provided some ballast. And while industry remained relatively insignificant for exports, mining remained a critical source of foreign exchange. Gold paid for large quantities of imported machinery and, after 1973, offset the increase in the price of oil which would otherwise have retarded South Africa's economy more severely—as it did other African countries.

The Anglo-American Corporation dominated expansion into the Orange Free State and Far West Rand goldfields. Ernest Oppenheimer, who established the group in South Africa and masterminded the take-over of de Beers, Rhodes's old diamond company in 1929, was succeeded by his son Harry in the 1940s. Initially, Harry followed in both Rhodes's and his father's footsteps in trying to marry business and politics: he became UP MP for Kimberley in 1948. But although politics remained close to his heart, Oppenheimer's taste was for cautious understatement rather than titanism; white politics did not look promising for a man of his relatively liberal views. He withdrew from parliament, though he became a major influence in and funder of the Progressive Party.

In raising large sums for the Orange Free State goldfield developments, Anglo-American remained a major interlocutor between London's City and South Africa. By the late 1950s it became the largest single gold producer, benefiting from the efficiency of new mines. By 1976, with a third of the country's gold mines, the company was by far the most powerful group in the industry. It also controlled over 80 per cent of world diamond production and had a major stake in uranium, coal, Zambian copper, and mining operations world-wide.

Anglo's growth into South Africa's largest corporation helps to illustrate the links between mining and manufacturing; together with other successful mining groups, it diversified energetically. When Anglo took over de Beers, it had acquired AE and CI, the biggest explosives, fertilizer, and later plastics producer in South Africa. Anglo developed a major presence in the metals industry, launched a merchant bank, and had an interest in the Nedbank consortium—the third largest in the country. Nor did it neglect public opinion: its newspaper company controlled the two largest selling daily papers (the Johannesburg *Star* and *Cape Argus*) and was integrated with a paper and pulp concern as well as the Central News Agency— South Africa's major newsagent and retail stationery chain. By the late 1970s over 150 Anglo-linked companies covered almost every sphere of mining, industrial production, finance, property, and agriculture, including the old Rhodes fruit farms. It was said that over 50 per cent of shares traded on the Johannesburg Stock Exchange were in Anglo companies. Other successful mining groups bought large brick, forestry, and paper concerns as well as the Cape's major fishing and freezing company.

Apart from foreign investment, mining capital, and the savings derived from agriculture, state involvement in heavy industry took on a new importance. Post-war public-sector growth reflected that in many industrial economies. State-owned monopolies continued to control electricity and water supply, railways and harbours, broadcasting, air travel, and much steel production. (Coal-mining remained private.) Manufacturing capital generated in this sector increased from less than 10 per cent in the 1920s to 25 per cent by the 1970s. But public-sector spending as proportion of the GDP—at about 30 per cent in 1975—probably did not rival that in Western Europe at least till the early 1980s. South Africa operated a relatively low tax regime and offered limited welfare provision. The most rapidly growing area of expenditure was defence.

The government pursued a policy of economic nationalism, especially with major new ventures in oil and armaments. While South Africa had large and relatively cheap supplies of coal, it lacked natural oil. Anxious about energy security, the state sponsored an oil-from-coal plant using a process developed in Germany before the war. The Sasol corporation, launched in 1951 in the northern Orange Free State, became significant after 1973 when OPEC raised prices and banned trade with South Africa. Iran continued to be a safe source until the Shah's fall in 1979. Oil refiners and distributors such as Caltex, Mobil, BP, and Shell kept supplies flowing. But the country's vulnerability was clear. In 1974 massive expansion of Sasol was planned at Secunda in the eastern Transvaal within reach of coalfields and electricity generating plants. Sasol produced around a third of oil supplies in the early 1980s and soon after consumed perhaps a quarter of coal production. Most of ESCOM's electricity generating capacity was also underpinned by coal.

After the UN Security Council imposed a ban on weapon exports to South Africa in 1963, Armscor was established as a parastatal company. By 1982 it had become one of the biggest industrial enterprises in the country and probably the largest arms manufacturer in the southern hemisphere. Whereas in 1966 perhaps 70 per cent of arms expenditure was on imports, by 1982 over 80 per cent of a hugely increased budget was spent within the country. As in the case of oil, it proved possible to circumvent embargos. French-style armoured cars and Mirage fighters as well as Italian-designed Impala aircraft were made locally; access was maintained to Israeli and American technology. Nevertheless, the South African version of some military hardware was distinctive, so that armoured vehicles such as Casspirs and Hippos, dramatically deployed when the army moved into the townships, epitomized the local military style. Armscor's contracts provided a major boost to the small local micro-electronics and computer industry, but in this, as in sophisticated airforce equipment, the country remained dependent on imports. Nuclear power and weapons capacity was developed with French assistance.

Urban and industrial expansion, as well as agriculture, had long been constrained by the problems of water supply and dam construction was a major preoccupation. The Vaal dam completed in 1938 secured Rand supplies. In the apartheid years, the Orange River Project, designed for irrigation as well as water (to Bloemfontein) and hydroelectric power, was a key undertaking. The main Hendrik Verwoerd dam, completed in 1971, was linked by a long water tunnel to eastern Cape valleys where irrigated land was put under crops and fruit. South African consortia were also involved in the Cabora Bassa hydroelectric power scheme on the Zambezi. These new mega-dams demonstrated conquest and control of nature's most unpredictable element. They were a metaphor for social change where Afrikaner corporate society had displaced the unruly frontier. Dams proved photogenic for newsreel films with resounding commentaries and bombastic music. They cele-brated a specifically Afrikaner contribution to industrial society and the modernization of agriculture.

It is important to appreciate the scale of these developments which confirmed South Africa's position as industrial power-house and entrepôt of the region. They were also a major factor in reshaping the country's social geography. To the original Witwatersrand was added an arc of satellite towns from the Far West Rand goldfields to the huge coal, electricity, and oil plants of the eastern Transvaal. The Orange Free State goldfields population, for example, was bigger than Bloemfon-tein's by 1970. In the 1970s these new heavy industrial zones ranked only behind six major cities in their size—though they in turn were soon to be outstripped by urban settlements which had little industrial base (Chapter 8).

But even in the boom years, there were signs of weakness. Economists now suggest that growth during this period was strong, but not as spectacular in international terms as suggested at the time. Although new patterns of consumption permeated many levels of society, manufacturers relied heavily on a limited white market. Throughout the 1960s industrialists complained of the shortage of skilled workers which both hampered expansion and raised the cost of white workers. Not many industries were able to export competitively and there were costs to the protection of industry and the high degree of monopoly in public and private sectors. South Africa remained dependent on imports for most sophisticated machinery—more so than some other southern, industrializing economies such as India. The country's import bill rocketed at the height of its boom. The lack of an educated work-force also inhibited industrial innovation. These weaknesses, some but not all linked to apartheid policies, were revealed when manufacturing growth slowed between 1975 and 1980 and subsequently stagnated.

White Society and Culture

The images of Verwoerd, Prime Minister from 1958 till his assassination in 1966, and Johannes Balthazar Vorster (1966–78), brood over the high apartheid years. Vorster rose to prominence as Minister of Justice responsible for much of the repressive political apparatus of the 1960s. His craggy features, glowering eyes, and impassive public face were the epitome of *kragdadigheid*—the uncompromising face of Afrikaner power. He had been interned in the Second World War for sabotage as a member of the OB, a point often made by his critics as he tightened security arrangements. His brother, conservative Moderator of the main Dutch Reformed Church, reinforced his image.

Reassessments of his premiership suggest he was not only less of an ideologue, but far more of a 'chairman' than either his forceful and visionary predecessor or his imperial successor, P. W. Botha. The beginnning of his period of rule saw the

National Party at the zenith of its power. In the 1966 election, it collected many English-speaking as well as the vast majority of Afrikaner votes. But by the mid-1970s the remarkable success of the government and Afrikaner organizations in controlling the ideas and identity of their own language group and many others was beginning to wane.

It was the best of times, materially, for white South Africans. This was reflected in demographic trends. By the 1950s over 80 per cent of them lived in urban areas and small towns, by the 1980s, over 90 (Table 3). White annual rates of population increase declined from around two per cent before 1950 to under one by the 1980s, somewhat to the consternation of the government. These figures take account of a net gain of white immigrants of over 20,000 per year between the early 1960s and 1984, peaking at 40,000 in 1975, the year of Mozambican independence. Birth-rates dropped as the population became wealthier. Like Europeans, white South Africans had fewer children, smaller families, and more disposable income.

Afrikaners benefited particularly from economic growth. The capital accumulated in farming flowed into financial institutions which helped greatly to diversify the range of Afrikaner commerce. New investment in education, especially at university level, expanded Afrikaner involvement in the whole range of professions. Those in agricultural occupations dropped from about 30 per cent in 1946 to 8 per cent in 1977 on the eve of the reform era. Afrikaners in blue-collar and unskilled work dropped from 40 to 27, while those in white-collar employment increased from 29 to 65 per cent (Giliomee and Adam, 169). Of half a million whites in public sector employment, the great majority were Afrikaners. In the private sector, the job colour bar 'floated' upwards as whites reaped the benefits of improved training and full employment.

Afrikaner women finally moved out of industrial employment where significant numbers had worked up to the 1950s. They were largely replaced by black men at lower wages. By 1970 only 3–4 per cent of employed white women worked in factories. Nevertheless, the number of white working women increased overall as, benefiting from protection, they were absorbed in clerical and secretarial jobs, nursing and teaching. The fragile social base for pre-war radicalism and worker organization, reflected in the Garment Workers' Union, was rapidly eroded. In major areas of women's employment like nursing and teaching, white women were tightly segregated from black.

Afrikaner entrepreneurs such as Anton Rupert, head of the tobacco multinational Rembrandt, spearheaded upward social mobility. Sanlam and Trustbank, amongst others, gave Afrikaners a better footing in a commercial world dominated by English corporations. Mining houses made space for Afrikaner-controlled corporations, notably Federale Mynbou, to buy into mining. Per capita income amongst Afrikaans-speakers, less than half that of English-speakers in 1946, had risen to 80 per cent in the late 1970s and was heading towards parity. The government not only filled the expanding state corporations and civil service with Afrikaners, but used state patronage to promote Afrikaner firms. Some analysts argued that whites came to enjoy a standard of living equal to that of the richest countries in the North. This statistic is a little misleading in that it compares the top 20 per cent of South African earners not with the top 20 per cent in Europe or the USA but the whole population of industrialized countries. Nevertheless, white South Africans had never had it so good.

Whites are often analysed in this period as agents of a repressive society, but they too have a complex social history. Images of them at the time are conflicting: they are portrayed as religious but militarized, racist but rich, narrow but hospitable. It is their otherness which is often stressed. But for all the peculiarity of this 'strange society', it was often familiar to Europeans and Americans. The apartheid period was one of suburbanization and the spread of a rather derivative consumer culture spliced on to the gnarled old settler stock.

White English-speaking middle-class culture still looked partly to Britain. Although immigrants into South Africa notoriously adopted apartheid ideas quite quickly, many retained strong links with their countries of origin. Afrikaners were getting richer and the English-speaking working class smaller, but class as well as cultural divisions remained significant in urban social networks. University education was one dividing line and universities themselves were sharply divided between Afrikaans and English. Afrikaners could isolate themselves socially because of their large range of cultural and educational institutions and their dominance of state employment. The strength of the Broederbond encouraged them to do so; Afrikaners who strayed politically or became anglicized could be the object of opprobium.

White living standards were most manifest in their houses and cars. Low density suburbs with modern detached houses in gardens, some with swimming pools, proliferated. Vehicle numbers nearly doubled every decade from 370,000 in 1940 to 1.3 million in 1960 and 3.8 million in 1980 (Table 4). At about twenty-one people per vehicle in 1950 and twelve in 1961, South African ownership exceeded that of many European countries, even if the black population—which owned only around 10 per cent of the total—is included (Andrews, 25). Per capita car ownership in West Germany only overtook South Africa in 1958. White car ownership in the boom years of the 1960s ranked behind only the most motorized countries—the USA (one car for 2.4 people), Australia, and Canada. The car culture in the apartheid years greatly facilitated the development of the suburbs and helped whites to insulate themselves from a common urban life.

From the 1960s British and American models were increasingly displaced by German. At the upper end of the market, successful Afrikaner businessmen and farmers bought Mercedes Benz, often white in colour. A small-town funeral, when a procession of cars followed the hearse to the cemetery, could be an extraordinary display of wealth that far exceeded the wildest pretensions of the small Wabenzi classes in independent African states. In the 1980s Japanese manufacturers captured much of the market. They were especially successful in sales of bakkies (pick-ups).

Jeremy Taylor's satirical hit song, 'Ballad of the Southern Suburbs', in the musical *Wait a Minim*, captured the essence of consumer culture and the primacy of the car in the less fashionable parts of Johannesburg. It started: 'Ag Pleez Daddy won't you take us to the drive-in?' In another verse children asked: 'Won't you take us off to Durban, it's only eight hours in the Chevrolet?' The celebrated chorus ran: 'pop-corn, chewing gum, peanuts and bubble-gum, ice-cream, candy floss and eskimo pie'. Cars and consumer spending reshaped South African shopping. The OK Bazaars (1927), started by Cohen and Miller, introduced mass retailing to South Africa. Now supermarkets, many developed by Jewish entrepreneurs with their fingers on the pulse of international marketing, proliferated. Chains such as Pick and Pay (1967) initially catered for a white suburban clientele. Some were later located near key transport spots and became accessible to blacks. Supermarkets were not segregated.

Consumerism brought with it new cultural influences. The USA did not become South Africa's primary trading partner, nor its main source of investment capital. Nevertheless, postwar American consumer icons and life-styles had great appeal for both whites and blacks. Sophisticated American advertising provided reference points to what was perceived as an international culture—an escape from both colonial British and Afrikaner heritage. Drive-ins, take-aways, hula hoops, and radio jingles all contributed to Americanization. For South Africans, also, things went 'better with Coca Cola'. To compensate, you could 'Brush your teeth with Colgate, fight tooth decay all day'.

Hollywood releases dominated the cinemas—Tarzan, Westerns, and the great epics. These were hardly threatening to white patriarchal culture and censors screened out material they thought politically suspect. Black urban leaders like Zorro took their names from cinema heroes. White children played cowboys and crooks rather than Boer and Zulu. When they were bought bows and arrows, the reference point was native American rather than the indigenous San. Jim Reeves's lugubrious small-town sorrow struck a specially deep chord with Afrikaners. American country and western styles—drawing on social experience similar to Afrikaners—seeped into local ballads, a market supplied by the smooth tones of Ge Korsten in *Die Hartseerwals* (Heartache Waltz). Beach holidays became increasingly popular; white women especially valued their suntans as evidence of leisure and style. The climate was suitable for adventurous youths, male and female, to develop their version of the Californian dream. The consumption of dagga (marijuana), long grown and smoked by blacks, increased significantly; it was one of the few expanding markets for homeland agriculture. British and American pop music and clothing fashions were dominant. These were all cultural borrowings that to some extent crossed racial boundaries.

In broadcasting, however, the government was determined to retain a monopoly. Hertzog had nationalized the radio in 1936 with the specific intention that there should be Afrikaans radio channels. The Nationalists were concerned that untoward 'liberalist' political messages might seep through and exercised tight control over the content of programmes. Largely for these reasons, the introduction of television was delayed until 1976 when the local film industry was more developed. The South African Broadcasting Corporation put out two national radio channels, one Afrikaans and the other self-consciously English, including imports from the BBC. In 1950 Springbok radio, a less sober bilingual national commercial channel, was launched. Current affairs and news on all these, as well as proliferating local FM and African-language programmes, toed the government's line. Radio was an important means by which the government could communicate its position to African people, many of whom were not literate.

Men were the major but not exclusive participants in a culture of smoking, drinking, and sports. Smoking was hardly new. African societies in southern Africa had widely adopted tobacco although snuff was more popular than pipes. The seventeenth-century Dutch became the most fervent tobacco consumers in Europe, even growing rough tobacco in Holland. The table-cloth in Cape Town, a blanket of clouds blown down the front of Table Mountain, was explained by an old tobacco folk-tale: a pipe-smoking contest between the Devil and Mynheer van Hunks, which probably reflected the guilt in a Calvinist Dutch culture about the centrality of the weed. In this context, the Rupert company's name for their brand leader, Rembrandt van Rijn, was particularly appropriate; it evoked a Dutch rather than British masterpiece and Rembrandt's seventeenth-century Dutch culture was wreathed in tobacco smoke. After the Second World War, cigarettes—including the ubiquitous Springbok brand—increasingly ousted pipes and chewing tobaccos (*twak*). Heavy smoking and high meat and alcohol consumption provided one reason why, in addition to sharing the demographic features of Western countries, white South Africans also came to share their health profile with high rates of heart disease and lung cancer.

White South Africans could not easily compete in the international cultural stakes; some of those with professional and artistic ambition left. But they could hold their own in sport—a means of male expression and self-fulfilment. It also provided a social cement in new urban communities. Horse-racing, a nineteenth-century sport, remained popular with whites and blacks in town; in the rural districts of the Transkei regular informal race meets were held. For middle-class English-speakers, tennis afternoons, swimming in private pools, golf and bowls at country clubs became central social events. Freed from much household drudgery by black domestic servants, white women could participate in many of these activities.

No serious attempt was made to revive Afrikaner pre-industrial pastimes. *Jukskei*, an old farm and trek game, was kept alive on the beaches of Strand where farm families came for holidays and spread at the time of the OB, but remained a minority activity for devotees. Rather, Afrikaners adopted British team games. In particular they made rugby their own. Stellenbosch, for many years crucible of Afrikaner intellectual life, also became cradle of South African rugby. It appealed as a 'sport for pioneers' which also allowed Afrikaners to beat the English at their own game. Rugby called for physicality, bravado, and team solidarity. Adopted as the main winter game in many educational institutions, it spread as new communities coalesced around schools, suburbs, police, and other institutions. The 1951/2 tour to Britain, when the Springboks won 30 out of 31 games and beat Scotland 44–0, confirmed the game's central status through the early apartheid years. As Afrikaner wealth grew and self-image modified in the 1960s and 1970s, they increasingly embraced more genteel pursuits such as cricket, tennis, and golf. Motorsports of all kind dispersed with the car culture. Football, king for most black South Africans, was more the game of British and European immigrants and of the older established white working-class areas. Apartheid was rigidly enforced in sport during Verwoerd's years.

In his book *Modernizing Racial Domination* (1971), Heribert Adam commented: 'one of the most striking features of South African cultural life is the relative isolation and ignorance about the changing world of ideas, which whites in particular hardly seem to notice.' The idea that Afrikaners were inward-looking, had missed out on the first enlightenment and most since then, was an old one. Certainly, censorship deprived white South Africans of much written and visual material which might have challenged their views. They defended their position with extraordinary vehemence both in public political argument and in everyday behaviour.

The imperative to stand alone, despite being the 'pole cats of the world' was broadcast through the media, through political speeches, and the churches with insistent regularity. Though 'overseas' was still a place many wanted to visit, it evoked an increasing defensiveness. Most whites were unable to see black South Africans during this critical period of the country's history. Homelands, passes, group areas, social amnesia, and powerful ideologies put them out of sight, literally and metaphorically. Whites believed that they knew 'their' Africans, and this justified their system against the attacks of ignorant outsiders. Many of them came across Africans only as servants and workers. Their school history taught them that whites had got to this part of Africa first. They believed that they were guarantors of Western values, technological society, and civilization; that they had invented the wheel and blacks had not. Events in Africa such as coups, wars, and one-party states were grist to their self-justificatory mill.

The political and cultural brokers of Afrikanerdom wished

to deliver wealth to their people as well as insulate them. To an extraordinary extent they did succeed. But there were greater paradoxes in their achievement than Heribert Adam might allow. It was not only racial domination that was modernized. Afrikaners chose modern architecture for public buildings and churches, proclaiming a desire to be international and forward-looking. Wealth brought the capacity to share in a Western culture of work and leisure which in turn provided a myriad routes out of the cocooned world. The church, racial ideology, the Broederbond, and *braaivleis* (barbecue) remained anchors. But by the 1970s a cultural secularism based on consumption, sport, leisure, travel, and personal freedom was beginning to fracture Afrikaner ethnic identity. It is an irony that television, launched only when the National Party felt it could control the medium in 1976, coincided with this gradual dissolution of unity and probably contributed to it.

Such paradoxes might be illustrated by growing divorce rates. The Dutch Reformed Churches, overwhelmingly the most important amongst Afrikaners, had long propagated a conservative view of the role of women, marriage, and the family. But in the 1960s, one white marriage in five was ending in divorce and by 1978, one marriage in 3.3. The demand on the courts was considerable and divorce laws were relaxed in 1979, despite the church. White women had achieved a degree of security in their access to property and employment and some of the sexual and economic freedom characteristic of capitalist societies. Although the state remained staunchly opposed to permitting abortion, contraception was widely available. Feminism was not strongly developed as a movement but the combination of high levels of education and relative freedom from domestic labour allowed white women to assert a degree of independence in a patriarchal world.

Even in the apartheid years, many different international currents of thought were being refracted through the complex prism of South African society. A strong minority white opposition survived and developed. The Liberal Party, which had attracted some black as well as white support, dissolved in the 1960s. Some of its constituency was absorbed by the Progressive

Party. Although their commitment was only to a qualified non-racial franchise, this was a challenging concept to whites. Helen Suzman, the redoubtable Progressive Party MP for the wealthy Johannesburg constituency of Houghton, maintained a relentless criticism of government economic policy, breaches of human rights, and apartheid. She was joined by six others after the 1974 election as the United Party fragmented. The Black Sash, a white women's movement launched at the time of constitutional protests in the 1950s, switched its attention to advisory work and publicity on passes, influx control, and removals. Organizations such as the South African Institute of Race Relations, church groups, and universities sustained a strong network of white anti-apartheid activity. Nadine Gordimer's novels and stories, some banned, captured the intense self-criticism and guilt of whites who recognized the immorality of their society.

There were always alternative views available even to Afrikaners. Social change and political challenges divided *verligtes* (the enlightened) from *verkramptes* (conservatives). *Verligtes* questioned the details of petty apartheid. They advocated a broader white nationalism, expressed greater desire for international acceptability, and were uneasy about the repressive security apparatus. Dissident writers associated with the *Sestiger* (Sixties) movement, and subsequently popular novelists such as André Brink, explored dangerous themes of cross-racial relationships, Afrikaner self-doubt, and the history of violence and expropriation. *Verligtes* certainly felt that they could initiate reform from above and within the parameters of racial separation. But Afrikaner as well as English intellectuals remained open to a surprisingly wide range of influences drifting in from 'overseas' which gave focus to a variety of social tendencies.

Class and Social Change in African Urban Communities

In the 1960s and 1970s banned groups and people could not express themselves publicly. It was particularly dangerous for African people to associate themselves with the ANC and PAC.

Fragmented community and church groups, homeland and ethnically based parties, black consciousness and trade union movements sprang up to fill the vacuum and take advantage of the limited openings afforded by government policy. It is important to record what was in fact possible at the height of apartheid—how people compromised, came to terms with their powerlessness, and expressed their interests. These years left a legacy of highly diverse associations. (Black political movements are discussed in Chapters 8 and 9.)

The contours of African social and political life, including the relatively quiescent decade after 1963, were moulded by demographic and social change as much as repression. Black people did not live by politics alone. Massive expansion of black employment in industry and, to a lesser degree, in white-collar and educational institutions meant that economic benefits of a kind did accrue to a significant minority, especially urban 'insiders', during the post-Sharpeville boom. Social scientists investigating fast-growing African urban communities at this time were struck by a growing class of professionals, traders, businessmen (especially in building and taxis), clerks, civil servants, teachers, and nurses who had access to higher salaries and tended to intermarry. The title of Kuper's study of the Durban locations in the early 1960s, *An African Bourgeoisie*, was misleading as few of the African élite controlled substantial businesses or properties. Amongst the few very rich were patent medicine manufacturers. But a wider range of people identified themselves self-consciously as élite or middle class.

Awareness of social differentiation was reflected in the language of the townships which became a biting commentary on division themselves. In Cape Town and Durban, the respectable middle class were called the 'ooscuse-me'. Though many were from a Christian background, a sense of class behaviour was overlaying the old rurally based distinction between Christian (Zulu *kholwa* or Xhosa 'school' people) and the traditionalists. Vilakazi argued that 'as part of this concern with individual rights and individual responsibility has come a high degree of "privatism" among the new *élite*' (p. 139). While national political leadership tended to come from this social stratum, by no means all were able or willing to identify with nationalist movements in the 1960s and early 1970s. Urban Location Advisory Boards, though they remained weak in the early apartheid decades, were just as important a focus of activity.

In the gregarious, congested, pre-apartheid inner-city locations such as Sophiatown, wealthier families lived together with the poor and it was difficult to maintain social exclusivity. But in large, dispersed new peri-urban townships, members of the middle class were beginning to live in identifiable areas. One élite neighbourhood in Lamontville, Durban, where a rare home-ownership scheme survived, was dubbed 'Nylon', possibly because it was built at the time when nylon stockings became available but also apparently because of its social transparency. (Nylon was one of the terms for lies and for police cars.) As elsewhere, careful choice of consumer goods signified the aspirations of the upwardly mobile. For blacks pushed into far-flung locations, just as for whites moving to the suburbs, cars were highly valued. An African anthropologist noted that 'a car is a very important badge of prominence . . . it's no use saying you have money if you can't produce a car' (Kuper, 112). New location houses were furnished with distinctive modern furniture and hire-purchase arrangements escalated.

In 1962 Africans were allowed to purchase manufactured liquor following a long period of prohibition—a move which reflected the strength of the wine interests and liquor producers in the country. Municipalities continued to run beerhalls for profit and new breweries mass-produced 'Bantu Beer' (a version of traditional beer). But middle-class men avoided municipal beerhalls and increasingly added lager, wine, and spirits to their patterns of consumption. The upwardly mobile in urban communities bought cigarettes rather than pipe tobacco or snuff. African women were far slower than white to start smoking.

Black middle-class urban society shared many social pursuits and patterns of consumption with white, though it did not merely replicate them. Church activities, mostly in established denominations or orthodox independent churches, occupied much leisure time, especially of women. Methodism, a badge of respectability and discipline, had been the most active mission denomination and probably retained its hold as the most widespread group of churches. Red-jacketed women from the Methodist *manyano* (women's union) proclaimed their presence forcefully every Thursday. In this church as in others they were a key nexus of women's organization which stretched beyond the confines of individual cities. The Independent Order of True Templars, a non-denominational Christian organization, attacked the destructive effects of drunkenness in urban society by advocating temperance and self-improvement; although led by the middle classes, it also attracted factory workers. Choirs, often based around the churches, hospitals, and educational institutions at the core of élite networks, were a major social expression, combining a specifically African vocal tradition, church music, and other new forms.

Some black women spent heavily on clothing; some straightened their hair and used skin-lightening cream. If it was true that 'Zulus used to admire light skins and they had special herbs for this purpose', the new fashion nevertheless spoke about the aspirations of an emerging class. Folk singer Jeremy Taylor joked that while white people wanted to tan themselves dark, black people wanted to be light. However, there was a dark side to these heavily advertised creams which contained dangerous chemicals and could discolour the skin. Nursing was one of the few opportunities available for salaried employment and black nurses set the pace in fashion. Ballroom dancing had been popular in the Cape cities after the war. The Zimbabwean political leader, Maurice Nyagumbo, later Secretary General of ZANU, was a devotee as a migrant hotel worker in Port Elizabeth. It was still an avenue for upwardly mobile working-class men in Durban in the early 1960s and 'a key . . . to the nurses home'.

Sociologists working in this period did not see a simple progress to 'Westernization' as predicted by the then fashionable modernization theories. They remained alert to the specifically African characteristics of urban society. Middle-class marriage ceremonies intricately intertwined Christian, traditional, and secular forms. Church weddings in white were frequently accompanied by bridewealth payment (though more in commodities and money than cattle) and elaborate gift exchanges between the families of the bride and bridegroom. Celebrations could include large open parties with beer, samp or *ngqushe*, and meat, private cocktail parties for friends, and receptions which provided material for the society pages of the *Golden City Post* or the *World* in Johannesburg. To a surprising degree, male initiation and circumcision were retained as a statement of Africanness in an urban environment.

Especially on the Rand, the *stokvel*, vividly described by Hellmann in inner-city slums in the 1930s, prospered across a range of social classes. It could take the form of a rotating credit society for a small group who pooled their savings regularly to provide one member with a payout at intervals. As always, it was difficult for people on relatively low incomes to accumulate sufficient themselves in order to make large purchases. This type of savings association could shade into a burial society, reflecting a deep concern for a decent death and well-attended funeral. But perhaps the most common form of *stokvel* amongst both rich and poor were weekend parties at which entry sums were charged and liquor sold. In the late 1960s at one of the frequent parties in a Rand location, a popular hostess could make a substantial profit of up to R300 on a Sunday. 'The patterns of the Stockfel and the reciprocity on which they were based pervaded all other . . . organizations and all forms of entertaining and hospitality' (Brandel-Syrier, 307).

Football rather than rugby was the leading black sport. Kuper argued that the committees of the Durban and District African Football Association, were 'in many ways, the major voluntary organization among Africans in Durban'. Initially played at mission schools, football caught on amongst the urbanized core in major cities. Like the *stokvel*, the game then crossed class boundaries. Squatter leader James Mpanza had been a keen player at school and the game spread in the post-Second World War squatter settlements and Johannesburg locations. It required few facilities and gradually displaced stick-fighting as the major sport of urbanizing black youth. By the 1970s the leagues were being professionalized and teams attracted a mass following; football was one of the first major sports to develop multiracial teams, leagues, and supporters. Cricket, which had been popular at Cape black schools at the turn of the century, faded with the heyday of the local African élite, but rugby did take root. When Steve Biko was portrayed in the film *Cry Freedom* playing rugby, this may have seemed out of place, but it was an accurate observation of the sports preferences of the black eastern Cape élite, even though it would not have been for much of the rest of the country.

Those Africans working in semi-skilled factory positions with some education and rising standards of living were increasing rapidly in number. Some shared the aspirations and associations of the middle classes, but many, especially the younger and less 'respectable', as well as the unemployed and self-employed, developed their own distinctive social practices and style. They could be intensely critical of the social pretensions of the élite and formed a potentially powerful political constituency. In turn the working class distinguished themselves from the urban criminal and youth *tsotsi* subcultures. As in the case of white youth, American cigarettes, films, jazz, pop music, and consumer patterns helped to redefine township styles. By the late 1970s Bob Marley and reggae music was one widespread accompaniment to youth protest.

Many African workers were still labourers, living in compounds and hostels, or domestic servants. The Mayers's study of East London, *Townsmen or Tribesmen*, demonstrated how rurally centred and encapsulated the lives of many migrants continued to be around 1960. In the next couple of decades, this type of labour migrancy became less significant not least because fewer men had prospects of accumulating rural resources. But some of those who did guarded their identities, their home groups, and their habits of consumption (including Sorghum beer) jealously. They were clearly perceived as different by urban location people and this social cleavage became an explosive point of tension in the 1970s and 1980s.

Amongst the most striking of the plethora of African associations were the independent churches which numbered an estimated 3,000 by the early 1970s with millions of members. About 900 were found in Soweto alone. In general, they were the churches of the working class and of poorer, more rurally oriented people with limited education. They were especially strong amongst women domestic servants. Zionist and Apostolic churches practising healing, river baptism, dancing, night communion, and drumming, grew and fragmented rapidly, throwing up a wide range of bishops, some claiming prophetic powers. While most churches had just a few hundred members, a few such as the Zion Christian Church (ZCC) of Lekganyane, based in the Transvaal, and Shembe's Nazarites in Natal did coalesce under leaders who could combine financial with prophetic skills. The ZCC had perhaps 200,000 members in 1970 and over a million by 1980.

Zionist churches (which had nothing to do with Judaism) originated in the late nineteenth-century USA but their religious forms were adapted in the African context. Church membership clearly provided an arena for social interaction, discipline, and belief in a world of rapid mobility, urban insecurity, and abrupt social change. Most churches had uniforms and developed a strong sense of identity. ZCC men donned oversize white boots with which they ceremonially stamped evil underfoot; Nazarites made extensive use of *izibongo* (praise poems), adapting them to new contexts. Aside from providing scope for intense religious expression, these churches were vehicles for the release of tension and frustration, 'comforting the uncomfortable', and some provided small material benefits in mutual aid and burial societies.

Some middle-class blacks tended to be disdainful of 'escapist' churches and uneasy with their fundamentalism. They were seen as politically conservative, concentrating on 'things celestial and heavenly'. Indeed Zulu Zionists were involved with homeland leaders in the development of Bantustan strategies. ZCC mass rallies at its headquarters near Pietersburg, northern Transvaal, attracted extensive publicity for their invitations to leading Nationalist politicians, including P. W. Botha, in the 1980s. But Zionist churches were not least attempting to defend an enclosed and inward-looking spiritual world for their followers so that they, like their predecessors in the 1920s, could keep the impact of white domination at arm's length and to some small degree shape the pattern of their incorporation.

Middle-class aspirations among the educated and religious fundamentalism among the poor did not necessarily preclude political reorganization. But given the repressive atmosphere, they helped to provide an alternative social focus in the 1960s and early 1970s, a phase of black political fragmentation. Whites expected deference from blacks and to a significant degree received it—at least in face-to-face relationships. Apartheid separated black and white communities more effectively than segregation had beforehand. But the rapidity of black urbanization created the social conditions for a gradually increasing similarity in consumer patterns and social practice. It also provided the basis for a new and more powerful black popular politics (Chapter 9).

8 Farms, Homelands, and Displaced Urbanization, 1960–1984

The Demography of Change

In 1948 when the Nationalists came to power, South Africa was still, demographically speaking, a predominantly rural society. The previous century had witnessed vast movements of population in the region which greatly modified its distribution but had not finally changed its balance. True, the people classified as white, Indian, and coloured were becoming fundamentally urban: at around 78, 78, and 65 per cent respectively in the 1951 census. It is also true that the epicentre of political conflict between white and black was moving to the cities. But to a significant degree white power still lay in the countryside and the small towns. About half of the urban Afrikaners lived in smaller towns and, politically, faced the country as much as the cities. Most important, perhaps three-quarters of the African population was still rooted in the rural areas, some 39 per cent in the reserves, and 35 per cent on the farms. This surviving rurality, it has been argued, had important implications for an understanding of social change, African political responses, and the nature of the state at the time.

During the next few decades the character of settlement again changed dramatically. By 1990 over 90 per cent of whites and Indians lived in towns. The constituencies behind white domination and the electoral base of the National Party had shifted more completely to the cities. And whereas in 1960, after more than a century of urbanization, the percentage of Africans living in towns reached 30, it probably doubled again within the next thirty years (Table 3). In absolute terms over the same years the number of Africans living in urban conditions increased from under 3.5 million to perhaps somewhere between 18 and 20 million. Hidden beneath the statistics are a multiplicity of stories of dispossession, forced movement, treks, and 'crying for land'. For African people, like Afrikaners in the previous half-century, this was a decisive phase of social change and it fuelled a radical politics which has been a major factor in recasting South African history.

These figures can be more easily understood if they are considered in the light of broader demographic changes. African births and deaths have not been fully recorded and some census counts of black people are thought to be underestimates, but the trends are clear (Table 2). The total African population grew from about 3.5 million in 1904 to 6.6 million in 1936, 8.5 million in 1950, over 20 million in 1980, and around 29 million in the 1991 census. The years between 1891 and 1904 were the last in which the white population grew much more rapidly than the black. Thereafter relatively high rates of growth, coupled with immigration, resulted in annual average white increases of close to 2 per cent to 1951. This was much the same as the black rate of increase and maintained the white population at over 20 per cent of the total (Table 1).

White rates of increase fell to less than one per cent annually in the 1980s and the white component in the total population declined to 19 per cent in 1960, 16 per cent in 1980, and perhaps less than 14 per cent in 1991. It will be an estimated 11–12 per cent of the total in the year 2000. Growth rates for those classified as coloured and Indian were considerably higher than those for whites so that they have remained about 8–9 and 3 per cent of the total population respectively. If racial classifications are abandoned in the census, it may not be possible to distinguish such figures in the future—especially as restrictions on sex and marriage across colour lines have been lifted.

African rates of increase, similar to those of whites in the inter-war years, diverged rapidly thereafter. While white rates declined, African rates probably peaked at over 3 per cent per year in the 1960s and 1970s. They subsequently fell to an annual average below 3 per cent in the 1980s and are no longer as high as in many other African countries (Table 2). (Overall growth rates have been about the same in Brazil since 1960 while in Zimbabwe they have been 3.1 and Kenya 3.6 per cent annually.) Nevertheless, these are high rates of demographic increase and the African population has become far younger (Figure 3). By 1985, 46 per cent of Africans were under 15 years old, as compared with 26.5 of whites. The children of the black baby boom of the 1960s hit their teens and early twenties in the 1980s, years of recession and youth insurrection.

Demographic change remains one of the most important but least explained phenomena in South African history. General explanations are more easily available than particular ones in that it is clear that South African patterns have been similar to those in much of Africa and Latin America. High rates of population increase tend to be linked with high infant mortality, poverty, and rurality. Historically, many African societies have valued large families. More recently, the rural poor sought social security and labour power through having more children. Moreover, there is strong evidence that, as elsewhere, social controls over both young men and women in African communities were increasingly eroded—resulting in high rates of teen-age and pre-marital pregnancy. Fewer African women were able to space their children. Previously widespread forms of non-penetrative sex (*metsha* in Xhosa) became unfashionable and men placed young women under considerable pressure to have sex. Alternative contraception was not easily available and abortion illegal.

High birth-rates were probably accompanied by lower death-rates and higher life expectancy for African people. While pockets of very high infant mortality remained, overall figures for under-5 mortality have halved between 1960 and 1990, from 192 to 90 deaths per 1,000 live births. Declining infant mortality rates, together with urbanization, help to explain why the rate of population increase seems to have slowed since the 1970s.

There is a profound irony hidden in these figures. A central element of apartheid planning was to keep the African population in the countryside and this had the effect of intensifying rural poverty. It seems that African families responded by having more babies, perceiving that they needed more potential workers and income-earners as resources declined. The 1960s was the last period when apartheid regulations did partly succeed in keeping people in rural areas. It was perhaps the last phase at which many families tried to hold on to their rural productive base. In this way government policies in the 1950s and 1960s may have helped to swell African numbers—which was certainly not their intention.

African population increase would have been fairly rapid even if urbanization had been facilitated. But comparative evidence suggests that as people concentrate in cities, and as services and welfare become available, they tend to have fewer children. The South African figures seem to bear this out. The perceptions of African families and individual women appear to have been changing in the last decade. In a world where everything has to be purchased there may be less imperative to seek security in children; too many can be a liability. Social advancement is increasingly conceived to lie in smaller families and contraception is also more widely available and acceptable in urban areas.

One other reason for rapid population increases may have been migration into South Africa by workers from the region. Despite the government's considerable success in deporting large numbers, many contrived to stay on and the foreign-born black population continued to grow. As in earlier years, foreign migrants established themselves in particular zones of employment: in the mines until the 1970s; as poorly-paid workers on the farms; in the hotel and catering trade where the skills and cordiality of Zimbabweans and Malawians were valued. The recent effects of immigration are unclear in that South Africa has absorbed many illegal Mozambican refugees.

Rapid urbanization in these years resulted not least from population growth. The homeland population has not declined, but rural districts could not support increases on this scale. Enormous pressures for housing, welfare, education, and employment have been released. Having been a relatively empty country, parts of South Africa have become crowded. One sixth the size of the USA, it now also has nearly one sixth the population. South Africa has wide open spaces on the white-owned farms but it can no longer be conceived geographically or culturally as a rural society.

The government's first response to its failure to contain urbanization was to tighten influx control in the 1960s. Between 1962 and 1967 convictions under the pass laws nearly doubled again to 693,661 annually. Statistics began to show that the African population of so-called 'white' urban areas grew far less quickly in the 1960s and 1970s. However, this evidence should not be taken to mean a decline in rates of urbanization. Rather, as the impossibility of keeping people in the countryside became clear, government strategy changed to one of displacing African conurbations outside the major metropolitan areas. Boundaries were changed and urban growth was contained within extended reserve or homeland zones. In order to understand the new social geography of the country, it is essential to turn first to the farmlands.

The White-Owned Farmlands

In many industrializing countries, the contribution of the agricultural sector to the national economy has tended to diminish rapidly. This was certainly the long-term trend in South Africa, but two qualifications must be made. Firstly, from about 1945 to 1960 commercial farmers experienced very favourable conditions internationally and domestically. Prices for primary products soared after the war. Whereas the proportion of Gross Domestic Product contributed by agriculture slipped from over 20 per cent in the 1920s to under 10 in 1945, it increased to 18 in 1950. Although it gradually declined again to 12 per cent in 1960 and 7 in 1980, these were years when mining and manufacturing were booming; farming output continued to expand fast.

Secondly, changes in agriculture had a disproportionate influence on population distribution and social developments. The white-owned farms probably absorbed a greater proportion of the black labour force than any other sector, whether mining, manufacturing, or domestic service, until the 1970s. In addition, homeland-based smallholder agriculture still drew in very large amounts of labour. The way in which African people were first held on farms, then dispelled from them, profoundly affected South African society in the apartheid era.

On the 77 per cent of land owned privately by whites, increases in arable crop and fruit production were especially dramatic. The era of sheep and cattle, when commercial agriculture could be considered primarily a pastoral activity, was over. Crop production was facilitated by the expansion of irrigated lands, following widespread dam construction. By the 1970s the proportion of South Africa's channelled water supply used for irrigation—rising to 75 per cent compared with under 50 per cent in the USA—was amongst the highest in the world. One of the many inequities of this period has been that production on white farms was prioritized over domestic water supplies for black families, most of whom did not (and many still do not) have access to tap water in their homes.

Between 1945 and 1960 maize production increased by 50 per cent, wheat a little more. Sugar production nearly doubled; fruit and groundnuts did so. Bananas in Natal, citrus and avocado pears in the Transvaal, pineapples in the eastern Cape all became subject to intensive large-scale commercial farming and greatly diversified the range of crops for domestic consumption and export. Between 1947 and 1961 the number of tractors increased from 22,000 to 122,218; by 1980 it had reached 300,000 or about four per farm (Table 4). Combine harvesters, first introduced in the wheat belt of the Cape, became common in the larger highveld maize districts from the late 1960s. The number of farming units declined from 117,000 in 1950 to about 66,000 in 1980. Land prices increased dramatically and so did the availability of credit. This overall process of concentration took place despite the fact that subdivision continued in more marginal districts.

The results for black tenants and workers, by far the majority of the farm population, were complex; it is difficult to generalize comfortably across all regions. In the initial phases of the process, up to about 1960, more rather than less labour was needed so that the number of farm-workers increased to about one and a half million. Mechanization allowed more land to be cultivated, but it was not yet so complete that machines displaced people across the whole range of agricultural activities. Large gangs were still required especially at harvest for picking fruit or maize, cane-cutting, transporting, and packing.

From the early 1960s the labour shortage, which had been so central a grievance for white farmers, gradually turned into a surplus. The number of farm-workers steadily declined, probably to about one million in the 1980s. Labour requirements also changed. Farmers wanted a core of permanent workers available all year round including skilled tractor drivers, dairymen, and others who worked with machinery. But they preferred migrant seasonal workers at times of peak labour demand.

Most skilled workers on the farms were black; agriculture was one of the few areas to which a systematic colour bar was not applied. Thus some of the staunchest supporters of apartheid were the least interested in protecting white labour on the farms. Farmers were even exempted from the provisions of an Act reserving skilled building work for whites. White tenants and workers drained from the farms even at the height of the apartheid era. By 1970 there were less than 20,000 white farm employees left. The number of whites living in the rural areas fell and Pretoria, which absorbed many rural Afrikaners, grew more rapidly than Cape Town or Johannesburg. Government promises to 'whiten' the white-owned countryside did not include featherbedding smaller farmers or white workers, both of whom were sacrificed on the altar of costs. As the number of rural whites declined, skilled black workers could find themselves in managerial-type roles, though few had any formal training. The wages of core black farm families actually increased.

Highly capitalized agricultural enterprises such as the sugar estates had long used African migrant workers. Large maize and potato farmers began to follow suit in the inter-war years and by the 1960s the fruit farms of the western Cape also employed a number of migrants, despite official discouragement of Africans in a Coloured Labour Preference area (Chapter 6). The labour bureaux, nearly 800 by 1970, and fully supported by the South African Agricultural Union (SAAU), were not least designed to channel migrant workers from homelands to the farms. Some highveld farmers kept 'labour farms' which they hired out to African tenants, drawing on their labour as required. Those who were less keen to compete for migrants could resort to convicts as casual labour.

The use of casual and prison labour eroded the remnants of paternalism on some farms and could result in atrocious working conditions. Despite occasional attempts at regulation by the state, agricultural employers were amongst the least controlled so that child labour persisted. Henry Nxumalo, writing for *Drum*, and Ruth First, on the Congress paper *New Age*, exposed abuses in powerful muck-raking journalism in the 1950s, concentrating especially on the eastern Transvaal district of Bethal. Long an intensively farmed district, Bethal became one of the potato-producing centres of South Africa and acquired a wide reputation for brutality. 'All over the eastern Transvaal, recruits spend fourteen hour days bent double scooping up potatoes with their bare hands; most now wore potato sacks after their clothes had been confiscated' (Bradford). Nxumalo's reports had some impact, precipitating a (suppressed) government inquiry and placing farm labour far higher on the ANC agenda. One of the first ANC commodity boycott campaigns in 1959 was of potatoes.

The result of these processes was that the government, the SAAU, and many leading farmers became far less concerned to immobilize labour on the farms in order to compete with mines and industries. Rather they relied on influx control to ensure that there was a continuous pool of workers in the homeland areas. Farmers were assisted by a steady increase in black unemployment in the economy as a whole through the 1970s—a result both of population increase and the inability of homeland agriculture to absorb more people. Foreign migrants, some illegals, also boosted labour supply. The abolition of the Masters and Servants Act, which had criminalized breach of contract, in 1974 facilitated labour mobility. By the early 1980s many farmers found even the labour bureaux unnecessary. While their perception of the corrupting influences of town and the lack of 'good boys' persisted, larger farmers, like urban industrialists, supported arguments for a freer labour market.

The position of labour tenants in many parts of the country had been weakened since the 1936 Native Land and Trust Act which required them to give six months' service per year. More was often demanded and rights to land or grazing diminished; migrant, casual, and prison labour further undermined tenancy. In 1964 pressure from farming organizations and officials resulted in legislation which would permit labour tenancy to be abolished in a whole district. As key arguments, officials cited efficiency and the technical and environmental benefits to be derived from owners controlling the whole farm. In the absence of a policy of protection for white farm-workers, reduction in the number of African tenants was seen as a way of countering *beswarting* (blackening) of the platteland. 'If farmers were to introduce a system of *cash wages*', so a government commission argued, 'and hire strong young labourers at a higher monthly wage, the number of Bantu in the rural White areas would greatly diminish' (Greenberg, 95). It estimated that 1.8 to 2.4 million Africans could be encouraged or compelled to leave the farms.

By the early 1980s this dire prediction had almost been fulfilled. In 1967 the government announced its intention to end black tenancy within three years and by 1969 these regulations had been applied in most of the Orange Free State and Transvaal. Natal proved to be a more difficult area. Outside the sugar, banana, and wattle belts, undercapitalized farmers feared that they would lose their labour supply and rents. A compromise was reached, lasting till 1980, whereby existing tenancy contracts would be respected but no new agreements allowed. Although various forms of tenancy survived in a disguised way, the axe had finally fallen on the descendants of those who had been at the forefront of South Africa's agrarian revolution.

Faced with unpalatable options or more secure prospects elsewhere, some black tenant families moved voluntarily; many more were pushed. The Surplus People Project (SPP), which pooled the research skills of young academics and activists in the early 1980s, calculated that about 1.1 million people were removed from the farms by 1982. A further 600,000 were forced off 'black spots'. These were farms which were owned by African people, many of them since the nineteenth century, but fell outside the designated homelands and therefore became susceptible to appropriation.

Simkins's detailed computations, on which many other sources are based, suggest that the percentage of the total African population on farms declined from 34.9 in 1951 to 31.3 in 1960 and 20.6 in 1980. However, because the rural population was growing so quickly there was a small increase in absolute terms from 3.4 million to 4.2 million between 1960 and 1980 (about 1 per cent per annum). If the black farm population had been maintained at 31 per cent of the total number of Africans, as it was in 1960, then there would have been at least 6.5 million Africans on the farmlands by 1980. SPP figures suggesting removals of close on two million therefore look reasonable, even though there was not an absolute decline in population on farms. Farms removals slowed in the 1980s, partly because the state could find nowhere else for people to go. By then, community protests against removals were also making more impact. Saul Mkize's death, resisting removal from Driefontein in the Transvaal in 1983, marked a turning-point. But by the early 1990s, the movement off the farms was gathering speed again.

Displaced Urbanization

Population movements were taking place in this period at a pace and on a scale which were unprecedented for Africans since Union. The 'surplus people' and internal refugees of South Africa were not able to choose freely where they went. Megalopolises did not immediately sprout as in Brazil or Mexico where the major cities grew so fast. Indeed from 1960 to 1980, the very years in which Africans were leaving the farms most rapidly, their proportion in what were classified as the 'white' urban areas actually declined from 29.6 to 26.7 per cent. (This still represented an absolute increase of over two million people.)

Settlement, planned and unplanned, was partly diverted to

areas defined as within the boundaries of the homelands, where the population grew from 4.2 million in 1960 (39 per cent of all Africans) to over 11 million in 1980 (52.7 per cent). Less than half of this seven-million increase would have taken place 'naturally'. Very few of those absorbed into the homelands obtained agricultural land. The great majority were drawn into closer settlements and new towns of various kinds.

Some found their way into existing rural villages and home-steads. Widespread rehabilitation and Betterment had resulted in more concentrated settlement patterns in the old reserves. By about 1980 up to half of the families in many rural homeland villages were without land. New arrivals could apply for plots when they became available, but few received them. Secondly, some of the surplus people moved into 'growth points' or expanded urban settlements within the homelands, such as Butterworth in the Transkei or Mafikeng in Bophuthatswana, where decentralized industries were being located and urban location-style housing built. Thirdly, homeland boundaries were redrawn to take in existing urban locations near major cities which then became large new townships. For example, Umlazi, formerly under the Durban municipality, became part of Kwazulu and Mdantsane, near East London, became part of the Ciskei. Lastly, government expenditure on African housing was frozen in areas classified as white and diverted through homeland budgets or the South Africa Development Trust. By the late 1980s the latter had established seventy-four new towns with a total population of over two million.

Millions of people found themselves in barely planned rural slums which were urban in respect of their population density and lack of agricultural opportunity, but rural in relation to facilities, services, and employment. These were the dumping grounds of apartheid, first documented extensively by the Catholic priest Cosmos Desmond in his book, *The Discarded People* (1971), after a journey through the 'labyrinth of broken communities, broken families and broken lives which is the South African Government's removals policy'. They have since received extensive media attention so that images of soulless self-built shanties have become indelibly associated with apartheid. Especially in their earlier years, these were 'wretched and desolate' places like Limehill in Natal—the first to come to Desmond's notice.

There is not enough water and not enough land for even a meagre subsistence farming. There is no industry and no work within daily reach. The inhabitants struggle against disease on the edge of starvation. It is impossible to say whether the physical degradation or the mental torture of living in such a place is the more terrible.

It was rivalled by places like Sada, Dimbaza, and Ilingi in the eastern Cape.

Although infrastructure and industry were extended to some resettlement towns, early rural slums were replaced by others on a far larger scale. In the 1970s that part of Bophuthatswana nearest to Pretoria became the biggest single 'close settlement' site with an estimated 750,000 people. This Winterveld area continued to grow because it was just about close enough to employment centres for daily commuting. Another striking example, Thaba Nchu, was also in Bophuthatswana—that island of it in the middle of the Orange Free State. Thaba Nchu had survived along with QwaQwa as one of only two small African reserve areas in the Orange Free State. From 1968 the government tried to stabilize the size of Bloemfontein's main location; in some smaller Orange Free State towns the African locations were razed to the ground. Sotho-speakers were supposed to go to QwaQwa and Tswana-speakers to Thaba Nchu. But Thaba Nchu had for a long time housed a diverse population and many Sotho- and Xhosa-speakers found it more attractive as it was closer to Bloemfontein and the Orange Free State goldfields.

By the 1970s services in Thaba Nchu were under control of the Bophuthatswana homeland government. Hard pressed to provide even minimal facilities, officials tended to favour Tswana-speakers. Politicians from QwaQwa, looking for a broader constituency, took up the cause of the dispossessed Sotho-speakers in Thaba Nchu. The central government, anxious to reward Bophuthatswana Chief Minister Lucas Mangope, who had taken Pretoria's offer of independence, agreed

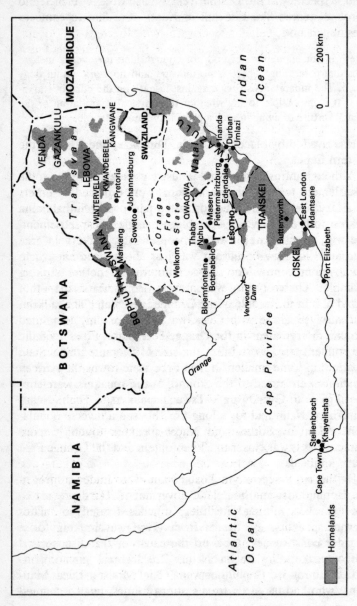

MAP 2. *Homelands and Urbanization*

to purchase some farms adjacent to Thaba Nchu in order to house the troublesome 'Sotho-speakers'. Initially this 10,000-hectare enclave, called Onverwacht (unexpected) or Botshabelo (place of refuge), was to become part of QwaQwa but it never did.

By 1980, a year after its establishment, over 100,000 people had crowded into Onverwacht. Residential plots were supposedly available on production of a reference book and QwaQwa citizenship card but this was largely ignored and people of all backgrounds made their homes there. 'The stands were 30 metres by 15 metres, each consisting of a patch of bare ground with a tin prefabricated toilet whose number—painted on the toilet door—was the new address' (Murray, 226). Within six years, by 1985, Botshabelo housed between 300,000 and half a million and had outgrown the Orange Free State capital Bloemfontein, established for over 130 years, and Welkom, the province's largest mining centre. Over the same period of time, QwaQwa itself grew from a largely rural black enclave of under 30,000 in the 1960s, tucked in near the northern corner of Lesotho, to another huge settlement approaching half a million. Those of Botshabelo's people who could get work commuted fifty kilometres each way by bus to Bloemfontein daily or went for longer periods to the more distant Orange Free State goldfields. New industrial sites were being constructed between Bloemfontein and Thaba Nchu, but the major local employer in 1985, the Country Bird battery chicken farm, had only 500 workers.

Displaced urbanization in places like Winterveld, Onverwacht, and QwaQwa seemed to solve a central problem for white South Africa. African people could not be kept rural and there was no longer any major economic advantage in perpetuating long-distance migrancy. But many African closer settlements, at least till the early 1980s, remained out of the major established cities and out of sight. African workers in these areas could reach employment centres daily and it became government policy to encourage 'commuting' rather than labour migration. This did not mean commuting in the sense of half-hour car journeys from the northern suburbs of Johannesburg to the city centre—or even hour-long train rides from closer townships like Soweto. 'Commuting' workers generally had to travel further, and in less convenient transport, as is illustrated by the case of KwaNdebele in the Transvaal.

Ndzundza Ndebele people had resurrected their identity and managed to regain land in a segregationist state (Chapter 4). A separate homeland did not, however, seem feasible for this small territorial authority until the government recognized that it might serve also as a zone for displaced urbanization. Additional farms were bought around the settlement in the 1970s and it too grew wildly from about 32,000 in 1972 to about 300,000 by 1985. It became a haven not only for former farmworkers but also for about 50,000 refugees from the Winterveld, Bophuthatswana, who felt victimized as non-Tswana.

Those of its inhabitants who could find work had to travel about 100 kilometres daily to Pretoria or East Rand towns. They were dependent on the Putco (Public Utility Transport Corporation) bus service. Begun as a small family business by immigrant Italians who ran buses from Alexandra to Johannesburg at a time when whites were being favoured with licences (Chapter 4), it expanded to become the largest bus company in the country. In 1984 its 3,500 vehicles serviced these far-flung dispersed towns, helped by a heavy subsidy from the South African government which was determined to make commuting work. In 1975 Putco ran two buses a day from KwaNdebele; in 1984, 263. Commuters could spend over six hours on noisy vehicles with hard seats designed for short hauls, leaving home at 4 a.m. and returning at 9 p.m. In his vivid indictment of government policy, American journalist Joseph Lelyveld remarked that the people of KwaNdebele were 'a nation of sleepwalkers'.

Nationally, transport difficulties were partially relieved in the 1980s by the rapid proliferation of microbus taxis, largely owned and driven by blacks. Between 1970 and 1989, microbus numbers increased from 24,000 to 174,000 (Table 4). Journey times were dramatically reduced. Taxis, which had carried very few black passengers in the 1970s, carried 30 per cent of commuters in 1989 and over 40 by 1992. Bustling taxi ranks became a new feature of most urban centres as did conflicts over custom and routes.

Given the high rate of population increase and rapid mechanization of farms, South Africa could not have escaped some degree of rural devastation and urban poverty in these decades. Yet the stark division of wealth in the country, the lack of social welfare, and the imperatives of apartheid exacerbated the trials of displaced people. Communities were dislodged and scattered. The benefits of city living, taken for granted by many whites, were absent from most new settlements. Recreational and health facilities, as well as employment, were minimal. There were economic costs, in high fares and transport subsidies, as well as serious social, environmental, and aesthetic costs in this form of urban development.

Social Division and Politics in the Homelands

Debates about the homelands have been central to critiques of apartheid. The very word 'homeland' has stimulated unease because it seemed to lend legitimacy to the state's policy of balkanization and exclusion. Opposition forces preferred to retain the word 'reserves' or use Bantustan, the term with central Asian overtones coined in the 1950s which has stuck in critical literature. Defending the language of separate development—and trying to make it a reality—was a feature of the Nationalists' task. The arguments for independence used by both the South African government and homeland leaders drew on a more widespread anti-colonial rhetoric. Britain could be seen as conquering the Transkei, and Afrikaners decolonizing it. Ideas of 'tribe' and chieftaincy had some attraction for African politicians uncertain about the possibility of any real gains under apartheid. And there were significant legacies in popular consciousness which gave Bantustan politicians some purchase.

Glossy brochures and books illustrated the undoubted beauty of some old reserve areas, as well as investments made into them, but underplayed their poverty. Tables showed that the bigger homelands would not be the smallest states in the world, nor the poorest: the Transkei and KwaZulu, it was argued, were not essentially different from Lesotho, Botswana, and Swaziland. The South African government quickly forgot that it, like its predecessors, had worked hard to incorporate these territories up to the late 1950s. Now their independence, constrained as it was by Pretoria's power, was seen as a model for the homelands.

Critics emphasized that Bantustans were not the whole of the historic African homelands and, more especially, that economically and politically they were inextricably part of South Africa. On the one hand, they and their people had made a central contribution to the development of South Africa and on the other, their people were incapable of producing enough food or achieving 'viability' given the historical skewing of the nation's economy. Millions of Africans lived in the cities and farmlands and the policy was used to justify diminishing their rights. Even after consolidation, a number of homelands remained disconnected islands surrounded by a sea of 'white' South Africa.

There is little doubt that the apartheid system, as developed up to the mid-1980s, had the effect of increasing the social chasm and income differentials between the rural homelands and urban areas. Poverty was externalized more systematically to the homelands. One indicator, among many, of these inequalities were the rates of mortality of children under 5. A number of countries which had a lower *average* per capita income than South Africa also had lower mortality rates in 1990: these included Iraq (before the Gulf War), Zimbabwe, Botswana, and Vietnam. South Africa's rates were so high, despite its wealth, because the distribution of wealth was so uneven. Although overall national estimates of under-5 child mortality declined from 192 to 90 per 1,000 between 1960 and 1990, figures of up to 300 were cited for some rural homelands in the 1960s and 1970s. Another indicator was the high rates of child malnutrition, tuberculosis, and other diseases of poverty in the Bantustans.

Homeland economies were primarily based on remnant smallholder agriculture and money from migrant workers. Evidence from the larger homelands such as Bophuthatswana,

Transkei, and KwaZulu suggests that total agricultural production did not decline greatly. Their problem was not so much that output went down, but that their population went up so rapidly. Whereas Betterment schemes were initially designed in part to control soil erosion and improve the prospects of agriculture, they increasingly became a means of rehousing displaced populations. Even where Betterment plans were relatively successful, they seldom prevented environmental degradation. Perhaps the major problem reported by anthropologists was that the new villages themselves became the site for ecological damage. Cattle, sheep, and goats still often had to be brought back nightly because of theft and inadequate maintenance of fencing, but they were now being returned to more concentrated village settlements than before.

Few villages had piped water, with the result that the streams, springs, and boreholes near concentrated settlements could be overstretched. In pre-colonial times, African settlement on the East Coast had been dispersed not least in order to minimize this problem. The supply of water was a critical issue not only for health reasons but also because women had to spend so much time and effort in collecting it. Surveys in the Transkei in the early 1980s suggested that on average women and children spent about three hours per homestead every day fetching water. Distance from water-sources was of major significance to a household's well-being. Per capita consumption of water, over 200 litres per day for white city-dwellers, could be as little as ten for rural blacks. The drought years of the early 1980s revealed the maldistribution of water with frightening clarity.

Few of the buildings in new rehabilitation villages or displaced towns were initially linked to the national electricity grid, fuelled by South Africa's plentiful supply of cheap coal. Indeed, only in the 1970s was progress made with the electrification of major black townships such as Soweto. Many rural people, and those living in a semi-urban situation, had to find their fuel from coal and especially timber. Firewood was collected by women in strenuous and time-consuming journeys. 'One of the clearest images of . . . poverty in the country is the sight of a group of elderly black women, each carrying home on her head a load of firewood weighing up to 50 kg., passing underneath the high tension cables that carry the electric energy between the towns (and farmsteads) of the Republic' (Wilson and Ramphele, 44). In one part of KwaZulu, the average distance walked in collecting one headload was over eight kilometres and the average time for collecting a load 4.5 hours. Women, who made up the majority of adults in the homelands, suffered particularly from the squeeze on rural resources.

Lack of electricity and affordable fuel aside from firewood could have a devastating effect on the environment around large new settlements. In 1976/7, 40,000 people moved from Herschel, which was about to be incorporated into the Transkei, to an area called Thornhill in the Ciskei near Queenstown where some farms had been bought from white owners. 'From the air this area stands out as a reddish patch of bare soil, virtually devoid of vegetation', Wilson and Ramphele noted. 'In 1976 . . . [it] had a good cover of thorn trees and bush. By 1981 hardly a tree was to be seen on the slopes of the hill' (p. 45). While systematic farm planning and subsidy probably improved the condition of farmlands, environmental ills were concentrated in the homelands.

Population movements, environmental problems, poverty, and unrewarding labour characterized many homelands at the height of the apartheid era. Although pockets of strong rural traditionalism and community life survived, not least because of the lack of modern services, it was less characteristic overall. Neo-traditional dress of blankets, beads, and head-dresses, faded away. The period from the 1960s to the 1980s marked a new phase of incorporation of the old African chiefdoms, so that they lost much of their distinctiveness and increasingly reflected the predominant urban and wage-based culture. In retrospect, the rural revolts and protests of the 1950s proved to be a last attempt to defend the autonomy of the reserves. Many elements of African culture did survive or were reinvented in some form both in town and countryside—for example bride-wealth, Sotho and Xhosa male initiation, Zulu 'traditional weapons' and women's headgear, communal labour, and African medicine. But the social bonds which some state ideologues argued they were attempting to preserve tended to erode.

It is inadequate, however, to leave an analysis of the homelands at that: a picture so often presented of social and environmental devastation. They should not be viewed purely in terms of their functionality to the capitalist system or as exhibiting the scars of underdevelopment. In 1980 over 50 per cent of the African population lived within new homelands and their particular pattern of politics and development had important implications for the country as a whole. For the homelands policy to work, even to the extent that it did, local co-operation was required and there were beneficiaries of the system.

The Transkei, flagship of homeland development, was granted self-government in 1963 and elections were held for a legislative assembly. Chief Poto, who led a Democratic Party opposed to many elements of apartheid, won 38 out of 45 seats. But Kaiser Matanzima persuaded the majority of *ex-officio* chiefs in the new assembly to support him. He could play on the insecurities of the chiefs and élite who had been so threatened in the rebellions of the 1950s and early 1960s. The state of emergency, imposed in these years, remained in force. Matanzima's Transkei National Independence Party (TNIP) subsequently improved its showing amongst an electorate which recognized that it had no alternative and he effectively introduced one-party rule. His path was followed by the other homeland leaders who, with Pretoria's support, veered away from representative forms of government. In this respect, they were more rather than less like independent African states to the north. Starting in 1976, four homelands—Transkei, Bophuthatswana, Ciskei, and Venda—accepted independence. Although the South African state took the trappings of independence seriously, homeland governments received little recognition beyond Pretoria.

The KwaZulu government, under Chief Mangosuthu Buthelezi, used the homeland system to its full potential, but stopped short of accepting independence. This gave him considerable bargaining power with the state which was keen to push him in this direction. Deeply conscious of the historic might of the

Zulu, Buthelezi's aims were larger than a localized authority. Far more than other homeland leaders, he was able to canvass popular support as a vocal critic of some elements of apartheid up to the late 1970s. His Inkatha movement, which emphasized cultural renewal and invoked popular Zulu symbols, was far more effective than Matanzima's TNIP, both locally and nationally. Whereas ethnicity in the earlier part of the century often involved defence of rural resources and an old way of life, it was now also mobilized in competition for new resources and control over new local states.

Pretoria funnelled large quantities of money into the homelands which emphasized emerging social differentiation. Expanding bureaucracies and educational institutions boosted the number of homeland citizens earning reasonable salaries. In the Transkei alone, there were 20,000 in state employ in 1980 and 14,000 teachers taught nearly 700,000 pupils (Southall, 182). All but a few hundred top posts and advisory positions were Africanized. Nationally, the homelands benefited disproportionately from funding for African secondary-school expansion so that by the 1970s perhaps two-thirds of high schools were within their boundaries. A central tenet of apartheid was to divert the ambitions of the African educated classes from major cities so that they would help guide the journey towards separate development.

Business as well as bureaucracy provided opportunities. Africans had been permitted to apply for trading licences in the reserves since the 1930s, but few were able to get key sites or credit from the merchant houses who supplied rural traders. Up to the 1960s trade in most African reserves was still controlled by the dispersed network of white-owned stores. Subsequently, as part of homeland development strategy, state corporations were established which bought out white traders and leased or sold the sites to blacks. Trade and transport proved the most secure routes, along with public employment, for accumulation in the homelands.

Although agriculture was not a major growth area, it mirrored more general social differentiation. Surveys from the 1980s suggest that only about 10 per cent of families in the

Transkei were significantly involved in agriculture and perhaps 5 per cent made a living from the land. As a proportion this number was small, but 10 per cent meant 60,000 families—almost as many as the total number of white farming units in South Africa. In KwaZulu, sugar outgrower schemes for smallholders provided scope for renewal and commercialization of agriculture. Families with significant wage income were often the most successful agricultural producers as well. But large numbers of homeland dwellers, even if they had little other income, were unable to accumulate rural resources.

Up to the 1960s urban and industrial development within the reserves had been minimal and the old magisterial towns remained relatively small administrative, transport, and trading centres. Three processes began to change this. One was the growth of new towns through displaced urbanization. Another was the extension of homeland boundaries to include existing and growing urban townships. Thirdly, while Verwoerd initially disallowed white investment in the homelands, he encouraged industrial decentralization to border industries. These were sited in 'white' territory, but serviced by a black labour force resident in the homelands. The Nationalists pumped subsidies into border industries over many years and also passed a Physical Planning Act which was in part designed to restrict new employment of Africans in the established industrial centres.

In the late 1960s direct investment by outsiders was allowed in the homelands in order to enhance their economic viability. Some industrialists, especially foreign investors, did choose to exploit subsidies and low wage rates in the homelands. In the 1970s decentralized industries grew more quickly than those in the older metropolitan centres. Most, but not all, of the homeland factories made products, from matches to clothing, which required limited skills and were cheap to transport to the main urban markets. Some of the most significant outcomes of investment were casinos, constructed notably by the Southern Suns hotel group, in order to circumvent strict South African gambling laws. Sun City, in a segment of Bophuthatswana, was a glitzy and highly successful hotel, entertainment, and gam-

bling venture within easy reach by car from the Rand. White
South Africans were its main customers.

Large funds and subsidies managed by Development Corporations and homeland governments opened the way for kick-
backs, property speculation, and corruption. Newspaper
reports of dubious dealings in the Bantustans were legion, a
fertile source for investigative journalism. As Streek and Wicksteed argued of Matanzima's Transkei: 'his involvement in
corrupt and suspect practices set an example to civil servants
and other government employees, and it is not surprising they
have done well out of independence' (p. 234). The Bantustan
system created networks of economic and political patronage,
with little outside control, reaching down from key figures in
Pretoria into homeland administrations so that many South
Africans, white and black, found some self-interest in it.
Nevertheless, by the early 1980s *verligtes* were expressing
severe doubts about the expense and unworkability of the
system. Homeland politicians were under increasing pressure
as the youth rebellion of the 1970s became a general insurrection in the 1980s. Their politics became more involuted and
violent, capped by a few military coups. While some leaders
turned more explicitly to ethnic mobilization, many of the
homeland élite began to look to national movements.

The legacy of displaced urbanization, homeland poverty, and
homeland politics deeply influenced social developments in
South Africa. Although the country was spared the terrifying
famines of Africa in the 1970s and 1980s and the vortex of civil
war, it had many of its own internal refugees. Industrialization
and transport had diminished outright famine but by no means
solved the problem of widespread malnutrition. The uprooting
of so many people undoubtedly compounded poverty and
contributed to the volatility of black politics. Similarly the
entrenchment of homelands with their systems of reward
through ethnic identification helped to fuel division between
and within African communities.

In the 1980s when the government finally lost control over
urbanization, the major established cities again experienced
explosive growth (Chapter 10). Nevertheless, the new towns of

the apartheid era will remain part of the urban landscape. QwaQwa, KwaNdebele, and Botshabelo will probably remain almost entirely black cities and in this sense the legacy of apartheid will be a long one. But given the problems of large metropolitan areas, there may be long-term benefits to a more dispersed pattern of urbanization—even if these are now hard to discern amidst the poverty and unemployment. In a post-apartheid era, interlinked conurbations may become corridors of growth where the environmental impact may be more containable than in the older metropolitan areas. They could provide an important stimulus to the surrounding rural districts. One example may be the Bloemfontein–Botshabelo–Thaba Nchu axis, stretching to Maseru in Lesotho, across the centre of the country, already home to over two million people.

9 Black Political Struggles and the Reform Era of P. W. Botha, 1973–1984

The ANC and the Politics of Exile

From the late 1970s, after three decades of power, the Nationalists were showing signs of vulnerability. The major reason was the growth of political opposition on a number of fronts. In this respect, the Natal strikes of 1973 and the Soweto protests of 1976 were turning-points. By the early 1980s domestic opposition was beginning to link more effectively to the banned political movements whose survival, largely in exile, proved to be of great importance.

The ANC, PAC, and others initially tried to work underground within the country. The ANC's armed wing, Umkhonto we Sizwe, initially concentrated on the formation of cells and sabotage. These were years of fallen pylons and bombs in public buildings. By minimizing civilian casualties, which it felt morally unjustified, Congress hoped that it might jolt the government into recognizing the need for negotiation. But armed struggle only increased Nationalist resolve, already strengthened by its victory in the Republic referendum. The PAC military wing, Poqo, was less inhibited and did kill some white civilians—actions which attracted more publicity and undermined the ANC's already uncertain strategy of using constrained violence to persuade. In 1964 a group of largely white student activists not based in the Congress movement launched their own sabotage campaign. After a few heady blasts, including the Johannesburg station explosion in 1964, they were arrested and station bomber Harris hanged.

Underground movements of all kinds were greatly hampered by the success of the security police in infiltrating them. Mandela was caught in 1962; in 1963 other key Congress underground leaders were captured at a farm owned by white

Communist Party members in Rivonia, north of Johannesburg. Perhaps 10,000 people were arrested in the early 1960s. Opposition movements still had relatively open recruitment policies and security police were able to find spies, black and white, or extract information from those arrested. Increasingly ruthless methods were used, including torture, which had not been so significant a part of the police repertoire before. The long and sorry saga began of deaths in detention, of prisoners alleged to have thrown themselves out of windows or hanged themselves in their cells. Legislatively sanctioned imprisonment without trial and house arrests were accompanied by an increasingly uncontrolled cop-culture—smashed windscreens and windows, dead cats on gateposts, threatening phone calls, and eventually political killings. Critical film-makers later created an image of blue-eyed police sergeants with searing stares, hard voices, and harder hands; they did, in a sense, exist.

Trust and betrayal became a central nexus in radical opposition politics and the stakes could be very high. It was difficult to be heroic in an atmosphere of suspicion. Nor were activists safe outside the country. Cross-border raids began in 1961 and the web of informers spread abroad with the exile movements. The state succeeded not only in discovering and imprisoning many key political leaders but also in defusing any rapid remobilization. Under Vorster and General van den Bergh the security police, now extended into the ominous Bureau of State Security (BOSS), became a highly effective instrument.

It has been argued that the ANC, Communists, and PAC underestimated the intransigence of the government, and overestimated both the readiness of the people to revolt and the likelihood of international assistance. In abandoning non-violent mass action or worker organization they thus fatally weakened themselves. Yet there seemed few options left other than a return to cautious reformism or working through the Bantustan system. By the mid-1960s, it was clear that stuttering sabotage would have to be replaced by a more systematic, better-funded military effort based outside the country. Reflecting the methods of liberation movements in the region, the ANC shifted its strategy to guerrilla struggle. Three small expeditions were sent through Rhodesia with Zimbabwean liberation movement units in 1967/8. They engaged fiercely but unsuccessfully with Rhodesian forces and South African police. With no bases in neighbouring countries, there was little scope for an externally based war as in Zimbabwe. South Africa's remnant peasantry, difficult to reach and tightly policed, could not provide a platform for sustained guerrilla struggle.

By contrast, the international diplomatic campaign, led by Tambo who had been sent overseas to open an office in 1960, made more effective progress. The ANC gained access to the United Nations; helped found national Anti-Apartheid movements; and mobilized funds and resources from the Eastern bloc, African allies, and Scandinavian countries. In the cold war era, the USA and Western European governments tended to see the ANC as revolutionary and to avoid it. A rapidly growing South Africa was seen, although increasingly uneasily, as a good investment and a bastion against communism. But anti-apartheid forces in these countries were able to claim some of the moral high ground. Boycott campaigns involving such varied targets as Outspan oranges, Cape fruit, cultural exchanges, and the arms trade met with some success. As in the case of anti-slavery campaigns over 150 years earlier, it became increasingly difficult to justify apartheid in Western countries.

One of the most significant boycotts was in sport. In a post-colonial age, segregated sport became a major international issue. Demonstrations began in 1960 in Aotearoa (New Zealand). Verwoerd and Vorster invited reprisals when they refused permission for Maori members to tour with an All Blacks rugby team in 1965 and for ex-Capetonian coloured cricketer Basil D'Oliveira to join the English cricket team in 1968. In the same year, pressure from African and Asian countries resulted in South Africa's exclusion from the Olympics. When a South African rugby team visited Britain in 1970, the sports boycott came of age in the Stop the Seventy Tour campaign. South Africa's response was to tough it out and play with those who would play with them. International control boards in rugby, where the former white dominions were more dominant than in cricket, athletics, and football, took more than a decade to isolate white South Africa. But the boycott brought the issue of apartheid into arenas which were not usually forced to confront such questions. For many white South Africans, whose identity was bound up with sport, creeping international isolation began to have its effects.

Exile movements, dispersed far from their constituencies, searching for diverse international support and fearful of infiltration, are prone to factionalism. Specific organizational and ideological issues did threaten the unity of the ANC: not least the role of the Communist Party and whites, and also the relative weight that should be placed on class or national struggle. Socialist ideas did permeate the ANC in exile, but difficulties were partly defused by the fact that the CP continued to work within the limits of a nationalist rather than explicitly socialist struggle. An attempt was made to specify what was implied by a national democratic revolution, based on the Freedom Charter, at a major ANC conference in Morogoro, Tanzania, in 1969. The conference also agreed to allow non-racial membership and to reactivate internal opposition. If the language of the exile movements seemed sometimes rigid, this was hardly exceptional in the context of left politics in the 1960s and 1970s. There were splits to the Africanist right and socialist left and it was perhaps necessary to police a tight political line when ideological and personal differences could rapidly have produced fragmentation.

The Communist Party not only helped to maintain organizational continuity but also to provide a conduit for funding and training in the Eastern bloc. When Mozambique and Angola were liberated and Marxist governments came to power in 1975, the ANC readily found new bases for operation closer to South Africa. By contrast, the PAC fractured and all but collapsed in exile. ANC prisoners, in particular those on Robben Island near Cape Town, also managed to sustain discussion and political planning. 'The ANC's survival through the bleak 1960s and early 1970s (albeit in a much-weakened form), had a cumulative—and pivotal—result for the movement. Its long-established traditions and symbols of resistance survived with it, and it would be repopularised—to considerable effect—during the resurgence of militant internal resistance' (Barrell in Johnson). At home Congress, like its imprisoned leaders, could remain a powerful memory, standing for a non-racial democracy and 'one man one vote' (in the language of the time), unsullied by the compromises of local politics.

Internal Remobilization: Black Consciousness

While the hiatus in internal black political organization after 1961 was sharp, that in opposition political thinking was less so. By the late 1960s a set of ideas which came to be called 'black consciousness', originating in the churches and educational institutions, were being reformulated. Black consciousness was more an intellectual orientation than a political grouping, difficult to capture analytically because it was represented by a scattering of proponents and small organizations rather than a single party. Protagonists asserted a confidence in being black in the wake of bannings, everyday racism, and dehumanization. They took on the government in the ideological sphere precisely at the moment when its economic success was cresting and the relentless propaganda in favour of apartheid and retribalization seemed to be gaining ground. Their concentration on ideological issues also reflected their caution about open and therefore vulnerable party organization. Moreover, they took issue with the deference and uncertain cultural direction of the African élite.

Use of the word 'black' was in itself a challenge to apartheid's ethnic and racial terminology and an alternative to the negative 'non-white' (*nie-blanke*) or 'non-European' which was in common currency. Terminology has been important in the political debate and the government's adoption of 'Bantu' rather than native or African was an essential part of its policy. As in the USA, where African-Americans shifted from 'Negro' and 'coloured' to black, the use of this word in South Africa set down claims to rights and evoked a new and unified identity. (Black was borrowed from the USA but had been in use in

African languages: *abantu abamnyama* meant ordinary or black people in Xhosa.) Steve Biko, the medical student who was one of the key protagonists of black consciousness, used the term non-white as late as 1969, switching to black around 1970. Black specifically included coloured and Indian people as well as African. Coloured intellectuals disdainfully prefaced that racial categorization with 'so-called' if they used it at all. This insistence on black was so successful that Botha's government itself renounced Bantu and adopted the term, for African people at least, a decade later.

The amalgam of ideas which made up black consciousness drew on the heritage of Africanism in the ANC and the PAC as well as the strong sense of being African that persisted in the rural areas, in African Christianity, and in everyday associational forms. But the eclectic new black consciousness was not essentially a local populist ideology and found much of its additional weaponry in the resounding language of the US civil rights and Black Power movements of the 1960s. Literature of liberation struggles, such as the writings of Frantz Fanon, and images of Che Guevara filtered back despite banning of individual works. Biko drew directly on Fanon in his critical article on psychological liberation: 'Black Souls in White Skins'.

In the 'orthodox' churches, which still had very considerable international connections and networks, specifically South African anger was given further focus by international liberation theology. In the 1960s major Christian denominations were coming to terms with decolonization and debates about Third World poverty. The language of Christianity and its political messages were changing. Anglicans, Catholics, and Methodists all threw up individual leaders, both black and white, who maintained a specifically Christian critique of apartheid policy and practice. The Christian Institute, formed in 1963, headed by the renegade Dutch Reformed Minister Beyers Naude, together with the South African Council of Churches, provided a focus for opposition groupings. Hammanskraal, the Catholic seminary north of Pretoria, became a centre for black consciousness meetings and one of the first specific groupings was the University Christian Movement founded in 1967.

If one organizational focus of the movement lay in the churches its central impetus came from educational institutions and student politics. In 1959 African entry into 'white' universities was further restricted and 'tribal' recruiting policies imposed on Fort Hare, Alma Mater of many nationalists. New ethnic universities, derogatorily called 'bush colleges', were established within homeland boundaries, in the western Cape for coloured students and at Durban Westville for Indians. They were peopled with conservative Afrikaner academics while their administration fell under ethnic education departments. Although black university education expanded, it did so in increasingly segregated spheres.

The National Union of South African Students (NUSAS) had survived as a single non-racial organization and a platform for politicized students both from the English-speaking and black campuses. (Afrikaner students had their own national union.) The English-speaking universities remained important nodes of opposition political culture. Carried by the surge of student protest in Europe and the USA and the mood of the anti-Vietnam movement, students developed a new sense of urgency about political and social change from the late 1960s. The University of Cape Town sit-in of 1968, triggered by a particularly South African issue—the blocking of Archie Mafeje's appointment as lecturer in Anthropology, apparently under pressure from the government—was one key turning-point.

Despite this radicalism, inter-racial political activity was limited and NUSAS conferences were dominated by the large and articulate white delegations. If the presence of blacks was appreciated, they were more marginalized than they wished. Black students broke with NUSAS in 1968 and launched the South African Students Organization (SASO) in 1969. Biko argued that white liberals 'are claiming a monopoly on intelligence and moral judgement and setting the pattern and pace for the realisation of the black man's aspirations' (*I Write What I Like*, 21). Blacks should liberate themselves. Black students also felt that they confronted particular problems in their new institutions, where both intellectual control and discipline were heavy handed. Their debate was not just with white students, but also an attempt to reach back into the communities and counter the ethnicization of black politics through the rapidly evolving Bantustan system.

In 1972 the Black People's Convention was launched as an umbrella body for the black consciousness groups coalescing in many different spheres. Awareness of the emerging trade union movement led in 1973 to the formation of the Black Allied Workers' Union (BAWU), though some were opposed to the idea of a specifically worker organization. A flagship community health project in the eastern Cape, launched under Mamphela Ramphele, probably expressed the movement's social aspirations more closely. Black consciousness literature and journalism flourished. In 1974 a major rally celebrated the collapse of the Portuguese Empire. At this time, leaders began to receive the same treatment of banning and imprisonment experienced earlier by Congress. A Turfloop student leader was forced into exile and then killed by a parcel bomb in 1974. The movement needed a high profile and access to the media in order to mobilize support, but this exposed its leaders to retaliation.

While churches, university students, and writers were at the ideological heart of black consciousness, school students proved to be its most effective political vanguard. Between 1950 and 1975, the number of African children at school rose from around one million to over 3.5 million and the proportion at secondary school from 3 to over 8 per cent. Secondary expansion was especially dramatic between 1965 and 1975, when it increased nearly fivefold. Class sizes averaged over 60 in Soweto and reached 100. Under-trained teaching staff in acutely under-resourced schools found it difficult to cope and corporal punishment was commonplace. Schools became sites of expansion, of expectation, of deprivation, and of explosive political potential.

The school-based South African Students Movement (SASM) was strongest in Orlando, the old heart of Soweto and a politicized area since the 1950s. It included leaders with some experience: the average age for black students completing matriculation in the late 1960s was 20. They challenged the authoritarianism of the Department of Bantu Education which had cowed teachers and dismissed political activists and aimed to find a channel for 'needs and grievances' by the formation of Student Representative Councils which were widespread in the universities.

One of SASM's campaigns was against interschool music competitions, a major extramural interest and commitment of African teachers, which students felt was disrupting education because they took so much time and energy. Choral music was heavily featured on black radio programmes and while it had strong roots in African churches, it was an activity that was not perceived to threaten the apartheid order. A clear generational challenge was involved, as also in the scholars' campaign against liquor which reflected awareness of the disruption it caused to education and social life. SASM incorporated the idea of 'the system' into their vocabulary to express the whole oppressive regime which seemed to impinge on their lives. By the mid-1970s some SASM organizers made contact with ANC members such as Joe Gqabi, later killed by a letter-bomb, who were coming off Robben Island.

SASM activists were catalysts in the Soweto marches which rocked the country in 1976, a time of regional crisis and economic recession (Chapter 7). Government was reluctant to maintain high subsidies on vital consumer items like maize and bread for the urban poor. This, coupled with rising unemployment and urban crowding, exacerbated the effects of the downturn in Soweto. But the protest was specifically against the inequalities of Bantu Education and the introduction of Afrikaans, 'the language of the oppressor', as a teaching medium for some subjects including maths.

After successfully resisting the arrest of one of its officials, SASM established an Action Committee with representatives from Soweto schools and organized a demonstration for 16 June 1976. Protesters were to converge from different points and march to Orlando stadium. It was the police overreaction which gave the student struggle its kickstart and helped launch over a year of action. School boycotts and attacks on govern-

ment buildings, police informers, and beerhalls were not
new tactics in themselves but achieved a fresh intensity and
provoked unprecedented retaliation leading to hundreds of
deaths.

Two striking features of 1976 were the spread of protest to
'coloured' schools in the western Cape and attacks not only on
Municipal beerhalls but also shebeens and liquor stores. Students were not fighting for the right to brew and sell liquor but
arguing that 'we can no longer tolerate seeing our fathers' pay-
packet emptied in shebeens'. Mbulelo Mzamane captured the
urgency of the rebellion and the simultaneous informality and
portentousness of its language in his novel *The Children of
Soweto* (p. 126).

> Listen our parents
> It is us, your children
> Who are crying;
> It is us, your children,
> Who are dying.
> *Amandla!*

We, the children of Soweto, hereby call upon you all to join us in
mourning our martyrs massacred in Soweto by Vorster's fascist
stormtroopers . . .

You yourselves have been eye-witnesses to all the atrocities perpe-
trated against us by the System (p. 143).

Vorster hit out against 'agitators' in the year following
Soweto so that black consciousness organizations, the South
African Council of Churches, and many individuals, black and
white, were banned. The Soweto *World*, which had supported
the students, was closed. In 1977 Steve Biko was arrested and
died after torture at the hands of the police. Perhaps 12,000
youths fled the country. It was difficult for organizations to
mature and develop nationally or to elaborate specific programmes. But anger and symbols of resistance survived: the
clenched fist, the slogan *amandla awethu* (power to us, the
people); the picture of Hector Peterson, one of the first to be
shot, being carried away by anguished scholars. There was a

strong belief amongst many black youths that 'the system' was so unjust that it could not last.

Trade Unions

Along with other Congress-linked groups, the SACTU federation was weakened by repression in the early 1960s and survived actively only in exile. A number of its organizers went underground as Umkhonto we Sizwe cadres. While white unions prospered under apartheid, and some tradition of multiracial activity was maintained in the moderate TUCSA federation, the 1960s—when real wages generally increased—was a period of deunionization for African workers. Strikes, however, had never been dependent on unions and the balance began to shift in the early 1970s. In 1971 a partially successful strike by Ovambo migrant workers in Namibia gained considerable publicity. In 1972 Durban stevedores stopped work. And in 1973 the industrial areas around that city were hit by a wave of strike action.

Interviews with Natal factory workers in 1973 revealed a clear memory of organization from the 1950s. Former members of SACTU remained in the work-force, but were not keen to develop formal union organization. Most of the workers were Zulu-speaking and in addition to singing the black national anthem *Nkosi Sikelel' iAfrika* (God Bless Africa), some expressed their solidarity in shouts of *Usuthu* for the Zulu royal family and brandished 'traditional' sticks. A speech to workers by Zulu King Goodwill Zwelithini at the end of 1972 raised hopes for wage rises. Later surveys found that informal leadership networks of *stokvels* and migrant home-groups were important nodes of mobilization.

The strikes followed a well-established pattern of non-unionized black worker protest but focused attention on the scope for unionization. They also coincided with new intellectual developments. The political traditions and social composition of white South African society were sufficiently diverse to produce, throughout the apartheid era, succeeding generations of dissidents. Most came from middle-class English-speaking families, including a disproportionate number from Jewish backgrounds. Post-1968 radicalization, together with the difficulties of coping with black consciousness ideas and a rediscovery of socialism, helped to refocus white radical student thinking.

Socialist and New Left currents which swept through British and American universities were expressed in the work of expatriates such as Legassick, Trapido, and Wolpe. Their analysis provided a means of conceiving South Africa as a peculiar capitalist society, in which class as much as race was a primary social division. That cohort of intellectuals at home and in Britain played a significant role in decolonizing minds. The years from 1968 to 1974 were a particularly fertile period for white as well as black student politics and many new radical initiatives were generated, from literacy groups to the South African Voluntary Service. White radicals, linking with older unionists, made their most significant impact in worker organization where black consciousness seemed to be hesitant.

In 1972 the Workers' Benefit Fund and Institute for Industrial Education in Durban, the Urban Training Project (Johannesburg), and the Wages Advisory Committee (Cape Town) were launched. Durban activists had some involvement in the 1973 strikes. By the mid-1970s fully-fledged African unions such as the General Workers in Cape Town and the National Textile Workers in Durban were established. Some Indian textile workers, inheritors of a strong union tradition, recognized the advantages of co-operation and joined the new independent union. The African Metal and Allied Workers Union (MAWU) made rapid strides in a few Natal factories, including Leyland, and by 1975 had extended to the Rand. Strong links remained between academics, the new unions, and service organizations which retained a non-racial leadership.

From the start, great emphasis was laid on democratic structures, shop-floor organization, and elected shop stewards. These were seen as a means of averting some of the weaknesses of black trade unions in the past where either the leadership was insufficiently controlled or mass membership had mushroomed then collapsed in the face of repression and failure. The ICU in the 1920s was held up as an example not to follow. The issue of representativeness was all the more important because government and industry attempted to meet the challenge of unions by developing appointed Works and Liaison committees to provide an alternative channel of communication between employers and black workers.

With the exception of some of those in the Cape, the independent unions tended to be industrial rather than general, concentrating their energies on work-related issues and avoiding open political alignment. While their political potential was patent, they were anxious to walk before they could run. Indeed, the government adopted a relatively cautious approach of containment and did not ban them outright. A survey of union members in 1976 found that workers 'contrasted SACTU's concentration on politics on a national level, with the present unions' concern with the day-to-day issues in the factory, and their stress on the need to resolve complaints through shop stewards, and not at the trade union offices' (Webster in Maree). The unions had remained careful during the Soweto protests of 1976, although there was widespread sympathy and stayaways were organized in response to calls from the scholars.

Unionists also suffered in the spate of bannings and detentions after 1976 and organization was weakened by industrial recession. But they had sunk sufficiently strong roots to survive. They minimized strike action and concentrated on international companies which were vulnerable to adverse publicity. By the late 1970s a small number of new unions were being recognized for negotiation purposes because of the extent of their shop-floor support. In 1979 and 1980 the independent Unions formed two federations, FOSATU and CUSA. The former was explicitly non-racial while CUSA restricted itself largely to black workers and black leadership. BAWU, associated with the Black Consciousness Movement, which had not developed much in the 1970s, split in 1979. One of its successor organizations SAAWU proved especially successful in the eastern Cape, a historically politicized region where black communities were both relatively well educated and relatively poor. It campaigned on community issues and challenged the Ciskei administration, which had recently taken independent status.

Crisis, Reform, and the UDF

Up to the early 1970s, Afrikaner *verligtes* emphasized the positive elements of separate development which many still felt might be attained. It was only a minority, such as a few church figures at Potchefstroom University for Christian Higher Education, who questioned the morality of apartheid. With white confidence shaken by Soweto in 1976 harder questions began to be asked about the feasibility of grand apartheid, the viability of the homelands, and the consequences of mass removals. Elsa Joubert's book, *The Long Journey of Poppie Nongena*, first published in Afrikaans (1978), caught this mood. It was the 'true' story of an Afrikaans-speaking black woman, marginalized by apartheid. Although Joubert denied a political intent, and many reviewers saw the story as a personal tragedy with a Christian ending, it was difficult to escape the devastating indictment of the effects of pass laws, influx control, and resettlement, which separated husband and wife, children and parents. It was widely read, serialized in the press, and made into a play.

In 1978 a political scandal broke that played strangely on whites' self-image. Vorster's security chief and information supremo misused public money in a campaign to persuade the world of the government's credentials. The 'information scandal' was not the first example of corruption, but it came at a difficult time and undermined some of those many who still believed in the morally superior character of the Afrikaner establishment. This spelt the end of Vorster, already a sick man, and P. W. Botha came to power. A long-established party official from the Cape and Minister of Defence he was a proponent of Armscor and the military.

Botha faced a regional context which had changed radically. Up to the mid-1970s white rule was cushioned by the circle of settler and colonial states around it. In the Portuguese colonies of Angola and Mozambique, the metropolitan government itself, rather than settlers, had underwritten the large military effort entailed in controlling an increasingly hostile African population in the 1960s and 1970s. In 1974, when a coup in Portugal—prompted not least by the costs of the colonial wars—displaced the Fascist government, decolonization followed rapidly. Rhodesian settlers had made their Unilateral Declaration of Independence from Britain after the break-up of Federation in 1965 and fought their own campaign against the black Zimbabwean liberation movements. But from the mid-1970s the intensity of the war became more severe and despite South African assistance and an 'internal settlement', settler rule succumbed in 1979. In 1980 a black Zimbabwe African National Union (ZANU) government under Robert Mugabe was elected.

Pretoria increasingly perceived itself to be subject to a 'total onslaught' from the north and the hinterland was seen not so much as a source of labour, or avenue for possible expansion, or even as a trading zone, but as a potential threat. The South West Africa People's Organization (SWAPO) was able to mount an increasingly effective challenge from bases in Angola. South African strategists were deeply concerned that the ANC was finding nearby military bases from which to prosecute its own armed struggle. Because of its proximity and its socialist government, Mozambique was seen as the major potential threat. South Africa fostered the rebel Renamo organization, initially launched by the Rhodesian security forces, to challenge the fledgling Frelimo state.

Vorster had tried hard to develop diplomatic and economic contacts with some African states in order to counteract regional isolation. He had some success with Malawi under the conservative and capitalist President Banda. Botha made renewed attempts to develop a 'constellation' of Southern African states, using both sticks and carrots. But an alternative organization linking the black governments of the region, the Southern African Development Co-ordination Conference, though beset by problems, confirmed the frontline states' commitment to find a political and economic future outside

South Africa's orbit. While Pretoria had long demanded that foreign powers should keep out of its internal affairs, it now felt that the 'total onslaught' justified almost any tactic, short of outright war. Political and economic destabilization became one of the least salubrious features of Botha's rule. Whereas armed struggle was the weapon of liberation movements until the late 1970s, it increasingly became the instrument of counter-revolution. South African intervention exacerbated and internationalized civil conflicts with tragic consequences for the people involved.

Regional pressures contributed, along with internal challenges, towards government 'reform' in the period from 1978 to 1984. In 1978 P. W. Botha warned whites to 'adapt or die'. Piet Koornhof, a Broederbonder on the *verlig* wing of the party, declared in Washington in 1979 that 'apartheid is dead'. Most Nationalist politicians were far more cautious at home, but recognized the need to reform. As the army rather than the police became central to the security and power structures of the country, so it was recognized that 'hearts and minds' had to be courted more assiduously (Chapter 10).

The Soweto school revolt of 1976 forced reconsideration of urban black living conditions. Electrification of Soweto and other townships became a more urgent priority which had many social implications. In 1979 tentative schemes were reintroduced for black private property in the urban areas, twenty years after the government had tried to abolish this. Koornhof's much-quoted aphorism also indicated that the party was beginning to deracialize its ideology and project a more incorporative image—a state which was national in the broader sense rather than simply an Afrikaner state.

Afrikaner businesses, along with industry in general, openly criticized restrictions in the labour market and state monopolies. As the free-market ideology of the Thatcher and Reagan era permeated South African politics, reformers found its combination of more liberal economic policy and conservative social philosophy matched well with their developing perception of the country's problems. Conservative dominance in the West provided something of a respite for white South Africa to work out a reformist strategy while its rulers could participate in a shared rhetoric against Communism. To a greater extent than before, the government clasped the business community to its bosom. Highly publicized conferences were held in Anglo-American's Carlton Centre, Johannesburg, and in Cape Town. Business interests were incorporated into commissions and advisory bodies. The Urban Foundation, a privately funded welfare body set up by both English and Afrikaner magnates, became a testing ground for new urban initiatives. 'The ghost of Hoggenheimer, the capitalist caricature against which the NP used to rail, [had] been laid' (Charney).

The rising union movement, together with the slowing of growth, persuaded the government towards examining economic restructuring. A proliferation of government commissions on key issues helped to expand the intellectual and ideological environment for reform. The Riekert Commission (1979) addressed the issue of skill shortages and 'manpower' requirements. While adhering closely to apartheid ideas, it argued that those Africans who did qualify to stay in the cities should have stronger rights as well as greater mobility between urban centres and more control over township government. The Wiehahn report (1979) advocated some limited recognition for African trade unions as long as they registered and subjected themselves to regulation. The government responded rapidly by passing a new Industrial Conciliation Amendment Act. De Lange (1981) was the most radical—arguing for a single national Department of Education and gradual equalization of education expenditure. His report had little immediate impact but together with the surge in school boycotts, helped push the government into massive new expenditure on African education. Rapid though the expansion in this area had been in the three decades to 1980, the scene was set for a further doubling in total enrolment, and trebling in secondary enrolment, over the next decade. The large gap between average expenditure on white children and that on black began to narrow.

The government had always recognized that it could not rule the country without cultivating some black allies. Whereas in the years up to the mid-1970s it had concentrated on the homeland leaders, attention was now switched to the urban black middle class. Africans were being offered gradual dismantling of job protection, incorporation in township local government, and the prospect of greater upward mobility. The language of the market seemed to provide increasing scope for blacks to identify with a national capitalist society. Movements like Inkatha, begun essentially as a vehicle for homeland politics in KwaZulu, now found some constituency amongst those aiming for an internal settlement who felt that the exile movements were too closely associated with sanctions and socialism.

Divisions were also apparent in state policies towards those it defined coloured and Indian. In its quest to create a new race and nation the government established a partly elected Coloured Person's Representative Council in 1968. It was to have control over local administration and services within coloured group areas. The Council was not completely boycotted. A new coloured Labour Party chose to mount opposition from within the system. After winning a resounding victory in a 1975 poll, it immobilized the Council and demanded full citizenship for coloured people.

In 1976 a government commission, cognisant of the unworkability of the segregated Coloured Council and deep anger over Group Areas and District Six, advocated a restructuring of the parliamentary system. *Verligte* thinking was moving towards some kind of group representation in a central parliament. The upper house of Parliament, the Senate, was abolished and a President's Council established in 1980. In 1983 a 'tri-cameral parliament' was approved in a whites-only referendum. Two new parliaments would be created for coloured and Indian people. While they would sit separately, their executives would participate on the President's Council, a kind of supra-cabinet from all three parliaments. At the same time, the Presidency was changed from a largely ceremonial to an executive post. The white parliament and National Party still dominated the President's Council and P. W. Botha became the new President.

A great deal of debate has been devoted to the question of

whether reform constituted 'real change' or whether it was merely a new language of white domination. The period certainly saw continuing efforts to achieve spatial segregation and homeland independence as well as militarization and intensive policing. Many of the reform initiatives could be contained within the policy of separate nations and the apex of the system, the tri-cameral parliament, stopped short of extending political rights to Africans. But reform was sufficiently significant to tear at the heart of Afrikanerdom, for so long educated in the righteousness of its cause. Disagreement within the state and party became more marked—no longer simply a debate between *verligte* and *verkrampte*.

Large sections of the bureaucracy had a particular commitment to protecting the concept of a white state and were uneasy about shifts in ideology. Amongst them were those who had actually implemented and learnt to justify policies such as influx control, labour bureaux, and Bantu education. Many felt 'it would be chaotic' if Africans had full freedom of movement and employment throughout the country. The older, shrinking constituencies of the National Party such as white workers were left behind, together with Nationalist solicitude for the '"little man" in the fields and factories' (Charney). When white miners, now largely Afrikaans-speaking, struck to defend job reservation in 1978, the government backed management. In the 1981 election, support for far-right groups increased significantly.

In 1982 Transvaal party leader Dr A. Treurnicht left with fifteen MPs to establish the Conservative Party. While the Nationalists remained in secure control of the white parliament, their support gradually declined. The Broederbond, perhaps less influential than at its height, was also deeply divided. Initially its leadership leaned towards the Conservatives, but it then put its weight behind the Nationalists. The government also lost support in the maize-producing regions of the Transvaal and Orange Free State where drought, high interest rates, and the threat of diminished subsidies put farmers under particular pressure. The Conservatives and their allies were unashamed in returning to the well-tried political language of racial preservation and the integrity of the *volk*. They hoped that the events of 1982 might herald a repeat of 1914 and 1934, when an exclusivist Afrikaner party broke from those advocating a more inclusive idea of nationalism and started on the long road to power. But the changing class character of white society, as well as the new balance of power in the country as a whole, made this an unlikely outcome.

Reform not only split Afrikaners, it provided new opportunities and new dilemmas for popular opposition. Legislation in 1979 extended the definition of 'employee' in the Industrial Conciliation Act to all black workers, except those from 'internationally recognized' foreign countries. Unions could be recognized if they registered with the state, and their members would have the right to strike. But they would be subject to constitutional and financial regulation—for example, they would have to provide full details of membership and office bearers. The legislation triggered an impassioned debate about the value of registration. FOSATU, the Rand and Durban-based Federation which had the largest number of negotiating agreements, decided to approve registration, once it had assurances that migrant workers would be included. It argued that unions needed more stability and muscle and had to take advantage of political space offered. Western Province unions felt that they had grown successfully without registration, which might hamper democratic structures and freedom of action. Unions were dependent ultimately upon 'the organised strength of the workers in each factory' (Maree, 182). SAAWU rejected the whole structure of labour legislation.

In 1979 and 1980 a new wave of protest swept the country, reaching its height in the educational institutions. The boycotts and burnings, while similar to those of 1976, were probably more widespread and students developed a wider range of demands including a single education system. Consumer boycotts proved particularly difficult for the state to counter and put white businesses in selected towns under some pressure. A rash of strikes from 1979 raised the question of the relationship between shop-floor militancy and the community issues in which workers were also involved. Already under pressure to follow SAAWU's lead, other Unions were pushed somewhat reluctantly into broader political action. In the late 1970s a rash of new township community associations and issue-oriented 'civics', together with a lively grassroots press, arose in response to government arrests and repression of movements. The links established by Oscar Mpetha, a leader of the Cape-based Food and Canning Workers Union and the ANC in the 1950s, were typical. Released from Robben Island in 1978, he threw himself back into union activities and helped to organize the Nyanga (Cape Town) Residents' Association in a bus boycott.

During a dispute at Fatti's and Moni's, the major pasta factory in Cape Town, the African Food and Canning Workers Union had called for community boycott of the firm's products in order to strengthen their bargaining position. Activists went into the supermarkets, filled trolleys with pasta, and then left them at the check-out counter. A dispute at the Ford factory near Port Elizabeth centred on the political role of a worker, Thozamile Botha, in the militant local Port Elizabeth Black Civic Association which helped to organize a strike. In 1981 strikes on the East Rand extended linkages between unions and community organizations. Demands for union recognition at Colgate Palmolive resulted in a boycott of that firm's products.

Strikers, especially on the East Rand, took up a wide range of issues—from health conditions to unfair dismissal and demeaning language—on which they had seemed powerless before. White supervisors still used derogatory terms. Indeed unionists felt that racial feeling may have intensified at this time, partly because the emergence of black shop stewards helped to undermine the old lines of authority through white supervisors. Job reservation, already under pressure from employers, was further eroded by union demands. As in the late 1940s, these were factors contributing to the emergence of the white hard right.

Although there were divisions in the union movement, the government seemed less intransigent. Strikes and wider protests helped the more regulated FOSATU and CUSA unions to grow from 70,000 signed up members in 1979 to about

320,000 in 1983. SAAWU, which kept less systematic records, probably exaggerated its claim of 300,000 members. MAWU, the main FOSATU union in the key metals sector, had 10,000 members in 1980 and 30,000 by 1982. Whereas initially membership tended to be strongest amongst those with secure urban rights, more vulnerable migrant workers became an important source of growth. In 1982 CUSA relaunched a National Union of Mineworkers which soon became the biggest in the country with over 100,000 members. Many industries remained unorganized and areas such as agriculture and domestic service were hardly touched. Overall membership was probably not more than 10 per cent of the total black work-force. But unions emerged one of the most effective areas of organized black resistance.

Reform from above, a response to intense political pressure from below, is a notoriously difficult exercise which often raises the expectations of the oppressed and unleashes further powerful forces for change. Oppositional culture in the townships which had found focus in a bewildering range of student, union, and community groups, gradually coalesced in the early 1980s. Some Black Consciousness leaders formed the Azanian People's Organization which explicitly took the PAC name for the country. But many activists saw black consciousness as a phase and moved towards a 'Charterist' or Congress-oriented position. Perhaps three-quarters of those who escaped the country in 1976–7 were shepherded into ANC sanctuaries. Many received training and some were able to return, relaunch the sabotage campaign, and form internal MK cells. A string of these were exposed in the Transvaal in 1978, but MK guerrillas managed to blow up petrol tanks at Sasolburg.

COSAS (Congress of South African Students) had become the major vehicle for student protests at the heart of the 1980 schools rebellion. It subsequently launched Youth Congresses in many centres which incorporated both school-leavers and the young unemployed. As student organizations abandoned black consciousness, they re-established connections with the well-resourced and radical NUSAS groups on English-speaking campuses. More importantly, youth and trade union activists fed into civics in the township communities where they lived together. Banned activists, together with those coming off Robben Island, cemented links with the Congress tradition. Radical members of the Natal Indian Congress, which refused to participate in the Indian elections, provided a further link in the emerging mass movement.

By 1983 the need for some national organization was patent. In August the United Democratic Front (UDF) was formed at a mass rally in Mitchell's Plain, a new coloured township on the Cape Flats. The movement was explicitly non-racial in the tradition of the ANC and also drew on Congress's Christian heritage: radical churchmen such as Alan Boesak and Frank Chikane joined the platforms and became leading representatives; Anglican Bishop Desmond Tutu, who won the Nobel Peace Prize in 1984, also identified with the UDF. So did Winnie Mandela, who had experienced frequent harassment and banishment during her husband's imprisonment, and had become an international symbol of the survival of the Congress tradition. Albertina Sisulu, formerly a major figure in the ANC Women's League, and wife of the incarcerated Walter Sisulu, became joint president. The UDF looked strongly like an internal wing of Congress, though it did not associate with the armed struggle.

While its first campaigns were organized against the elections to new ethnic parliaments and local councils, the UDF's character changed in the mid-1980s. The cycle of insurrection and repression based around schools, universities, factories, and townships which began in 1976 rose to a crescendo between late 1984 and early 1986. This marked the turning-point for the apartheid state. Some organizations identifying with the UDF took a more militant path. The ANC itself was becoming a focus for opposition forces and demands for Nelson Mandela's release from prison became a central unifying call both in the exiled ANC, the external anti-apartheid movements, and at home.

In conclusion, we should return to the debate about apartheid and its gradual erosion (Chapter 7). South African industrial growth under apartheid was initially impressive.

Multinationals, mining houses, the state, and agricultural interests were all of great importance in generating capital for investment. This element of the radical argument seems justified. Apartheid did not initially inhibit manufacturing and both local and foreign investors responded favourably to stability even if this was produced by repression.

Yet acute skill shortages, technological dependence, and lack of competitiveness evident from the late 1970s has strengthened the case that apartheid came to inhibit growth and that rates of development may have been more impressive without it. Capitalists, Lipton argued, lived with apartheid rather than advocated it. They began to attack it more vociferously not necessarily 'because they were liberals—though some of them were', but because 'apartheid labour policies . . . conflicted with their interests and this had dynamic implications for the whole system'. In general, radicals have accepted that apartheid-induced weaknesses were an important reason for economic crisis and reform from the late 1970s.

Both radicals and liberals have recently taken ideology more seriously in explaining segregation and apartheid and most scholars have also recognized the complexity of interaction between economic interests and political systems. However, in identifying and addressing the crisis of the late 1970s, radicals laid more stress on political struggle and trade unionism, rather than on the workings of the market, in highlighting the contradictions and costs of apartheid.

10 Insurrection, Fragmentation, and Negotiations, 1984–1992

Urban Government and the 1984–6 Insurrection

If the renaissance of black opposition in the 1970s paved the way for political change, the insurrection of 1984–6 made the process difficult to reverse. White authority partially collapsed during the 1980s and early 1990s, but has not yet (at the end of 1992) been totally displaced. Afrikaners have been reluctant to sacrifice power and whites in general protective of their wealth. The Nationalist Party actively pursued a settlement which might satisfy their conception of black aspirations but fall short of democratic government in a unitary state.

At the same time, imminent political change also intensified divisions in black politics. The ANC and its allies, with social democratic and socialist ideas, appeared to carry majority support. But homeland-based movements, others with an ethnic or conservative outlook, as well as state-supported vigilante-type organizations, tried to stake their claim. The erosion of state authority has been attended by increasing civil disorder and crime. Any successor government which emerges from this uncomfortable interregnum will inherit a difficult legacy.

A decade of political mobilization lay behind the insurrection of the mid-1980s, but its intensity was fuelled by economic recession and the intricacies of managing the black urban population. The question of how to govern the new urban millions was starkly posed in the early 1980s. Up to the mid-1970s apartheid logic dictated that the old black Urban Advisory Councils were relatively neglected. In 1971 city locations were placed under official Bantu Affairs Administration Boards (BAABs) which would both govern them and implement state policy on removals and urbanization.

As part of its attempt to meet the challenge of 1976, the government passed a Community Council Act (1977) which established a new tier of elected municipal councils under the authority of the BAABs. The state hoped that 'black councillors would be able to absorb and defuse discontent' (Seekings). Its initiatives were in keeping with the belated belief that a stable urban black middle class with a greater stake in the system could be essential to the success of reform. In 1982 black local authorities received augmented powers to run their 'own' affairs. Unpopular white BAAB officials, whose image was so deeply bound up with bureaucratic terrorism, were gradually withdrawn from the fractured coalface of urban government.

Although attempts at reform and devolution extended African rights outside the homelands, they further politicized local government. Potentially, urban African people could now exercise some control over matters such as housing, rent, and services which had been the province of authoritarian officials. The central question for politicized urban communities was whether they should participate in state structures which fell far short of granting full civil rights. An initially lukewarm response to the councils cooled further in the early 1980s. In the first round of elections in the late 1970s, the government claimed a 39 per cent turn-out of registered voters. In 1983, when the UDF co-ordinated a campaign against the elections, perhaps 12 per cent voted. The number of Sowetans who voted in the second election rose from 6 to 10 per cent, but was still under the national average. When elections were held for the Indian and coloured houses of the tri-cameral parliament in 1984, about 13 and 18 per cent respectively voted. The overwhelming decision of black people seemed clear: 'reform' was inadequate and inoperable.

Community Councils, which did take office, were immediately placed in a difficult financial position. The government aimed not only to decentralize responsibility for spending revenue, but also for the far more fraught task of raising it. This would enable the central state to abrogate some of its fiscal commitments for urban black welfare. The major inheritance of the Community Councils was vast sprawls of low-quality township housing; rents were a major source of income. As the urban population exploded in size, councillors faced a housing crisis. In 1979 the Greater Soweto Council raised rents in a vain attempt to break even. When recession, inflation, and a new Sales Tax bit from 1983, rent increases became more widespread.

Some councillors compounded their difficulties by using their position to their own best advantage. They had access to sites, licences, information, and excellent opportunities in such fields as supermarkets, liquor outlets, and taxis. Like Afrikaners, they benefited from their relationship with state institutions, but they were widely seen to be corrupt. Popular politics in the urban areas aimed not least at preventing the government from finding allies to work 'the system'. Intense and sometimes violent pressure was put on those viewed as sell-outs in the locations. As in earlier contexts, conflict turned inwards against those perceived to betray the community. Especially on the Rand, rent boycotts became a key form of political action, both because these could mobilize large numbers of people and because they struck at the heart of the reforms imposed on Africans.

Up to the early 1980s, apartheid planning ensured that much urban growth took place in displaced towns, like KwaNdebele and Botshabelo, sited within homeland boundaries or away from the main cities (Figure 1). Since that time, patterns of population movement have changed radically again so that millions moved towards the main cities. Pass laws proved incapable of arresting the process and were less vigorously enforced; by 1986 some of the major influx control regulations were rescinded. Durban, said to be one of the fastest growing cities in the world, doubled in size to about three million in less than two decades. Cape Town soon rivalled it. Khayelitsha (new home) and neighbouring informal settlements on the Cape Flats, which hardly existed in 1980, were estimated to house three-quarters of a million people by the end of the decade. Cape Town's demographic composition began to resemble that of the other major centres. Many new townspeople lived in location backyards and informal shack settlements.

The Rand and southern Transvaal remained by far the largest urban zone and for the first time since tight controls were enacted in the 1950s, squatters returned to the area in large numbers. In Katlehong, south of Germiston, one of the major areas of insurrection, the estimated number of shacks rose from 3,000 in 1979 to 44,000 in 1983, far outnumbering the houses. By 1988 perhaps half a million people lived there. Under pressure from central government, a prevaricating Community Council attempted to remove squatters in 1984. Here and elsewhere there was defiance and confusion in shack settlements.

In August and September 1984 protests against the inauguration of the tri-cameral parliament and rent rises ended in pitched battles between youths and police. Councillors were killed in Sebokeng, south of Johannesburg on the Vereeniging road; the mayor of Sharpeville died on his doorstep after shooting two demonstrators. Insurrections in places like Katlehong, Sebokeng, Tumahole (in the Orange Free State), Boipatong, and Bophelong (near Sharpeville) branded the new social geography of the country into the national and international consciousness. It was here, as well as Alexandra, Sharpeville, and Soweto that the key political events were played out.

Thus the crisis in South Africa, as in so many other parts of the Third World, had agrarian and demographic as well as political and economic roots. Proponents of segregation and apartheid always argued that their policies depended not least on controlling urbanization and they were probably right. By the 1980s unemployment and poverty could no longer be externalized to the homelands and remnant smallholding could no longer give a significant number of people either income or social support. Most perceived themselves to have the best opportunity of a job or informal sector income in the big cities. African people presented themselves in their millions and demanded to be incorporated in the social order—to be made not only subjects of the state but citizens.

Problems of urban government were compounded by the

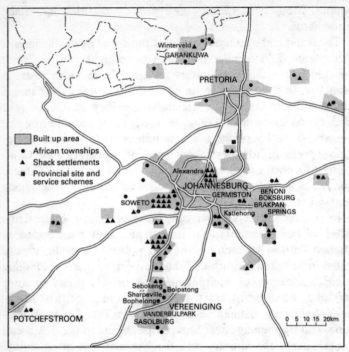

MAP 3. *Townships in the Pretoria–Witwatersrand–Vereeniging Region*
Source: Urban Foundation, 1990

longevity of the economic downturn. Gold prices, which had
helped the country through the oil crisis and recession in the
1970s, declined in 1983. Expensive imports and debt repayments became a financial drain. When Europe began to climb
out of its early 1980s recession, South Africa, especially its
manufacturing industries, stagnated. Despite enormous
advances in manufacturing, there were insufficient areas of
specialist advantage or independence to cope with international
competition.

Economic problems, especially high unemployment, helped
to fuel political turmoil in the mid-1980s which in turn exacerbated economic difficulties. After signing a non-agression Nkomati Accord with Mozambique in March 1984, Botha had been

received in European capitals and sanctions looked vulnerable. But the 'fruits of Nkomati' shrivelled before the year was out as insurrection triggered a flight of capital and tightening application of sanctions through disinvestment (Price, 221). Simultaneously, the rand collapsed to less than half its previous value against the dollar and pound sterling; chronic inflation set in and the foreign debt grew. The government responded by hiking interest rates to over 20 per cent which had the effect of slowing recovery. High interest rates also impacted on the indebted agricultural sector and contributed to rural Afrikaner disaffection. One indicator of farming problems was the falling number of tractors (Table 4). Burdened with heavy expenditure on border wars, the government cut public spending. While this was justified by a longer-term commitment to privatization, following the British and US example, precipitate action compounded unemployment, estimated at up to 30 per cent. Overall standards of living fell.

Popular struggle reached a nation-wide crescendo in 1985 and did begin to achieve its aim of ungovernability. Militant youths seemed always on the move, dancing the toyi-toyi, jog-trotting in large crowds through the streets, lending an urgency to the movement. BAAB offices, police stations, and shops were burnt. The most spectacular manifestation of protest involved 'necklacing' those identified as informers by placing a tyre doused with petrol around the victim's neck and lighting it. The cast-offs of industrial affluence were being recycled to purify society by fire and death.

COSAS, a key UDF affiliate, renewed school boycotts. Popular committees and people's courts sprang up which did, in some zones, briefly take on the governance of their own communities. Widespread seminars developed their own 'street sociology and pavement politics'—working hard to define what the national democratic struggle and people's culture meant for activists on the ground. Youthful rebels saw themselves as a 'comrades' movement, aligned with the ANC and fighting—when necessary as part of the armed struggle—for its aims.

Green, black, and gold ANC banners appeared at rallies

where *Nkosi Sikel' iAfrika* and the slogan *Amandla awethu* resounded. The term 'Viva', drawn from Mozambique, prefaced long lists of names and organizations as a history of struggle was relived. Frequent funerals became the site for emotive speeches, expressions of solidarity, and widespread political co-ordination. Death legitimized struggle and provided heroes. At the funeral of Matthew Goniwe, an eastern Cape activist, and three others widely believed to have been killed by the security forces, the red flag of the Communist Party was also unfurled. People's power gradually rolled back the boundaries of what the government had to consider acceptable. In response, the government moved large numbers of troops into the townships. The township war escalated as the state's heavier armoury was countered by street barricades and Molotov cocktails. In a terrifying incident filmed in Cape Town, police hid themselves on a lorry, waited till they were stoned, and then shot at their assailants.

In 1985 Western financial institutions expected Botha to hasten the pace of reform. Confronted by a rising right wing and angered by youth insurrection, Botha failed to deliver in his 'Rubicon' speech and confidence collapsed again. A business delegation, led by Gavin Relly, Chairman of Anglo-American, met the ANC in Lusaka and firms in South Africa committed themselves more whole-heartedly to African home-ownership, training, and renewal through the Urban Foundation. For powerful sections of the white élite, as well as for the UDF and Comrades, the locus of future political legitimacy began to crystallize.

While the externally based ANC itself called for ungovernability, it was not able to establish formal internal organization and a number of Congress and UDF members were uneasy with the excesses of people's courts. Often composed of youths, they extended their jurisdiction to major crimes and political trials. In Alexandra township, Johannesburg, activists recognized by 1986 that some rebels were not only 'ungovernable to the enemy', but 'ungovernable to their own organisations' (Carter, 126). Comrades aiming to develop 'governability within ungovernability' found it extremely difficult to set up liberated zones in city locations where the security forces remained active. Some UDF militants justified violence, yet the movement had to be careful not to make itself even more vulnerable to state retaliation by openly espousing armed struggle. Zwelakhe Sisulu, son of the imprisoned Walter and later editor of the UDF-oriented *New Nation* weekly, argued that when 'bands of youth set up so-called "kangaroo courts" and give out punishments, under the control of no-one and with no democratic mandate from the community, this is *not* people's power'.

Responses to the collapse of schooling culminated in the formation of a National Education Crisis Committee (NECC) in March 1986. It envisioned alternative education and syllabuses and tried to set in place some means to achieve this—emphasizing education for liberation, rather than liberation before education. It could thus encourage the youth to return to school without appearing to support the existing educational system. A host of organizations dealing with matters from labour, human rights, and industrial health to land, ecology, and economic policy found sharper focus in this insurrectionary period. A basis was laid for opposition intellectual energies, both black and white, to concentrate increasingly on future reconstruction rather than just protest.

Strikes, including major action organized by the revived National Union of Mineworkers, reached a crescendo in 1986 and 1987 as workers both expressed their political outrage and struggled to meet the rising cost of living. Successful stayaways cemented links between the independent Unions and the UDF civics. In 1985 most of the independent unions came together as the Congress of South African Trade Unions (COSATU). Its leaders were less cautious about congregating 'around the honeypot of popular activity' than FOSATU had been (Murray, 192). COSATU supported disinvestment and sanctions as well as nationalization. A delegation met the ANC in Lusaka. Cyril Ramaphosa, general secretary of the NUM, argued that working-class interests and redistribution of wealth should be pushed to the centre of popular struggles. But political unionism, less factory-based, had its costs. In Natal, a number of unions had been able to straddle the political divide between Inkatha and UDF. COSATU refused to hold back in its criticism of Inkatha and as Buthelezi retaliated against youths and workers, conflict spilled over into violence.

Despite some dramatic city-centre demonstrations and occasional attacks on white people or their property, the insurrection remained largely confined to black townships and rural districts. Penetrating into white areas in large numbers was difficult; township conflicts and battles for local space were the immediate priorities. Nevertheless, the insurrection made an unprecedented impact on white lives. Even restricted media coverage brought home black anger. Stay-aways, strikes, and extended consumer boycotts sucked in large numbers of police and troops. The sheer tenacity of the popular movement demanded attention to its widening demands: the release of political prisoners, abolition of apartheid, and a unitary non-racial democratic political system.

The State: Militarization, Vigilantes, and Retreat

In July 1985 Botha declared a state of emergency which gave the security forces even more formidable powers. The government's capacity to ride out the challenge drew on and fed into an increasingly militarized pattern of authority. During the first phase of Botha's rule from 1978 to 1983, the military role in government expanded. This was a new development, justified by the perceived external threat. Although former generals had ruled South Africa till 1948 and Smuts was not averse to using the armed forces to impose order, civil and military functions had largely been separated following Union. D. F. Malan and Verwoerd, hostile to the English-dominated Second World War defence establishment, initially continued the tradition.

By the 1970s the military, especially the army, was Afrikanerized and broadly sympathetic to the Nationalist project. The security apparatus began to impinge on the civil state, blurring divisions and shaping the nature of government. Botha introduced General Magnus Malan, Chief of the Defence Force, into the cabinet as Minister of Defence. During the 1980s the

State Security Council, a supra-cabinet, became the lynchpin of an elaborate hierarchy of committees forming a parallel state structure. There was not a military coup, but a more surreptitious extension of military influence. Estimates suggest an increase in defence expenditure in the budget from about 6 per cent in 1960 to 15 per cent in 1980 and subsequently to between 17 and 20 per cent. By the late 1980s, Armscor, at the apex of a pervasive 'military–industrial' complex, could claim to be the largest single exporter of manufactured goods.

The ideas of the South African officer class were influenced by counter-insurgency techniques developed to contain the guerrilla struggles of the late colonial period in Vietnam, Malaysia, and Algeria. The term 'total strategy' was borrowed from the French general Beaufré, who emphasized that in modern warfare the whole society should be involved in a 'dialectic of two opposing wills'. The state should engage at every level with a perceived revolutionary onslaught and attempt to win the 'hearts and minds' of the common people. It was a strategy which reflected Botha's difficulty in recognizing the scale of the political problem and justified simultaneous reform and repression. The government believed it could restore a new legitimacy as apartheid began to crumble.

Total strategy also fitted well with the reinvented traditions of the Afrikaner commando—a people's army defending a nation at war. The period of national service demanded from young white men was extended from nine months to two years after 1977. Men could be recalled for camps or commando service over many years. The number of servicemen who could be mobilized increased to over 400,000. Military service sometimes entailed long terms of duty on the Namibian border, even raids into Angola. Hostility to communism, terrorism, the ANC, and opposition movements was inculcated into servicemen. Many learnt a language of male bravado and violence— of themselves as heroes fighting dehumanized targets. State-controlled radio and television became a conduit for total strategy objectives. Private gun ownership rocketed amongst whites in the 1980s. Existing school cadet programmes were expanded. War comics, while hardly unique to South Africa, became a staple of the corner shop. The local version portrayed the *Grensvegter* (border warrior) fighting against the predictable forces of darkness and disorder.

Thus when the insurrection reached its peak, the government was prepared. As reformist strategies promoted by the Department of Constitutional Development and Planning faltered in the face of mass opposition, so more aggressive, hardline 'securocrats' emerged as the dominant force. Protest was the work of agitators, they argued, and it could be halted by removing the leadership. The repressive apparatus of the state was unleashed on an unprecedented scale, but also with 'stamina and steady concentration' (Webster, *SA Review*, 4: 141).

In the first eight months of the 1985 emergency, 8,000 people were detained and 22,000 charged with offences arising from protests. In the year from June 1986—when a new emergency was imposed after the first had been briefly lifted because of international pressure—a further 26,000 people were detained. Reporting and especially filming of incidents was far more tightly controlled from mid-1985. Undoubtedly the power of the insurrection was augmented by its televisual representation locally and internationally. The government hoped to suppress graphic illustrations of police brutality which had so undermined the international acceptance of reform. Initiatives such as the Commonwealth Eminent Persons Group, which promised to facilitate multilateral negotiations, were apparently deliberately sabotaged when the security forces bombed the capitals of three frontline states in May 1986.

A network of Joint Management Centres was activated to co-ordinate military, police, and civil functions at a local level. Counter-insurgency advocates who gained Botha's ear convinced themselves that a soft economic and ideological war could win hearts and minds. 'There is presently only a limited section which is really interested in political participation,' Magnus Malan argued, 'I think for the masses in South Africa democracy is not a relevant factor' (Centre for Policy Studies). Joint Management Centres, sometimes displacing Community Councils, tried to upgrade facilities and living conditions in black townships, offering the promise of a taste of 'the good life' (Cock and Nathan, 163). The easing of pass laws, the abolition of the Mixed Marriages and racial sections of the Immorality Act in 1986 hinted at more far-reaching change. Freehold property rights for Africans in town were extended.

But faced with an everyday level of dissidence which they were barely able to control, the hard war predominated. Internal professional constraints in the security forces slackened. In addition to the firepower, mass arrests, beating, and torture, sinister evidence of political assassination accumulated. Black policemen, attacked or forced to move out of their homes in the townships, pursued their own vendettas with comrades. Hit squads, some involving white and black members of the security forces, now operated in the country as they had previously beyond its borders. In 1988 these activities were consolidated in the Civil Co-operation Bureau, ultimately under command of members of the Defence Force, whose disruption of the 'enemy' could involve anything from breaking a window to killing.

Faltering attempts to devolve civil authority to black clients were now accompanied by devolution of armed authority to homeland armies, municipal police, and 'kitskonstabels' (instant constables) in the townships. Local black powerbrokers and their supporters felt able to take the law into their own hands. These 'vigilantes' had diverse social origins; what they had in common was hostility to the youthful comrades and a readiness to use violence for political ends. By identifying with the state and police they earned the disdain of rebellious youth.

The clearest early manifestations of this new axis of urban conflict were attacks by migrant workers, urban outsiders living in hostels, on youth rebels in 1976. One issue was access to liquor. Over the next decade, political and generational cleavages deepened, facilitated by the security services. The deathrate escalated. In 1985 and 1986 informal local vigilante groups mushroomed, giving themselves names such as Mabangalala, Witdoeke, or A-Team. To a greater extent than before they had access to firearms. Some were connected with homeland leaders, councillors, taxi-owners, and police; some were groups

...men ('fathers') or hostel-based migrant workers. As
...DF forces they disrupted areas of opposition, removed
...ters, and attacked individuals.

'Warlords' could build more organized private armies or
posses. In 1985 Simon Skosana, bent on achieving homeland
independence for KwaNdebele, attacked communities resisting
incorporation into his sphere. Vigilantes controlled by a former
squatter leader destroyed much of the shack settlement at
Crossroads near Cape Town in 1986 after clashing with comrades for control of the area. Over 60,000 people were made
homeless. For the security forces, such client groups were a
cheap form of reasserting control. The state could dissociate
itself from their excesses, point to the dynamic of 'tribal' or
'black on black' violence, and project itself as the sole guaran-
tor of stability. Few in the opposition believed that the security
forces were not involved.

Natal was a major site of violent conflict within and between
black communities as Inkatha attempted to cement its authority
over Zulu-speaking areas. Buthelezi, stoned and insulted by
black consciousness youths as early as 1978 during the funeral
of the PAC leader Robert Sobukwe, appealed to tradition and
the patriarchal order of Zulu society. Inkatha's Youth League
was instructed not to boycott schools which, leaders argued,
were under KwaZulu and not Bantu Education control. Buthelezi increasingly distanced himself from the ANC and UDF
as he attempted to forge an image as a moderate leader with
a national constituency. His stance against armed struggle,
sanctions, and socialism won considerable support from the
government, from liberal business leaders in Natal, and
internationally.

Inkatha's political practice, however, involved extending
one-party government in KwaZulu. The movement used its
control over housing, pensions, and water in major townships
such as Umlazi and KwaMashu (part of Durban but under
KwaZulu control) to demand membership and loyalty. Civil
servants and teachers found it difficult not to join. Inkatha
leaders like Thomas Shabalala of Lindelani, a shack settlement
north of Durban, increasingly resorted to violence to enforce

political authority. The single incident during the insurrection which resulted in the greatest number of deaths was a battle south of Durban between Inkatha-organized *impis* and squatter communities from the Transkei. Inkatha also attacked a National Education Conference in Durban in 1986.

Between 1987 and 1990 the fiercest clashes took place in the peri-urban townships and settlements around Pietermaritzburg. When people in Edendale township tried to resist incorporation into KwaZulu, it became a battlefield between *amaqabase* (comrades) and Inkatha *impis* brandishing 'traditional' weapons. While Inkatha seemed to forfeit the popular support that it had won in its earlier anti-apartheid days, it probably achieved a tighter hold on local politics. Inkatha fighters were better armed and less likely to attract police hostility; most of the 4,000 dead in three years of township carnage in Natal were youths. This phase of violence was not largely ethnic in character in that most protagonists were Zulu-speaking. Cleavages were between rural and urban, between generations, between people with different political beliefs and different ideas about Zulu identity and tradition.

To some extent, Botha regained control of the country after 1986. Despite divisions in Afrikanerdom and splits in the government over strategy, the security forces, including the black police, had remained loyal. Though white South African daily life was affected, it was not yet significantly threatened. But his was a tenuous hold, based on increased militarization and unpopular black allies who were not fully under state control. The civil institutions on which the state had relied to control blacks were crumbling. Decentralization of armed authority resulted in a degree of fragmentation after decades of centralization.

Economic crisis and sanctions also hurt. Although South Africans were experienced in circumventing trade sanctions, tighter exclusion from international capital markets, disinvestment, and arms embargos were less easy to counter. Armscor production was sufficient to suppress internal insurrection, but Cuban soldiers and Soviet weaponry in Angola eroded the state's capacity to neutralize opposition on the Namibian border. A major South African offensive launched in 1987 was designed to support Angola's UNITA rebels and undermine SWAPO as negotiations over Namibian independence broke down yet again. South African air supremacy was challenged and the foray resulted in a severe military set-back at Cuito Cuanavale in southern Angola. The government and armed forces were beginning to appreciate the costs, at a time of economic recession, of fighting beyond its borders. The death-rates of white soldiers caused concern and momentum against military adventures built up in the press, in the white End Conscription Campaign, and amongst Afrikaner intellectuals.

International realignments undermined South Africa's claim that it was the last bulwark against communism. In 1988 the Soviet Union and the USA began to defuse regional super-power conflicts. Gorbachev offered to withdraw Soviet involvement and put pressure on the Cubans, but in turn demanded American insistence on free elections in Namibia. The South African government's acquiescence was a critical moment in the shifting balance of power in the region. SWAPO won 57 per cent of the Namibian vote in 1989 and took office in what had been Africa's 'last colony'. As ANC guerrilla activities and the township revolt again escalated in South Africa, and opposition forces amalgamated in the Mass Democratic Movement, the securocrats' blend of reform and repression faltered. A stalemate had been reached in which the opposition could not unseat the government by force and the government could not reassert full control.

Violence and Negotiation

By the late 1980s a single political party had been in power for forty years under an almost seamless succession of Prime Ministers. Botha had, however, moved away from the West-minster-type parliamentary system which had served the Nationalists so well. Constitutional reforms such as the executive presidency, the tri-cameral parliament, and the State Security Council diminished the authority of the National Party itself. Agencies of the state became less accountable, even to the Party, a process emphasized by devolution of power to homelands and urban councils. The scope for corruption and violence was greatly extended. Botha had become autocratic and ill-tempered in his relationships with his own supporters.

The Nationalists, having shed much of their right wing to the Conservatives, had more freedom of action. The Broederbond, formerly split over reform, came out strongly for extending the process and ending statutory discrimination. When Botha suffered a stroke in January 1989, he decided to separate the office of President and National Party leader, both of which he held. In the elections for party leadership F. W. de Klerk, the Minister for National Education, succeeded against Botha's preferred candidates. In August de Klerk also displaced Botha as President. He represented sections of the party which wanted greater control on the executive and further progress in controlled reform rather than the erratic repression of Botha's last few years. This might restore economic growth and international acceptability.

In the white election of 1989, the Nationalists lost twenty-seven seats. Their vote fell below 50 per cent and the Conservative Party consolidated itself as the largest white opposition group. Afrikanerdom's political fragmentation, together with the decline in economic protection for whites, fuelled paramilitarism. Its potential was uncertain because the security forces were one seat of reaction which might turn against the government. As institutions they did not. While the far right demonstrated its potential to disrupt and disorganize political change, it did not seem capable of winning power. The liberal Democratic Party (formerly the Progressive Reform Party) also expanded its vote in 1989 and de Klerk could count on over two-thirds of the white electorate in favour of reform. This number remained stable in a white referendum over continued negotiations in 1992.

De Klerk's background as a politically astute conservative did not prepare his supporters for the pace at which he would act. He was determined to seize the initiative from opposition forces and keep his party and constituency in the political vanguard. He sought to develop a power base and constitutional system which, while it might end the overall political dominance of whites, would protect their position in the country. Botha had already recognized that the key might lie with Nelson Mandela who, ill with tuberculosis, had been moved from Robben Island on to the mainland. Given greater freedom to communicate in the late 1980s, he made it known that there was scope for discussion. Congress itself had projected Mandela as a symbol of unity and hope; he was the most easily recognized icon of a new South Africa both at home and abroad. After meeting de Klerk, Mandela published a forceful statement on the desirability and possibility of a negotiated settlement.

Mandela's release in February 1990, together with the unbanning of the ANC and other black political movements, set in train a new phase of politics which remains unresolved. For the Nationalists, this step was a final recognition that they could no longer hope to win legitimacy by relying on black allies outside Congress and the democratic movements. It was also an admission that a political settlement required negotiations with the popular movements. Mandela's slow walk to freedom, followed by a cavalcade of cars, was an emotional moment, a televised event of almost religious intensity—the raising of a man from another world who seemed to carry the promise of salvation.

A wave of optimism was unleashed, the signal for symbolic reclaiming of the country. Blacks were able to move into spaces and institutions which had been barred to them. Pent-up forces of protest were released and, by the middle of 1990, more black councils were inoperative than at the height of the insurrection of the mid-1980s. Rent, school, and consumer boycotts were renewed and a 'rebel' tour of British cricketers forced to go home. Nevertheless, the ANC initially found it difficult to use the political space that opened up. Congress leaders had to act cautiously in that they still had no formal access to power and their movement, publicly exposed, could still be dismembered. There was no easy walk to democratic elections and they faced acute problems of transforming a liberation movement into a potential governing party.

The ANC hierarchy, many returning from exile, had to find common ground with the UDF, unions, civics, and highly committed but volatile comrades. Organization forged in the struggle had to be reassembled as democratically elected local ANC branches. The role of the Communist Party, to which a number of ANC and MK leaders belonged, had to be resolved in the face of strident state rhetoric. Against international trends, it was successfully relaunched internally at a mass rally in 1990 and, led by almost mythical former exiles such as Joe Slovo, seemed to be growing. While all these groupings shared a desire for some form of democratic South Africa, they had different degrees of trust in negotiations. The first full ANC conference took place only in July 1991.

Buffeted by the stormy politics of the early 1990s, Mandela could not hope to live up to the heroic image which had been constructed around him. But he and the older, non-Communist leaders like Sisulu held control of the movement and worked hard to maintain its moral ascendancy and popularity. The prison years had added to his personal stature and capacity to deal with the media. He could appear as 'communal patriarch, working-class hero, and liberal democrat', appealing simultaneously to a radical mass movement and, as the voice of reason and constraint, to an anxious white population and broader international community (Lodge, in Meer). When Winnie Mandela's involvement in a criminal trial threatened to undermine the movement's moral authority, she was sidelined.

In the negotiations about negotiations which continued haltingly from 1990, the ANC aimed for a representative national convention and unitary democratic state. They nevertheless compromised on key issues. Against some internal opposition, Congress suspended the armed struggle in 1990. Its leaders recognized that guerrilla warfare was not their strongest suit; victory in the short term seemed a chimera, while the costs of political violence were potentially great and the lessons of Mozambique stark. Chris Hani, leader of MK, committed himself to negotiations and was able to represent and contain more impatient elements in Congress until his assassination in 1993.

The language of democracy rather than socialism has been more strongly emphasized. Both the collapse of communist systems and the realities of a weakened South African economy influenced ANC economic thinking. Ideas such as the nationalization of mines have been put in abeyance. The difficulty of running so complex an industry, of dealing with a powerful and politicized union, and of stabilizing the labour force have made the potential costs of state responsibility more apparent. By 1991 Congress tended to stress 'growth with redistribution' and a mixed economy rather than nationalization.

The position of COSATU unions, a critical force for change in the 1970s and 1980s, was weakened by protracted economic recession and high unemployment (perhaps 40 per cent of blacks). Though they remain amongst the most organized groups within the Congress alliance and Ramaphosa of NUM became ANC General Secretary, their influence has perhaps been less central and their demands more constrained. While the ANC continued to advocate sanctions because of the uncertainties of the negotiating process, it became more acutely aware of the need to facilitate investment. The region was suffering not only from a high debt burden and again from drought, but also, like much of the rest of Africa, from marginalization in the international economy.

De Klerk, on his side, gradually dismantled racial legislation. The Separate Reservation of Amenities Act was revoked in June 1990; the Land Act, Group Areas, and Population Registration a year later. Since the late 1980s, breaches of racial legislation had been less actively policed so that a few white residential areas like Hillbrow, Johannesburg's city-centre flatland, went 'grey' and then largely black. Even the National Party opened its membership to blacks. While the legacy of apartheid remains starkly obvious, there was some scope for social practice to change.

Nationalists have, however, tried to entrench basic protections for whites and a capitalist economic system prior to any transfer of power which might result from elections. The government has been reluctant to countenance a democratic constitution in the kind of unitary state which proved so valuable for Afrikaner self-advancement. While de Klerk has frequently met Mandela, the government insisted that formal negotiations which took shape in the Convention for a Democratic South Africa (CODESA) at the end of 1991 included representatives of a wide range of political groups, including homeland governments and ethnic parties. It has argued that some form of power-sharing would be most conducive to stability. Nationalists as well as homeland representatives have supported a strong regional tier of government at CODESA. Regions would include both formerly white and black areas, but decentralization might mean that Nationalists and their allies could retain more influence at a local level in some areas.

Guarantees over private property have been central to government concerns. During the 1980s privatization resulted in some contraction of the state sector. Parastatal corporations such as ISCOR (iron and steel), SATS (railways), and SASOL (oil) were wholly or partly privatized. Education spending increased but by 1992 education policy foresaw gradual withdrawal of central control and greater capacity for state schools to run themselves, raise their own fees, and shape admission policies. Similarly, the government has disposed of state land to private concerns and homeland governments. To some extent it has attempted to pre-empt future redistribution of resources by placing these in private hands. Race in itself would no longer disqualify ownership. But a new government might find itself with more limited control of the economic levers of the country than has been the case for much of this century. While demands for services and redistribution will clearly be enormous, so too will the budgetary constraints.

Government actions suggest that it initially saw protracted negotiations as more likely to favour its interests and increase divisions within the opposition. Violence has also delayed a political settlement. De Klerk promised to diminish the influence of the security forces and dismantle Joint Management Councils; arms expenditure declined in real terms. But disorganizing violence, often against ANC supporters, persisted. Congress argued that a 'third force'—a term borrowed from the Algerian independence struggle—linked with the security services was deliberately provoking violence in black communities in order to delay political settlement.

The violence that has scarred South Africa since 1990 includes but is not limited to this nexus of conflict. Inkatha supporters responded to renewed Congress mobilization in Natal after Mandela's release by attacking ANC strongholds in Pietermaritzburg. In 1991 the movement launched a campaign for support in southern Natal; the resulting violence left many homeless. Revelations brought to light evidence of secret funding by security services, but Inkatha had its own strategies and goals to pursue.

From 1990, the Rand rather than Natal was the crucible of conflict. Masked gunmen killed at random on black commuter trains, previously used as vehicles for political mobilization by youths during the emergency. Taxi wars over transport routes escalated. Inkatha started a recruitment drive in hostels and hostel-dwellers armed themselves against township residents. As in Natal, ANC comrades who felt that the state and vigilantes knew only the language of violence, resisted and took pre-emptive action against perceived enemies. Meetings between Mandela and Buthelezi in 1991 had little impact.

By the early 1990s seven million people were estimated to live in informal settlements which were absorbing large new inflows of people both from township backyards and from the countryside. Politicized rivalries over scarce resources in volatile and impoverished shack cities resulted in a sequence of clashes. In a number of cases, hostilities broke out between squatters and hostel-dwellers or migrants. Participants and the media sometimes saw allegiances in ethnic terms—for example between Zulu and Xhosa—though such identities were often fluid amongst the mobile urban poor. For the first time, guns poured into the urban locations. They were traded across the border from Mozambique, released to vigilantes, or brought in by MK networks. A market for firearms developed and new weaponry exacerbated conflict and resulted in higher death-rates.

In July 1992 a massacre of residents at the ANC stronghold of Boipatong, south of Johannesburg, led the ANC to withdraw

from CODESA. The ANC's determination to break the homeland governments prompted a march against the unpopular
military supremo of the Ciskei, Brigadier Gqozo, whose forces
killed a further twenty-nine people. Late in 1992 vigilante
activity appeared to be easing and the ANC resumed participation in the talks. But the Azanian People's Liberation Army
(APLA), the armed wing of the PAC, tried to outflank Congress by staging dramatic attacks on white civilian targets along
the old colonial faultlines of the eastern Cape Border region
and the Orange Free State. They hoped to attract radicalized
youth frustrated by delays in negotiations and the ANC's
suspension of the armed struggle. Violence, vengeance, and
the politics of fear sapped the optimism generated by Mandela's
release. As policing loosened, a crime wave swept white as well
as black communities. Attacks against whites, both on farms
and in suburbs, became less unusual. Politicized security forces
and a Kalashnikov culture threatened to engulf the country; a
Lebanese or Yugoslavian future was invoked. Violence seemed
to be an increasingly fragmenting force, raising the spectre of
civil disintegration.

The government and the ANC together increasingly tried to
assume the responsible middle ground on these issues as
alliances and positions fluctuated. Buthelezi, formerly an
uneasy ally of the Nationalists, talked to white conservatives
and intensified his separatist rhetoric in a bid to secure regional
power. The Conservative Party seemed to be winning over
more Afrikaners. Mangope in Bophuthatswana also hedged his
bets about the future. However, the Congress-oriented Transkeian Military Council ruler, Holomisa, has given sustained
commitment to reincorporation of that large and important
area. It seems clear that the homelands will be reincorporated,
although the reshaping of diverse civil services in particular
presents difficulties. Despite the frequent delays in negotiations, they resumed late in 1992. Many of the major issues
of conflict have been defined and some progress made towards
settlement. An election date was set for April 1994, although
the powers of the regions remained unresolved. The very
fluidity of politics was reflected by ubiquitous use of the word

'players' to describe participants in political and economic negotiations.

A range of other groupings and interests, such as major corporations, the Democratic Party, and churches, declared themselves broadly sympathetic to deracialization and some form of liberal democracy, if not more radical change. Institutional change is preceding a political settlement. Large companies speeded up recruitment of blacks. Universities, which remain vital intellectual centres whose strength as civil institutions should not be underestimated, incorporated more black students. The University of the Western Cape, formerly a segregated institution for coloured people, has offered greatly expanded access to higher education and become a centre of reconstruction thinking. The legal profession, long powerful in the country, produced an influential human rights lobby as well as support, through the Legal Resources Centres, for unions, rural land claims, and opposition groups. Some English-language newspapers have remained a significant independent critical force. Such institutions remain a potential anchor for a democratic political culture.

In the past South African whites worked hard to link race, culture, and politics—justifying their dominance by the need to protect what they saw as a distinctive identity and 'civilization'. But along with settler populations elsewhere, some have increasingly turned away from identifying themselves as exclusively European or Western. Clearly language, race, and culture will remain powerful forces amongst blacks as well as whites. But the divisive potential of race and ethnicity can be defused if it is recognized that political rights and culture need not be one and the same. Common political and civil rights can provide a new social foundation in which some individual cultural freedom is also possible.

A democratic settlement will no doubt involve costs and not only for whites. One of the arguments of this book has been that the remnant autonomy of rural African communities has been insufficiently understood in analyses of South Africa. Some languages, for example, are likely to receive less protection as a new state attempts to forge a national identity. While there should surely be no rapid dismantling of communal tenure in the homelands, ethnic land claims might come under scrutiny.

Democracy will also require political constraint by citizens, black and white, as well as the state. The white right and Inkatha are only two of the threats to a stable civil order. The instruments and techniques of mass struggle which have proved essential for undermining white power might be less appropriate in a more democratic order. And perhaps only a democratic system can guarantee that there is not a repetition of the period of Afrikaner rule: so that a history of oppression does not result in a future of repression.

There is a great deal that divides South Africans. But in addition to sharing the same country, they may have more in common on which to build than at first seems apparent. Years of enforced ethnicity has produced a strong intellectual reaction against overemphasis of local identities. A few years of intensive negotiations has changed the political culture. Gradual deracialization is beginning, slowly, to affect the pattern of everyday social interaction. Sports bodies have largely been integrated. Both white and black have a tradition of hospitality. Many people of all backgrounds are familiar with more than one language—thus providing scope for cultural fluidity. English is increasingly a shared language of national politics.

The media, especially some television, is beginning to reflect and promote a more inclusive South African identity. While it can celebrate images of violence and unobtainable luxury, television has enormous power to project shared symbols. Its reach is extending as the townships become more fully electrified. Christianity remains a surprisingly powerful force. And it may be in the aisles of the new cathedrals, the supermarkets, as well as the old, that a common society is ultimately forged. Deep divisions of wealth and poverty persist, but these are no longer simply congruent with race and a common consumer culture is increasingly generalized. Massive urbanization has eroded the particularisms of black and white.

While decisions about anthems and flags, symbols which have been so divisive in the past, must await a new government they are surely not irresolvable issues. Symbols can be reworked and invested with new meaning. *Nkosi sikelel' iAfrika*, the ANC anthem composed in the early part of this century and widely used since, lays less definite claim to the land than *Die Stem* but its broad sentiments are not dissimilar. South African flags have a history of crowded compromise and more could undoubtedly be crammed in. Yet the ANC flag of green, gold, and black does include two of the colours of the formerly all-white rugby team. The ox-wagon and the springbok, appropriated by Afrikaners, were never simply theirs and are surely available for broader reconstruction.

Political fragmentation, chronic disorder, and economic relapse are still possible. The ideas and social conditions for conflict between narrow ethnic nationalisms and intransigent sectional groups are by no means absent. But there is some prospect of a freer society, a stable social order, and a relatively democratic system under a majority black but non-racial government. As long as poverty can be addressed, as long as ideas of citizenship are kept broad and inclusive, there may yet be a culturally diverse nation in the state of South Africa.

Appendix 1. *Tables*

TABLE I: *Total population and percentage by race as designated in census*

	Total population	White	Coloured	Asian	African
1904	5,174,827[a]	21.6	8.6	2.4	67.4
1911	5,972,757	21.4	8.8	2.5	67.7
1921	6,927,403	21.9	7.9	2.4	67.8
1936	9,587,863	20.9	8.0	2.3	68.8
1946	11,415,925	20.8	8.1	2.5	68.6
1951	12,671,452	20.9	8.7	2.9	67.5
1960	16,002,797	19.3	9.4	3.0	68.3
1970	21,794,328	17.3	9.4	2.9	70.4
1980	28,979,035[b]	15.7	9.1	2.8	72.4
1991	38,268,720	13.2	8.6	2.6	75.6
2000	47,591,000[c]	11.4	7.9	2.4	78.3

a In 1904 censuses were taken in all the colonies which came together in the Union of South Africa. There were census counts in the Boer republics and British colonies in 1890/1, but the former excluded the African population.

b It is important to note *which* figures are given in these tables as there is a great deal of variety in the numbers reported in different published sources on South Africa, including other general histories, for 1980 and 1991. Between 1976 and 1981 four black homelands, Transkei, Bophuthatswana, Venda, and Ciskei accepted independence from Pretoria. Most official statistics subsequently exclude their population from the total given for South Africa. e.g., the official census figure for 1980 is about 25 m. and for 1991, about 31 m. As a result, the proportion of whites in the population does not decline so markedly from 1970 in official statistics issued in these years. Figures in tables here *include* all the homelands so that there is a reasonably consistent geographical base to the population statistics from 1904 to 1991. Figures reported for the independent homelands in 1980 and 1991 vary significantly so that these numbers may not correlate exactly with other sources. The 1980 and 1991 census figures have been adjusted for undercounts. The upwardly revised figures, now generally accepted and used, are reported here.

c Projected figures published by the Urban Foundation and widely reported.

TABLE 2: *Average annual increase over previous census year*[a]

A

	Total % increase	African population	% increase	White population	% increase
1891				620,619	
1904		3,490,291		1,117,234	4.63
1911	2.07	4,018,878	2.03	1,276,319	1.93
1921[b]	1.49	4,697,285	1.57	1,521,343	1.76
1936	2.19	6,595,597	2.29	2,003,334	1.86
1946	1.76	7,830,559	1.73[c]	2,372,044	1.70
1951	2.10	8,560,083	1.79[c]	2,641,689	2.18
1960	2.63	10,927,922	2.75[c]	3,088,492	1.75
1970	3.14	15,057,952	3.26	3,752,528	1.97
1980	2.83	20,984,758	3.37	4,551,068	1.95
1991	2.62	28,889,600	2.96	5,068,110	0.98
1993	2.42 (estimate)				

B

	Coloured population	% increase	Asian population	% increase
1904	444,991		122,311	
1911	525,466	2.41	152,094	3.12
1921	545,181	0.37	163,594	0.86
1936	769,241	2.32	219,691	1.90
1946	928,062[c]	1.89	285,260[c]	2.65
1951	1,103,016	3.51	366,664[c]	5.15
1960	1,509,258	3.55	477,125	2.97
1970	2,018,453	2.95	620,436	2.66
1980	2,624,007	2.66	819,202	2.82
1991	3,285,718	2.07	986,620	1.70

a The annual average figures for the period from 1911 to 1951 are taken from the government publication *Union Statistics for Fifty Years*. I have computed the other figures on the basis of census returns and estimates for the independent homelands.

b Many commentators have suggested that the 1921 figures are the most marked undercount in the earlier national censuses. This may not be so. The census was taken only a few years after the influenza epidemic of 1918, probably the major single demographic check of the 20th c. Influenza deaths have been estimated at roughly 5% of the black population and 2.5% of the white, totalling about 300,000 in all. If they are taken into account, then the 1921 census is likely to have been of the same accuracy as others and population growth would have been relatively and remarkably stable for the whole of the first half of this century at around 2% p.a.

c Some published figures differ from those given here because they are adjusted to take account of upwardly revised total estimates for the African population before this was done officially in 1980. (e.g. the figures published in Annual *Official Yearbook of the Republic of South Africa* in the 1980s.) This has the effect of somewhat increasing the upward curve in annual average increase of African people in 1946 and 1951 but reducing it in 1960. The series presented here shows a fall in the rate of black population increase in 1946 and 1951 which may be a little difficult to explain. Similarly the rise in 1960 and 1970 may represent an exaggeration, but there is a clear explanation for it. By contrast the 1946 figure for Coloured and Asian people has been revised upwards and the 1951 downwards in some series.

TABLE 3: *Proportion of population in urban areas*[a]

	All	(Total × 1,000)	White	Coloured	Asian	African
1904	23	1,199	53	49	36	10
1911	25	1,477	52	50	53	13
1921	28	1,933	60	52	61	16
1936	32	3,106	68	57	71	21
1946	38	4,384	75	61	71	23
1951	43	5,398	78	65	78	27
1960	47	7,473	84	68	83	32
1970	[48][a]		87	74	87	[33]
1980	54	15,704	88	75	91	49
1991	63	24,411	91	83	96	58[b]
2000	70	33,400 (estimate)				

a The term 'urban' is difficult to define and becomes increasingly so as the 20th c. progresses. Figures up to 1970 are taken from the census returns. The 1970 figure for the total urban population calculated on the basis of official census returns would be about 10.5 m. This is very probably considerably less than it was because some areas in which Africans were settled in urban conditions were classified as within homelands and counted as rural in the census returns. I have not found an attempt to recalculate the figure for 1970. Subsequent figures, which are probably closer to the position on the ground, were recalculated by demographers and are taken from the Urban Foundation series, *Policies for a New Urban Future: Urban Debate 2010* (Johannesburg, n.d., 1990?).

b Even though this figure is adjusted for the above areas and settlements, there are probably many other African people who live in rural closer settlements, such as Betterment or Trust villages, or in peri-urban areas who do not have land or rural employment, but derive a living from urban earnings or pensions or the earnings of migrant workers. This figure should not be taken to suggest that over 40% of African people have access to rural resources or farm employment.

TABLE 4: *Motor vehicles*

	Cars	Commercial vehicles	Tractors	Minibuses
1930	135,000	16,000	4,000	
1940	318,000	49,000	6,000[a]	
1950	471,000	124,000	48,000	
1960	895,000	212,000	119,000	
1970	1,553,000	435,000	223,000	24,000
1980	2,333,000	871,000	302,000	73,000
1989	3,275,000	1,228,000	181,000	174,000

a Figure for 1937.

Appendix 2. *Figures*

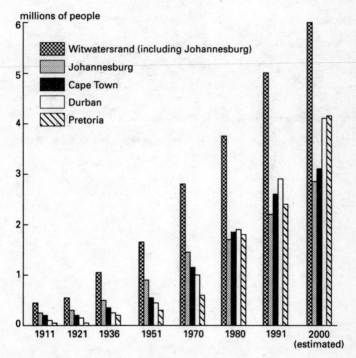

FIG. I. *Urban growth, 1911–2000. Main metropolitan areas*

Sources: Census and Urban Foundation.

Note: the figures are not based on the same geographic area in different years as the metropolitan areas expanded in size.

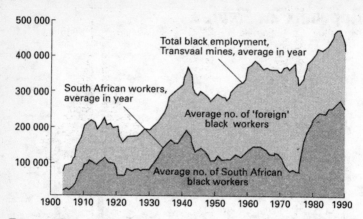

FIG. 2. *African employment in Transvaal mines*

Sources: Jeeves, *Migrant Labour*; Crush *et al.*, *South Africa's Labour Empire*.

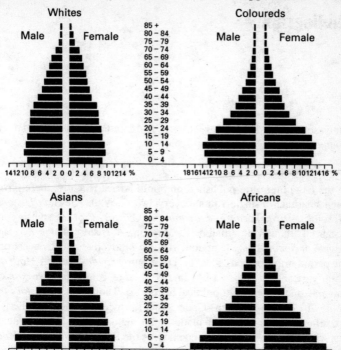

FIG. 3. *Age structure of population, 1980*

Source: *South Africa 1986. Official Yearbook of the Republic of South Africa*
(Pretoria, 1986), 30, taken from J. L. Sadie, 'Labour Force 2000' in *RSA 2000*
Human Sciences Research Council (Pretoria, 1981).

Bibliography

Only sources in English are listed. *JSAS* indicates the *Journal of Southern African Studies*.

Introduction

In the large literature published on South Africa recently, there have been a number of single-volume overviews. C. W. de Kiewiet's *History of South Africa, Social and Economic* (Oxford, 1941) is stylish and insightful, though now dated. P. Maylam, *A History of the African People of South Africa* (London, 1986) is innovative but strongest on the period prior to 1900. T. R. H. Davenport, *South Africa: A Modern History* (London, 1991, 4th edn.) is a large comprehensive work, valuable on the details of political history. L. Thompson, *A History of South Africa* (New Haven, Conn., 1990) provides a fluent synthesis. Exciting progress has been made in the field of popular illustrated histories. Despite its alarming claim to be the Real Story, *The Reader's Digest Illustrated History of South Africa* (1989) is the best of them; see also S. Spies (ed.), *An Illustrated History of South Africa* (Cape Town, 1986) and N. Parsons, *A New History of Southern Africa* (London, 1982). For single-volume works on political economy which include a strong historical dimension see B. Magubane, *The Political Economy of Race and Class in South Africa* (New York, 1979) and M. Lipton, *Capitalism and Apartheid, South Africa, 1910–1986* (London, 1985), who approach the issues from different theoretical positions. C. Bundy, *Remaking the Past* (Cape Town, 1987) explains some of the new historical writing, and K. Smith, *The Changing Past* (Johannesburg, 1988) gives a longer perspective. Three edited volumes provide a good introduction to new historical work: S. Marks and A. Atmore (eds.), *Economy and Society in Pre-industrial South Africa* (London, 1980); S. Marks and R. Rathbone (eds.), *Industrialisation and Social Change* (London, 1982); S. Marks and S. Trapido (eds.), *The Politics of Race, Class and Nationalism in Twentieth Century South Africa* (London, 1987). B. Bozzoli and P. Delius (eds.), *History from South*

Africa (New York, 1990), vols. 46/7 of the *Radical History Review* includes interesting historiographical surveys.

Chapter 1

General overviews of African societies include Maylam, *A History of the African People* and Wilson's chapters in M. Wilson and L. Thompson (eds.), *The Oxford History of South Africa*, 2 vols. (Oxford, 1971). M. Hunter, *Reaction to Conquest* (London, 1936, 1964) remains valuable. Sansom's chapter in W. Hammond-Tooke (ed.), *The Bantu Speaking Peoples of South Africa* (London, 1974) is one of the few attempts to write comparatively about coastal and highveld kingdoms. J. Guy, 'Analysing Pre-capitalist Societies', *JSAS* 14 (1987) on the Zulu is the fullest analysis of the control of women. C. Bundy, *The Rise and Fall of the South African Peasantry* (London, 1979; Cape Town, 1989) remains the key text on this issue. W. Beinart, *The Political Economy of Pondoland 1860–1930* (Cambridge, 1982) explores change in an area less affected by colonization. J. Lewis, 'The Rise and Fall of the South African Peasantry: A Critique', *JSAS* 11 (1984) suggests that the peasantry's opportunities were very restricted. For Natal see S. Marks, *Reluctant Rebellion* (London, 1970), and N. Etherington, *Preachers, Peasants and Politics in South East Africa, 1835–1880* (London, 1978). Detailed monographs on African societies in the nineteenth and early twentieth centuries include: J. Guy, *The Destruction of the Zulu Kingdom* (London, 1979); J. B. Peires, *The Dead Will Arise* (Johannesburg, 1989) on the Xhosa cattle-killing; P. Delius, *The Land Belongs to Us* (London, 1983) on the Pedi; P. Bonner, *Kings, Commoners and Concessionaires* (Cambridge, 1983) on the Swazi; and K. Shillington, *The Colonisation of the Southern Tswana* (Johannesburg, 1985). Marks and Atmore (eds.), *Economy and Society* and Marks and Rathbone, *Industrialisation and Social Change* contain articles on incorporation, the origins of migrant labour from Mozambique (P. Harries), Cape liberalism (S. Trapido), and on early mining (R. Turrell, J. van Helten, and P. Richardson). W. Beinart and C. Bundy, *Hidden Struggles in Rural South Africa* (London, 1987) examines peasant movements; J. and J. Comaroff, *Of Revelation and Revolution* (Chicago, 1992) develops new approaches to the cultural conflicts during colonization.

On early mining, see R. Turrell, 'Diamonds and Migrant Labour in South Africa', *History Today*, 36 (1986), and essays in P. Warwick

270   *Bibliography*

(ed.), *The South African War* (London, 1981). R. Turrell, *Capital and Labour on the Kimberley Diamond Fields* (Cambridge, 1987), and W. Worger, *South Africa's City of Diamonds* (New Haven, Conn., 1987) are two important new books on diamonds. H. Wolpe, 'Capitalism and Cheap Labour Power in South Africa', *Economy and Society*, 1 (1972) is the major statement of the cheap labour thesis; critiques are included in Delius, Harries, and Beinart above and P. Harries, 'Capital, State and Labour on the 19th Century Witwatersrand: A Reassessment', *South African Historical Journal*, 18 (1986). For the gold mines and migrancy, A. Jeeves, *Migrant Labour in South Africa's Mining Economy, 1890–1920* (Kingston, Ont., 1985). B. Bozzoli, 'Marxism, Feminism and South African Studies', *JSAS* 9/2 (1983) examines the effects of rural patriarchy on migrancy.

Chapter 2

For general introductions to settler farming see F. Wilson, 'Farming, 1866–1966' in Wilson and Thompson, *Oxford History*, vol. ii, and W. Beinart, P. Delius, and S. Trapido (eds.), *Putting a Plough to the Ground: Accumulation and Dispossession in Rural South Africa 1850–1930* (Johannesburg, 1986). D. Denoon, *Settler Capitalism* (Oxford, 1983) is a useful comparative work. For the western Cape: R. Elphick and H. Giliomee (eds.), *The Shaping of South African Society, 1652–1840* (Cape Town, 1989); T. R. H. Davenport, *The Afrikaner Bond, 1880–1911* (Cape Town, 1966); H. Giliomee, 'Western Cape Farmers and the Beginnings of Afrikaner Nationalism, 1870–1915', *JSAS* 14/1 (1987); P. Scully, *The Bouquet of Freedom* (Cape Town, 1990); W. James and M. Simons (eds.), *The Angry Divide* (Cape Town, 1989). On the midland Cape and sheep, Union of South Africa, *Final Report of the Drought Investigation Commission* (U.G. 49—1923), and my unpublished paper: 'The Night of the Jackal: Sheep, Pastures and Predators in South Africa', African Studies Seminar, University of Cape Town, 1993. Olive Schreiner's novel, *The Story of an African Farm* (London, 1883) is a personal evocation of Cape rural society. M. Legassick, 'The Frontier Tradition in South African Historiography' in Marks and Atmore, *Economy and Society* is the key critique of the frontier legacy. M. Morris, 'The Development of Capitalism in South African Agriculture', *Economy and Society*, 3 (1976) proposed a transition from rent to labour tenancy on the highveld; S. Trapido, 'Landlord and Tenant in a Colonial Economy', *JSAS* 5 (1978) explored tenancy more widely. T. Keegan, *Rural Transformations in Industrializing South Africa: The Southern*

Highveld to 1914 (London, 1987) is especially instructive on sharecropping and poor whites. Solomon Plaatje, *Native Life in South Africa* (London, 1916) remains a major source on the effects of the Land Act but should be read alongside recent historical writing. W. M. Macmillan, *The Agrarian Problem* (Johannesburg, 1919) and *Complex South Africa* (London, 1930) are still fresh. J. Krikler, 'Agrarian Class Struggle and the South African War', *Social History*, 14/2 (1989) examines tenant struggles. In *Facing the Storm* (Cape Town, 1987), Keegan presents evocative oral testimony from black tenant families, as do T. Matsetela, 'The Life Story of Nkgono Mma-Pooe' in Marks and Rathbone, *Industrialisation and Social Change*, and M. Nkadimeng and G. Relly, 'Kas Maine, the Story of a Black South African Agriculturalist' in B. Bozzoli (ed.), *Town and Countryside in the Transvaal* (Johannesburg, 1983). H. Bradford, *A Taste of Freedom* (New Haven, Conn., 1987) is especially interesting on the 1920s. See C. van Onselen, 'Race and Class in the South African Countryside: Cultural Osmosis and Social Relations in the Sharecropping Economy of the South-Western Transvaal, 1900–1950', *American Historical Review*, 95/1 (1990), and C. Murray, *Black Mountain* (Edinburgh, 1992), for rural social relationships over a longer timespan. D. Opperman, *Groot Verseboek* (Cape Town, 1968) for poem. See general sources and L. Thompson, *The Unification of South Africa* (Oxford, 1960) for railways. The quote is from F. D. Lugard, *The Dual Mandate in Tropical Africa* (London, 1929). J. MacKenzie, *The Empire of Nature* (Manchester, 1988) is instructive on hunting, and J. Carruthers, 'Creating a National Park, 1910–1926', *JSAS* 15/2 (1989) on conservation.

Chapter 3

Important overviews on the densely covered period of the South African War and Reconstruction include: C. van Onselen, *Studies in the Social and Economic History of the Witwatersrand, 1886–1914*, 2 vols. (London, 1982); S. Marks and S. Trapido, 'Lord Milner and the South African State', *History Workshop*, 8 (1979); P. Warwick (ed.), *The South African War* (London, 1980). On Merriman, P. Lewsen, *John X. Merriman: Paradoxical South African Statesman* (London, 1982); quotes are from her *Selections from the Correspondence of J. X. Merriman* (van Riebeeck Society series, vols. xli and xliv, Cape Town, 1960–9). R. Rotberg, *Cecil Rhodes* (London, 1988) is the newest of many biographies. On mining and labour, see Chapter 1 and L. Callinicos, *Gold and Workers* (Johannesburg, 1980), and

Working Life, 1886–1940 (Johannesburg, 1987); F. Johnstone, *Class, Race and Gold* (London, 1976); N. Levy, *The Foundations of the South African Cheap Labour System* (London, 1982), and D. Yudelman, *The Emergence of Modern South Africa* (Cape Town, 1982). To some degree newer works contest D. Denoon, *The Grand Illusion* (Oxford, 1973), which saw less success in reconstruction. Detailed discussion of the origins of the war, which is avoided here, can be found in J. S. Marais, *The Fall of Kruger's Republic* (Oxford, 1961), and A. Porter, *The Origins of the South African War* (Manchester, 1980). See Thompson, *Unification* on constitutional history. Key government documents quoted include Great Britain, *Report of the Transvaal Labour Commission*, Cd. 1897 (1904), and *South African Native Affairs Commission Report* (London, 1905). John Buchan, *Prester John* (1910) remains revealing; quotes from Penguin edn. M. Legassick, 'The Making of South African "Native Policy", 1902–23: The Origins of Segregation', unpublished, Institute of Commonwealth Studies, London, 1972, and for comparative works: J. Cell, *The Highest Stage of White Supremacy* (New York, 1982), and J. MacKenzie, *Propaganda and Empire* (London, 1984). F. Reitz *A Century of Wrong*, partly written by Smuts, for whom see W. K. Hancock, *Smuts*, vol. i, *The Sanguine Years* (Cambridge, 1962). Many books on Afrikaner history are caught up in the ideology of Afrikanerdom. For a variety of views: W. de Klerk, *The Puritans in Africa* (Harmondsworth, 1976) which should be read alongside the demythologizing work of A. du Toit, 'No Chosen People: The Myth of the Calvinist Origins of Afrikaner Nationalism and Racial Idiology', *American Historical Review*, 88/4 (1983) and also L. Thompson, *Political Mythology of Apartheid* (New Haven, Conn., 1985), H. Giliomee and H. Adam, *Ethnic Power Mobilized* (New Haven, Conn., 1979) and I. Hexham, *The Ironies of Apartheid* (New York, 1981). Giliomee, 'The Beginnings of Afrikaner Ethnic Consciousness, 1850–1915' in L. Vail (ed.), *The Creation of Tribalism in Southern Africa* (Berkeley, Calif., 1991) ably summarizes the literature and Hexham, 'Modernity or Reaction in South Africa: The Case of Afrikaner Religion,' unpublished paper, 1981, looks at Afrikaner folk belief and popular religion, quoting L. Leipoldt, *Bushveld Doctor* (London, 1937). See Bundy, 'Vagabond Hollanders and Runaway Englishmen' in *Putting a Plough to the Ground* and R. Morrell (ed.), *White but Poor* (Pretoria, 1992) for new perspectives on poor whites and also T. Davenport, 'The South African Rebellion, 1914', *English Historical Review*, 77 (1963).

Chapter 4

On Plaatje, B. Willan, *Sol Plaatje South African Nationalist 1876–1932* (London, 1984), and Plaatje, *Native Life in South Africa*. On the African élite, A. Odendaal, *Vukani Bantu: The Beginnings of Black Protest Politics in South Africa to 1912* (Cape Town, 1981), and A. Ngubo, 'The Development of African Political Protest, 1882–1910', unpublished Ph.D. thesis (University of California, 1973). S. Trapido, 'African Divisional Politics in the Cape Colony, 1884–1910', *JAH* 9/1 (1968) discusses voting politics; see also his 'The Origins of the African Political Organisation', Institute of Commonwealth Studies seminars, vol. 1 (London, 1973). D. D. T. Jabavu, *The Black Problem* (Lovedale, 1920) gives a sense of eastern Cape preoccupations. M. Swan, *Gandhi: The South African Experience* (Johannesburg, 1983) is authoritative but critical. Quotes on Bambatha are from Shula Marks, *Reluctant Rebellion* (London, 1970). Other material on Zululand is drawn from S. Marks, 'Natal, the Zulu Royal Family and the Ideology of Segregation', *JSAS* 4/2 (1978); 'Class, Ideology and the Bambatha Rebellion' in D. Crummey (ed.), *Banditry, Rebellion and Social Protest in Africa* (London, 1986), and *The Ambiguities of Dependence in South Africa* (Johannesburg, 1986). For recent work on ethnicity Vail (ed.), *The Creation of Tribalism*, and P. Delius 'The Ndzundza Ndebele' in P. Bonner *et al.* (eds.), *Holding their Ground* (Johannesburg, 1990). Beinart, *Pondoland*, looks at chieftaincy. Bradford, *A Taste of Freedom*, concentrates on the rural ICU; see also Beinart and Bundy, *Hidden Struggles* on East London. J. Wells, 'Why Women Rebel', *JSAS* 10 (1983), and 'The Day the Town Stood Still' in Bozzoli, *Town and Countryside*, explores women's movements as do articles by Beinart and Bradford in B. Bozzoli (ed.), *Class Community and Conflict* (Johannesburg, 1987). C. Walker, *Women and Resistance in South Africa* (London, 1982), and (ed.), *Women and Gender in Southern Africa* (London, 1991) provide an overview. For an outline of the ANC see P. Walshe, *The Rise of African Nationalism in South Africa* (London, 1970), and F. Meli, *South Africa Belongs to Us* (Harare, 1988), a recent history of the ANC from within the movement. H. and R. Simons, *Class and Colour in South Africa, 1850–1950* (Harmondsworth, 1969) is a classic socialist analysis of black protest. B. Sundkler, *Bantu Prophets in South Africa* (London, 1948) is still valuable on African churches, and on Israelites see R. Edgar, *Because They Chose the Plan of God* (Johannesburg, 1988). New Nation and the History Workshop, *New Nation, New History* (Johannesburg, 1989) collates a series of newspaper articles on black politics written by historians. On gangs and male associations: van Onselen, *Social and Economic History of the Witwatersrand*, especially 'The Regiment of the Hills' and the 'Witches of Suburbia'; T. D. Moodie, 'Migrancy and Male Sexuality on the South African Gold Mines', *JSAS* 14/2 (1988), and Moodie, 'Collective violence on the South African Gold Mines', *JSAS* 18/3 (1992); P. la Hausse, 'The Cows of Nongoloza: Youth, Crime and Amalaita Gangs in Durban, 1900–1936', *JSAS* 16/1 (1990), and 'The Message of the Warriors' in Bonner *et al.* (eds.), *Holding their Ground.*

Chapter 5

Yudelman, *Emergence of Modern South Africa* remains most authoritative on the state and the mines. T. Dunbar Moodie, *The Rise of Afrikanerdom* (Berkeley, Calif., 1976), D. O'Meara, *Volkskapitalisme* (Cambridge, 1983), Giliomee and Adam, *Ethnic Power Mobilised*, and P. Furlong, *Between Crown and Swastika* (Middletown, Conn., 1991) are valuable on Afrikaners. I. Hofmeyr, 'Building a Nation from Words: Afrikaans Language, Literature and Ethnic Identity, 1902–1924' in Marks and Trapido (eds.), *The Politics of Race, Class and Nationalism*, moves in new directions on cultural history. Hancock, *Smuts*, vol. ii, *The Fields of Force* remains the best biography. M. Lacey, *Working for Boroko* (Johannesburg, 1980) offers a materialist interpretation of segregation; S. Dubow, *Racial Segregation and the Origins of Apartheid in South Africa, 1919–1936* (London, 1989) re-examines the ideologies behind segregation. Walker (ed.), *Women and Gender* for the vote and for essay by E. Brink on the *volksmoeder*. D. Innes, *Anglo American and the Rise of Modern South Africa* (Johannesburg, 1984) is useful on mining. On industry and unions: E. Webster, *Cast in a Racial Mould: Labour Process and Trade Unionism in the Foundries* (Johannesburg, 1985); J. Lewis, *Industrialisation and Trade Union Organisation in South Africa, 1924–1955* (Cambridge, 1984); B. Hirson, *Yours for the Union: Class and Community Struggles in South Africa, 1930–1947* (London, 1990); Callinicos, *Working Lives*; I. Berger, *Threads of Solidarity: Women in South African Industry, 1900–1980* (Bloomington, Ind., 1992). Union of South Africa, *Report of the Native Economic Commission*, U.G. 22–1932, is a central government document of the inter-war years, and Union of South Africa, *Report of the Native Laws Commission*, U.G. 28–1948, is important for understanding the Smuts government. E. Hellmann, *Rooiyard: A Sociological Survey of an Urban Native Slum Yard* (Cape Town, 1948) remains vivid on the slums; E. Koch,

'Without Visible Means of Subsistence' in Bozzoli (ed.), *Town and Countryside* provides further background. Novels include M. Dikobe, *The Marabi Dance* (London, 1973); P. Abrahams, *Mine Boy* (London, 1946); and *Tell Freedom* (London, 1954); P. Lanham and A. Mopeli-Paulus, *Blanket Boy's Moon* (London, 1953); A. Paton, *Cry, The Beloved Country* (London, 1948). On mine-workers: T. D. Moodie, 'The Moral Economy of the Black Miners' Strike of 1946', *JSAS* 13 (1986), and D. O'Meara, 'The 1946 African Mineworkers' Strike and the Political Economy of South Africa', *Journal of Commonwealth and Comparative Politics*, 13 (1975). Compare D. Hemson, 'Dock Workers, Labour Circulation and Class Struggles in Durban, 1940–59', *JSAS* 4 (1977). On squatters: A. Stadler, 'Birds in a Cornfield: Squatter Movements in Johannesburg, 1944–1947', *JSAS* 6 (1979), and P. Bonner in Bozzoli and Delius (eds.), *History from South Africa*; see also Bonner, 'Family, Crime and Political Consciousness on the East Rand', *JSAS* 14 (1988). On Betterment, W. Beinart, 'Soil Erosion, Conservationism and Ideas about Development', *JSAS* 11 (1984), B. Hirson, 'Rural Revolt in South Africa, 1937–51', Institute of Commonwealth Studies, collected seminar papers, vol. 8 (1977), and P. Delius, 'Sebatakgomo and the Zoutpansberg Balemi Association: The ANC, the Communist Party and Rural Organization, 1939–1955', *Journal of African History*, 34 (1993). T. Lodge, *Black Politics in South Africa since 1945* (London, 1983). Voting figures are from K. Heard, *General Elections in South Africa 1943–1970* (London, 1974).

Chapter 6

The early apartheid period has been very thoroughly covered. References on Afrikaner history for Chapter 5 are a good starting-point. Older books such as Gwendolin Carter, *The Politics of Inequality: South Africa since 1948* (London, 1958), and W. Vatcher, *White Laager* (London, 1965), have considerable interest as responses by concerned foreigners. B. Bunting, *The Rise of the South African Reich* (Harmondsworth, 1963) is a committed statement by an opposition expatriate. F. Johnstone, 'White Prosperity and White Supremacy in South Africa Today', *African Affairs*, 69 (1970) was an early radical reinterpretation of apartheid; Wolpe, 'Capitalism and Cheap Labour Power' remains important. H. Adam, *Modernising Racial Domination* (Berkeley, Calif., 1971) was one of the first to argue for the flexibility of apartheid. D. Hindson, *Pass Controls and the Urban African Proletariat* (Johannesburg, 1987) challenged the view linking apartheid largely to the extension of migrancy; D. Posel, *The Making of Apartheid 1948–1961* (Oxford, 1991) develops further the arguments about influx control and the Nationalist Party's labour policies. J. Lazar, 'Conformity and Conflict: Afrikaner Nationalist Politics, 1948–1961', unpublished D.Phil. thesis (University of Oxford, 1987) tries to marry O'Meara's materialist approach with Moodie's concern about ideology. I. Goldin, *Making Race: The Politics and Economics of Coloured Identity in South Africa* (Harlow, 1987) analyses Nationalist attempts to influence the labour market of the western Cape. J. Western, *Outcast Cape Town* (London, 1981) is especially interesting on the effects of the Group Areas Act, and A. Mabin, 'Comprehensive Segregation: The Origins of the Group Areas Act and its Planning Apparatuses', *JSAS* 18/2 (1992) on its origins. G. Pirie, 'Rolling Segregation into Apartheid', unpublished paper to the 1990 History Workshop conference, discusses the railways. J. Crush, A. Jeeves, and D. Yudelman, *South Africa's Labour Empire: A History of Black Migrancy to the Gold Mines* (Cape Town, 1991), is the best new overview on this question. For analyses of Bantu education: J. Hyslop, 'State Education Policy and the Social Reproduction of the Urban African Working Class: The Case of the Southern Transvaal, 1955–76', *JSAS* 14/3 (1988), and P. Kallaway (ed.), *Apartheid and Education: the Education of Black South Africans* (Johannesburg, 1984). Union of South Africa, *Summary Report of the Commission for the Socio-Economic Development of the Bantu Areas within the Union of South Africa*, U.G. 61–1955 (Tomlinson Commission) is the key government document on the homelands.

Lodge, *Black Politics*, is the fullest outline on the ANC in these years. A. Luthuli, *Let My People Go* (London, 1963) is a heartfelt autobiography; A. Sampson, *Drum* (London, 1956) describes his period editing the magazine. There is not yet a good biography of Mandela. F. Meer, *Higher than Hope* (Johannesburg, 1988) is celebratory but includes interview material. Mandela's speeches were published in *No Easy Walk to Freedom* (London, 1965). J. Guy and M. Thabane, 'The Ma-Rashea: A Participant's Perspective' in Bozzoli (ed.), *Class, Community and Conflict*, as well as Bonner, 'Family, Crime and Political Consciousness', and Bonner and Lambert, 'Batons and Bareheads' in Marks and Trapido, *The Politics of Race, Class and Nationalism*, are important on gangs, unions, urban politics, and the ANC. P. Delius, 'Sebatakgomo; Migrant Organization, the ANC and the Sekhukhuneland Revolt', *JSAS* 15/4 (1989) looks at links between the ANC and rural movements.

Chapter 7

For articles on apartheid and growth see Johnstone, 'White Prosperity', and others in Chapter 6. M. Lipton, *Capitalism and Apartheid*, is a thorough restatement of the 'liberal' position which is in many ways more materialist than recent 'radical' writing. Quote is from C. Desmond, *The Discarded People: An Account of African Resettlement in South Africa* (Harmondsworth, 1971). J. Saul and S. Gelb, *The Crisis in South Africa* (London, 1986) moved the radical argument onwards; see also S. Gelb (ed.), *South Africa's Economic Crisis* (Cape Town, 1991) for survey articles covering manufacturing, the economic crisis, and reform era. Debates are reconsidered in N. Nattrass, 'Controversies about Capitalism and Apartheid in South Africa: An Economic Perspective', *JSAS* 17/4 (1991), and T. Moll, 'Did the Apartheid Economy "Fail"?', *JSAS* 17/2 (1991). Overview books on the economy and political economy of South Africa are numerous: J. Nattrass, *The South African Economy* (Cape Town, 1988) is useful. The *Annual Yearbooks* published by the South African Government are a valuable source of statistics: figures on cars are from here and H. T. Andrews *et al.* (eds.), *South Africa in the Sixties* (Cape Town, 1962). The social history of white society is covered in popular rather than academic works. Peter Joyce (ed.), *Reader's Digest South Africa's Yesterdays* (Cape Town, 1981) is better on the earlier decades of the century but well illustrated and suggestive. J. Cock, *Maids and Madams* (Johannesburg, 1980) was a pathbreaking feminist analysis of domestic service. Jeremy Taylor's song was taken from the record *Wait a Minim*. R. Archer and R. Bouillon, *The South African Game* (London, 1979) is especially interesting on rugby. S. Burman and M. Huvers, 'Church versus State: Divorce Legislation and Divided South Africa', *JSAS* 12/1 (1985) analyses changing divorce laws. Adam, *Modernizing Racial Domination*, and Giliomee and Adam, *Ethnic Power Mobilised* analyse Afrikaner social and economic mobility. Studies of African social change in the 1950s and 1960s include: L. Kuper, *An African Bourgeoisie* (New Haven, Conn., 1965) on Durban; M. Brandel-Syrier, *Reeftown Elite* (London, 1971); M. Wilson and A. Mafeje, *Langa* (Cape Town, 1963) on Cape Town; A. Vilakazi, *Zulu Transformations* (Pietermaritzburg, 1965) on a rural community near Durban; P. and I. Mayer, *Townsmen or Tribesmen* (2nd edn. Cape Town, 1971). On churches, M. West, *Bishops and Prophets in a Black City* (Cape Town, 1979); J. Comaroff, *Body of Power, Spirit of Resistance* (Chicago, 1985). M. Nyagumbo, *Forward with the People* (London, 1980), sketches the life of a Zimbabwean migrant worker at an earlier period.

Chapter 8

A number of the sources noted in Chapter 6, including Hindson, Posel, and Lazar have been drawn on. The most striking early account of the population removals, especially in the rural areas, was Desmond, *The Discarded People*. A great deal of the research was systematized in the five-volume collation of the Surplus People Report, *Forced Removals in South Africa* (Cape Town, 1983); this in turn was summarized and given context in L. Platzky and C. Walker, *The Surplus People* (Johannesburg, 1985); Murray, *Black Mountain*, incorporates a deeper historical perspective and concludes with a chapter on Botshabelo. See also his 'Displaced Urbanisation: South Africa's Rural Slums' in J. Lonsdale (ed.), *South Africa in Question* (Cambridge, 1988). S. Greenberg, *Race and State in Capitalist Development: South Africa in Comparative Perspective* (New Haven, Conn., 1981) has comparative observations on agriculture. See also F. Wilson, A. Kooy, and D. Hendrie (eds.), *Farm Labour in South Africa* (Cape Town, 1977) for agricultural workers, and H. Bradford, 'Getting Away with Slavery', paper to the History Workshop, Johannesburg, 1990, for Bethal. M. de Klerk, 'Seasons that will Never Return: The Impact of Farm Mechanisation on Employment Incomes and Population Distribution in the Western Transvaal', *JSAS* 11/1 (1984) is important on maize farms. At a more general level, see Lipton, *Capitalism and Apartheid*, M. de Klerk (ed.), *A Harvest of Discontent* (Cape Town, 1991), and W. Beinart, 'Agrarian Historiography and Agrarian Reconstruction' in Lonsdale (ed.), *South Africa in Question*.

C. Simkins, *Four Essays on the Past, Present and Possible Future of the Distribution of the Black Population of South Africa* (Cape Town, 1983) is much quoted on population trends; the Urban Foundation series, *Policies for a New Urban Future: Urban Debate 2010* (Johannesburg, n.d. 1990?) is a valuable collation of demographic discussion and projection. Barbara B. Brown, 'Facing the "Black Peril": The Politics of Population Control in South Africa', *JSAS* 13/2 (1987) deals with some neglected elements of demography. J. Lelyveld, *Move Your Shadow: South Africa, Black and White* (New York, 1985) is a searing journalistic account of South Africa in the early 1980s with reportage from the homelands. A great deal of new material was presented to the Carnegie Conference on Poverty in South Africa (Cape Town, 1985), summarized in F. Wilson and M. Ramphele, *Uprooting Poverty* (Cape Town, 1989). R. Southall, *South Africa's Transkei: The Political Economy of an 'Independent' Bantustan* (London, 1982), and B. Streek and R. Wicksteed, *Render Unto Kaiser: A Transkei Dossier*

(Johannesburg, 1981) are interesting overviews on the Transkei. On industrial decentralization, William Cobbett *et al.*, 'South Africa's Regional Political Economy: A Critical Analysis of Reform Strategy in the 1980s', *South African Review*, 3 (Johannesburg, 1986); T. Bell, 'The Role of Regional Policy in South Africa', *JSAS* 12/2 (1986).

Chapter 9

Lodge, *Black Politics*, Meli, *South Africa belongs to Us*, S. Ellis and T. Sechaba, *Comrades against Apartheid* (London, 1992), and Stephen M. Davis, *Apartheid's Rebels: Inside South Africa's Hidden War* (New Haven, Conn., 1987), give a sense of the ANC and Communist Party in exile. See H. Barrell, 'The Turn to the Masses: The African National Congress' Strategic Review of 1978–79', *JSAS* 18/1 (1992). G. Gerhardt, *Black Power in South Africa* (Berkeley, Calif., 1978) includes an early exploration of black consciousness; see also Steve Biko, *I Write What I like* (London, 1978), and S. Nolutshungu, *Changing South Africa* (Manchester, 1982). Z. K. Matthews, *Freedom for My People* (Cape Town, 1983) on Fort Hare. M. Mothlabi, *The Theory and Practice of Black Resistance to Apartheid* (Johannesburg, 1984) is an overview before the insurrection of the mid-1980s; S. Johnson (ed.), *South Africa: No Turning Back* (London, 1988), and R. Cohen, Y. Muthien, and A. Zegeye (eds.), *Repression and Resistance: Insider Accounts of Apartheid* (Oxford, 1990), contain useful overview articles written afterwards. Mbulelo Mzamane's novel, *The Children of Soweto* (Johannesburg, 1982) best captures the mood of 1976; see also S. Sepamla, *Ride on the Whirlwind* (Johannesburg, 1981). N. Diseko, 'The Origins and Development of the South African Student's Movement (SASM): 1968–1976', *JSAS* 18/1 (1992) and her article in Cohen *et al.* analyse the politics of schools. For the trade unions, the *South African Labour Bulletin*, launched in 1974, is an invaluable source; J. Maree (ed.), *The Independent Trade Unions 1974–1984* (Johannesburg, 1987), includes articles and extracts from it, and see also S. Friedman, *Building Tomorrow Today: African Workers in Trade Unions, 1970–1985* (Johannesburg, 1987). Material on the Durban strikes is from the Institute of Industrial Education, *The Durban Strikes 1973* (Durban, 1974). Amongst a rash of new books covering black politics M. Murray, *South Africa: Time of Agony, Time of Destiny* (London, 1987) is especially interesting on unions and their political links, and Anthony W. Marx, *Lessons of Struggle: South African Internal Opposition, 1960–1990* (Oxford, 1991) on black consciousness. G. Mare and G. Hamilton, *An Appetite for*

280   *Bibliography*

Power: Buthelezi's Inkatha and South Africa (Johannesburg, 1987)
remains most informative on Buthelezi and Inkatha. R. Davies, D.
O'Meara and S. Dlamini, *The Struggle for South Africa: A Reference
Guide to Movements, Organizations and Institutions* (London, 1984) is
a general reference work. For material on reform, see Chapter 7.
Quotes are from C. Charney, 'Class Conflict and the National Party
Split', *JSAS* 10/2 (1984). The five volumes of the *South African
Review*, compiled and edited by Glenn Moss and Ingrid Obery (Ravan
Press, Johannesburg) contain valuable commentary on all aspects of
South African society while the annual South African Institute of Race
Relations' *Race Relations Survey* remains a treasure trove of detailed
information.

Chapter 10

In this chapter, I have been partly reliant on the press, especially the
Weekly Mail and the *Guardian*, on the large volume of contemporary
magazines and journals published in South Africa, on Moss and Obery
(eds.), *South Africa Review* and the *Race Relations Survey*. The
journals *Work in Progress* (Johannesburg) and *Transformation*
(Durban) carry important debates and academic analysis of contem-
porary South Africa. Recent issues of the *Journal of Southern African
Studies* have been valuable, especially articles in the two special issues:
S. Marks and S. Trapido (eds.), *Social History of Resistance in South
Africa*, 18/1 (1992); and W. Beinart, R. Turrell, and T. O. Ranger
(eds.), *Political and Collective Violence in Southern Africa*, 18/3 (1992).
Quotes are taken from C. Carter, 'Community and Conflict: The
Alexandra Rebellion of 1986' in *JSAS* 18/1. Murray, *Time of Agony,
Time of Destiny*, Marx, *Black Opposition*, and Davis, *Apartheid's
Rebels*, were all useful. W. Cobbett and R. Cohen (eds.), *Popular
Struggles in South Africa* (London, 1988) contains good coverage of
the insurrection, including J. Seekings, 'The Origins of Political
Mobilisation in PWV Townships, 1980–1984'. Volumes in the series
South Africa: Time Running Out summarize political developments:
R. Schrire, *Adapt or Die: The End of White Politics in South Africa*
(London, 1992); T. Lodge and W. Nasson, *All Here and Now: Black
Politics in South Africa in the 1980s* (London, 1992). Robert M. Price,
*The Apartheid State in Crisis: Political Transformation in South Africa
1975–1990* (Oxford, 1991) is interesting especially on the international
dimensions of the mid-1980s crisis: J. Baskin, *Striking Back: A History
of COSATU* (Johannesburg, 1991) on unions in the 1980s.

On militarization and the South African state, P. Frankel, *Pretoria's*

Praetorians (Cambridge, 1984); J. Cock and L. Nathan (eds.), *War and Society: The Militarisation of South Africa* (Cape Town, 1989); J. Cock, *Women and War in South Africa* (London, 1992). N. Haysom, *Mabangalala: The Rise of Right-wing Vigilantes in South Africa* (Johannesburg, 1986), and J. Cole, *Crossroads: The Politics of Reform and Repression* (Johannesburg, 1987) are key sources on early vigilante activity. Centre for Policy Studies, *South Africa at the End of the Eighties: Policy Perspectives 1989* (Johannesburg, 1989) is useful for a perspective of Botha's era; M. Swilling *et al.* (eds.), *Apartheid City in Transition* (Cape Town, 1991) begins to rethink the cities as does the Urban Foundation, *Policies for a New Urban Future*. H. Giliomee, '*Broedertwis*: Intra-Afrikaner Conflicts in the Transition from Apartheid', *African Affairs*, 91 (1992) explicitly challenges the link between class and political outlook amongst Afrikaners. On violence and political killings: A. du Toit and N. Manganyi (eds.), *Political Violence in South Africa* (Cape Town, 1991), and C. Charney, 'Vigilantes, Clientelism, and the South African State', *Transformation*, 16 (1991).

Index

Abdurahman, Dr A. 86, 93
Abrahams, Peter 122, 123
Adam, Heribert 139, 172, 178–9
African Food and Canning Workers
    Union 232
African National Congress (ANC)
    92, 99–103, 125, 128, 145, 148–9,
    153, 157, 159–60, 180, 195,
    213–17, 220, 226, 233–4, 236,
    241–2, 248, 250, 252–4, 256–7,
    260
    Umkhonto we Sizwe 212, 222
African Political Organization 86
Africans:
    ANC and politics of exile 212–16
    black consciousness 216–21
    chieftaincy, ethnicity and rural
        protest 92–98, 156–8
    class and social change 180–7
    crisis, reform and the UDF
        225–35
    élite and nationalism 84–91
    heritage 15–19
    land division 9–15
    mining and labour migration
        25–34, *see also* migrancy
    peasantries 14–15, 19–25, 32–3,
        37, 46–7, 51–2, 56, 93, 102, 129,
        158, 214
    struggles in the 1920s 98–108
    trade unionism 125–7, 222–4
Afrikaner Broederbond (1919) 27,
    37–8, 63, 85, 115–16, 140, 142,
    155, 174, 179, 230, 251
Afrikaners 22, 40, 45–6, 61–2, 104,
    114–15
    politics in war and depression
        109–17
    re-emergent 1890s–1920s 74–83

white society and culture 171–80
agriculture 208, 241
    African 10–11, 14, 15, 96–7, 129,
        208–9
    capitalist 19, 28, 56, 58, 101
    white 35–58, 77, 113, 119, 132,
        140, 150, 192–7, 241
    see also tenancy
alcohol 38, 44, 104, 143, 182, 220–1,
    247
    beer brewing 104–5, 121–3
All Africa Convention (1935) 125
Amafelandawonye movement 102,
    127–8
amalaita 105
Amandla awethu 221, 242
Amelika 99, 103
amenities, segregation of 142, 146
Andrews, Bill 81
Andrews, H. T. 174
Anglo-American Corporation
    167–8, 228, 242
animal disease 21, 32, 42, 50
animal slaughter 94–105, 102
anthem, national 109–10, 222,
    259–60
apartheid 93, 132, 190, 192, 194,
    198, 203–4, 206–8, 211, 214,
    216–17, 220, 222, 225, 227–8,
    234–36, 238–9, 244–45, 254
    economic growth and 163–71
    1948–1961: labour control and the
        homelands 149–58; legislation
        and reaction 142–49;
        Nationalist mission 137–42;
        Sharpeville and the Republic
        159–62
armaments 169–70, 255

Armscor 169–70, 225, 245, 249
Asiatic Land Tenure Act (1946) 146
Asinamali movement 128
Australia 25, 35, 39, 60, 111

Baker, Herbert 73
Bambatha Rebellion (1906) 68, 86,
    91, 94–5
Banda, Hastings 226
Bantu Affairs Administration Boards
    (BAABs) 236–7
Bantu Authorities Act (1951) 154
Bantu Education Act (1953) 153–4,
    156–7, 220, 248
Barolong community 54
Barrell, H. 216
Beaufré, General 245
beer, *see* alcohol
Betterment proclamation (1939)
    129–30, 154, 158, 198, 205
Bhaca people 98
Biko, Steve 185, 217–18, 221
bilingualism 109, 259
Black Allied Workers Union
    (BAWU) 219, 224
black consciousness 216–24, 233,
    248
Black People's Convention 219
Black Sash 180
Bloemfontein 72, 87–8, 121, 170,
    199, 201, 211
Boesak, Alan 234
Boipatong 239, 256
Bophelong 239
Bophuthatswana 156, 205, 207, 257
    Mafikeng 84, 198
    Sun City 209
    Winterveld 199, 201
Botha, Louis 54, 74–7, 80
Botha, P. W. 165, 171, 186, 225,
    227, 229, 241–2, 244–6, 249–52
Botha, Thozamile 232
Botshabelo 201, 211, 238
Botswana 17, 204
boycott 93, 96, 99, 102, 214–5,
    231–2, 238, 241, 244, 252
Bozzoli, B. 32
Bradford, H. 53, 195
Brandel-Syrier, M. 184

Brandt, Joanna 78–9
Brazil 139, 145, 189, 197
bridewealth 18, 31, 53, 117, 130,
    184, 206
Brink, André 180
Britain:
    gold standard 111
    imperialism 22–4, 32, 36–7, 39,
        44, 46, 59–63, 66, 74, 84, 86, 90,
        97, 161, 166, 203
broadcasting 176, 179, 246, 259
Buchan, John 68–9
bucket boys 99
Bulhoek 97
Bundy, C. 15, 21, 22, 27, 52
Bureau of State Security (BOSS)
    213
bureaucracy 63, 119, 139, 142, 162,
    208, 230
Burke, G. 79
Burton, Henry 84, 85
Buthelezi, Mangosuthu 207–8, 244,
    248, 256–7
Buthelezi, Wellington 102–3

Cape 10–11, 20, 23, 26, 30, 49, 53,
    57, 59, 64–6, 70, 72–3, 77, 92,
    100, 107, 110, 140, 143, 145, 166,
    168, 170, 185, 193–4, 218, 224,
    258
    African élite 84–6
    Afrikaners in 37–8, 114–15
    agrarian worlds 35–43
    franchise 24, 27, 55, 69, 75–6, 87,
        118–19, 180
    government 63, 83, 95–6, 132
    Herschel 22, 102, 108, 206
    Mitchell's Plain 234
    Sada, Dimbaza and Ilingi 199
Cape Town 26–7, 36–7, 39, 42,
    73–4, 86, 144–5, 151, 156, 159,
    176, 181, 194, 223, 228, 238, 242
    Crossroads 248
    District Six 146–7, 229
    Keeromstraat 115
    Robben Island 215, 232–3, 252
    Sea Point 156
    Simonstown 72–3
    university sit-in (1968) 218

capitalism 56, 58, 164–5, 179, 223, 229, 235, 254
Carr, St John 59
cars 166, 174–5, 182, Table 4
Carter, C. 242
casinos 209
cattle 17–18, 22, 31–3, 42, 48, 53–4, 117, 129, 193, 205
  dipping 50, 96, 113, 130
Chamber of Mines 60, 64, 66–7, 150
Charney, C. 228, 230
chieftaincy 11, 14–20, 23, 30, 51, 69, 87, 92–5, 97, 107, 117–18, 129, 154–8, 203, 206–7
Chikane, Frank 234
Chinese people 65–6
Christian Institute 217
Christianity 17, 24, 37, 40, 78, 84, 86, 94, 101, 103, 105, 116, 176, 186, 259
Ciskei 130, 156, 207, 224
  Thornhill 206
Civil Co-operation Bureau 247
class, social 23, 44, 93, 116, 138, 174, 181, 183, 185, 187, 223, 231, 237
climate 10–11, 16–17, 36, 39, 176
coal 91, 169, 205
Cock, J. 247
Colenso, Bishop 157
colonization 14–18, 20, 22–5, 33, 35–6, 38, 42, 46–7, 59–66, 68–9, 73, 85, 92, 94, 102, 108, 117, 119, 138, 157, 163, 175
coloured people 36–7, 75–6, 92–3, 143, 146–7, 188–9, 217, 221, 229, 237
Commission on National Health (1944) 125
communal tenure 19, 31, 33, 50, 88, 147, 156, 259
communalism 119
  see also ethnicity
communism 101, 119, 125–7, 139, 148, 213–15, 242, 250, 253–4
Community Council Act (1977) 237–9, 246
commuting 201–2, 256

compounds 28–9, 31, 44, 47, 98, 104, 106–7, 121, 126, 150, 185
Congress movement 148–50
Congress of South African Students (COSAS) 233, 241
Congress of South African Trade Unions (COSATU) 243–4, 254
Congress Youth League 128, 148, 160
conservation, *see* environmental decay
Conservative Party 230, 251, 257
consumerism 175, 182, 259
consumption 171
Convention for a Democratic South Africa (CODESA) 255, 257
cooperatives 39, 49, 113
Cornelius, Hester 116
Council of Non-European Trade Unions 126
Council of Unions of South Africa (CUSA) 224, 232–3
Creswell, F. H. P. 137
crime 28–9, 41–2, 53, 105–6, 123, 125, 131, 153, 205, 236, 257

Dadoo, Dr Y. 125
dams 170, 193
De Beers 26, 167, 168
de Kiewiet, C. W. 5–6, 113, 167
de Klerk, F. W. 251–2, 254–5
de Lange, 228
Defiance Campaign 143, 148
democracy 252–4, 258–60
Democratic Party 251, 258
depression 42, 102, 109, 111–13, 115, 129
Desmond, Cosmos 163, 198–9
diamond mining 25–9, 37, 39, 167
Die Burger 38, 114–15
Die Huisgenoot 115
Dikobe, Modikwe 122, 123–4
Dinuzulu 95
disease 73–4, 79, 118, 120, 146, 204
domestic service 32, 70, 74, 104, 121, 153, 177, 185, 192
Doornfontein 121–2
dress 21, 206
drought 42

Drum magazine 147
du Toit, S. J. 38
Dube, John 86, 87, 91, 93, 100, 107
Dubow, S. 117, 119
Durban 43, 64, 73, 104–5, 108, 121,
    126, 146–8, 151, 156, 181, 184,
    222–3, 238, 248–9
  KwaMashu 248
  Lamontville 182
  Umlazi 198, 248
  Westville 218
Dutch imperialism 9, 36–7, 39, 71,
    76, 176–7
Dutch Reformed Church 115–16,
    179

East Griqualand 96
East London 39, 107–8, 121, 185
  strike (1930) 104
economy and society in the 1960s and
    1970s 162–87
Edgar, R. 98
education 40, 69–70, 76, 87, 102–3,
    115–16, 118, 120, 125, 153–4,
    160, 172, 174, 179, 208, 216,
    218–20, 228, 231, 241, 243, 248,
    255
Eiselen, Dr W. 153
electricity 110, 205–6, 259
élite:
  African 69, 84–5, 90, 108, 153,
    157, 181–2, 185, 207, 216
  Indian 90–1
environmental decay 42, 50, 113,
    117–18, 129, 154, 205–6
ethnicity 75, 91–3, 97, 106, 114, 116,
    134, 139, 157, 199–201, 208–10,
    248, 256
  see also nationalism; tribe
exile, politics of 212–16, 222, 229

Fagan Commission (1948) 125
Fanon, Frantz 217
Fascism 131, 144
Federation of South African Trade
    Unions 224, 231–2, 243
fencing 42, 113, 129, 205
firearms 20–1, 96, 247, 256
  see also armaments

First, Ruth 195
First World War 77, 80, 98, 113
flag, national 109, 259–60
football 105, 184–5
Fort Hare 160, 218
Frame, Philip 165
franchise:
  African 46, 69, 84, 143
  Afrikaner 74, 137
  Cape 24, 27, 55, 69, 75–6, 87,
    118–19, 180
  coloured 76, 144–5
  foreigners 61
  Indian 90
  women 110, 115, 119
Franchise Action Committee
    (FRAC) 144–5
fruit 38, 193–4, 196
fundamentalism 186–7
Fusion coalition 112–15, 131, 134

Gandhi, Mohandas 90–1, 93, 148
gangs 104–5, 153, 175
Garvey, Marcus 99–100, 102
Gazankulu 156
Gemmill, William 150
Gesuiwerde 114, 116
Giliomee, H. 139, 172
Glen Grey Act (1894) 20, 27, 95
gold:
  mining 25–9, 31, 39, 59–61, 64,
    67, 75, 80, 82, 98, 106–7, 111–2,
    114, 124, 167–8, 199, 201, 240
  standard 25, 60–1, 111–12
Goniwe, Matthew 242
Gorbachev, Mikhail 250
Gordimer, Nadine 180
Gordon, Max 125
Gqabi, Joe 220
Gqozo, Brigadier 257
Graaff-Reinet 39
Grahamstown 39, 156
Great Trek (1836–8) 37, 45
  anniversary trek (1938) 116, 131
Greenberg, S. 196
Greytown 101
Group Areas Act (1950) 147–8, 229,
    254

guerrilla campaigns 3, 213–14, 233, 250, 253
Guevara, Che 217
Gumede, J. T. 87, 97, 100

Hani, Chris 253
Harrismith 87, 97
Heaton Nicholls, G. 119
Hellmann, E. 122, 184
Hendrik Verwoerd Dam 170
Hertzog, J. B. M. 54, 76–7, 79, 81, 109–17, 125, 131, 137, 176
Hofmeyr, I. 115
Hofmeyr, J. H. 37, 38
Hofmeyr, Jan 124–5
Hoggenheimer 78
Holomisa, B. 257
homelands 149–58, 197–8, 202–211, 218, 225, 227, 229, 236–40, 242, 244, 247–8, 250–1, 255–57
    see also reserves
homosexuality 106
Houghton, Hobart 124
housing 16–17, 41, 73, 121, 146, 153, 174, 198, 238
Huddleston, Trevor 147
hunting 20, 41, 50, 77

identity:
    African 16, 24, 123, 148, 153, 206, 216
    Afrikaner 45–6, 75–7, 83, 93, 120, 131–3, 139–40, 157, 162, 172, 179
    racial 19, 40, 87, 89, 91–3, 97, 105, 210, 256, 258–9
Iliso Lomzi 85, 87
immigration 70–72, 82, 173, 189, 195
Immorality Act (1950) 141, 247
Imperial Conference (1926) 109, 112
imperialism, *see* Britain; Dutch imperialism; Portuguese imperialism
Imvo Zabantsundu 24, 85, 89
Indian people 43–4, 66, 90–3, 125, 131, 146–8, 188–9, 217, 223, 229, 233–4, 237
Industrial and Commercial Workers Union of South Africa (ICU)
    100–2, 105, 107–8, 125, 128, 130, 223
Industrial Conciliation Act (1924) 81
Industrial Conciliation Amendment Act (1979) 228, 231
Industrial Development Corporation 165
industrialization 28, 82, 114, 120, 124, 139, 151, 156–7, 164, 198–9, 201, 209–10
    see also manufacturing
infant mortality 190, 204
Inkatha 107, 208, 229, 244, 248–9, 256, 259
insurrection, fragmentation and negotiation 1984–1992 236–60
International Workers of Africa 107
iron and steel 21, 110, 255
Isitshozi 106
Izwi Labantu 85

Jabavu, D. D. T. 125
Jabavu, J. T. 24, 85, 88
Jameson, Leander Starr 85–6
Jameson Raid 27, 59–60
Jews 36, 71, 222
Johannesburg 27–30, 39, 42, 59, 72, 74, 78–9, 98, 105, 121, 145, 166, 194, 223, 228
    Alexandra 127, 239, 242
    Doornfontein 121–2
    Hillbrow 254
    Klipspruit 74
    Orlando 122, 220
    Rivonia 213
    Sophiatown 146, 147–8, 182
    Star 61, 80, 168
    station explosion (1964) 212
    Triomf 148
    see also Soweto
Joint Management Centres 246, 255
Joubert, Elsa 225
Jukskei 177
justice, sense of 62

Kadalie, Clements 100–101, 107
Katlehong 239
Keegan, T. 48, 55
Khaylelitsha 238

Khoikhoi people 36, 39–40
Khoisan people 10, 36
Kimberley 22, 26, 28, 30, 72, 82,
    84–5, 167
Kingwilliamstown 39
Koornhof, Piet 227
Korsten, Ge 176
Kruger National Park 110
Kruger, Stephanus Johannes Paulus
    31, 38, 50, 59, 60–1, 137
Kuper, L. 181, 182, 184
KwaMashu 248
KwaNdebele 211, 238, 248
KwaZulu 157, 206–7, 209, 229, 249

labour:
  African 28, 30, 32, 64–5, 112, 140,
    153, 181
  child 44, 195
  gender division of 18, 21, 32, 52
  indentured 43–5, 65, 91, 97
  market 92, 117, 124, 132, 142,
    149, 227–9, 235, 254
  racial division of 26
  waged 29–31, 37, 57, 65–7, 82, 98,
    101, 126, 132, 150, 153, 181, 194,
    209, 222
  women 103, 172–3, 206
Labour Party 77, 110, 133, 144
land:
  access to 14, 19, 23, 93, 96, 118,
    129
  alienation 9–15, 22, 33, 87–8, 119
  see also communal tenure; tenancy
Land Act (1913) 119, 130, 254
language 258–9
  African 16, 153, 156
  Afrikaans 36, 38, 76, 109, 115,
    154, 174, 176, 220
  diversity of 89
  Dutch 75–6
  English 75, 124, 174, 176
  Fanakalo 106
Lebowa 156–7
Legassick, M. 45, 223
Leipoldt, Louis 78
Lelyveld, Joseph 202
Lesotho 17, 26, 31, 51, 150, 201,
    204, 211

Lewsen, P. 59, 60
Liberal Party 179
liberalism 24, 58, 68, 85, 99, 119,
    124, 134, 179–80, 218, 251, 258
Lipton, M. 235
literacy 56, 89, 115, 154, 176
Lodge, T. 253
Lovedale school 84, 102
Lugard, Lord F. D. 48
Luthuli, Albert 159, 161
Lydenburg 130

Mackenzie, J. 41
Macmillan, Harold 156
Macmillan, W. M. 82
Madikizela, Solomon 158
Mafeje, Archie 218
Maine, Kas 51
maize 17–18, 22, 33, 47–9, 51–2, 97,
    104, 111, 193–4, 220, 230
Makabeni, Gana 125
Makiwane, Elijah 27
Malan, D. F. 114, 116–17, 132–3,
    137, 139–40, 143, 154, 244
Malan, Magnus 245, 246
Maliba, Alpheus 130
malnutrition 118, 204, 210
Mandela, Nelson 92, 128, 160, 212,
    234, 252–3, 255–6
Mandela, Winnie 234, 253
Mangope, Lucas 199, 257
Mantanzima, Kaiser 157, 207–8, 210
manufacturing 82, 113, 124–6,
    149–51, 163–9, 171, 192, 234,
    240
Maputo 64
Marais, Jan S. 38
Maree, J. 231
Marketing Act (1937) 113
Marks, J. B. 125, 126
Marks, Sammy 51
Marks, Shula 92, 95
Marley, Bob 185
marriage 18, 69–70, 73, 77, 141, 181,
    184, 189, 247
  divorce 179
  polygyny 18
Masekela, Hugh 147
Mass Democratic Movement 250

Masters and Servants Act 195
Matsetela, T. 52
Maxeke, Charlotte 88
Mayer, P. and I. 185
Mbeki, Govan 159
Mdantsane 198
Meer, F. 160
Merriman, Agnes 59
Merriman, John X. 37, 59–60, 63, 85
Metal and Allied Workers Union (MAWU) 223, 232
Mfengu people 23, 39, 84, 92–3, 97
Mgijima, Enoch 97–8
migrancy 14, 23, 25–34, 40–1, 53, 57, 66, 73, 98–9, 103–5, 118, 120–2, 125–7, 150–3, 155, 163–4, 185, 191, 194–5, 201, 204, 222, 231, 233, 256
militarization 244–51
Milner, Lord A. 63, 64, 65, 70, 71, 137
Mines and Works Act (1911) 80
mining 25–34, 53, 57, 59–67, 71–2, 78–82, 91, 98, 110, 112, 120, 124, 126, 149–51, 163, 167–8, 173, 191–2, 230, 254
miscegenation 57, 68–9, 141, 146
missions 17, 24–5, 37, 103, 153, 183
Mixed Marriages Act (1949) 141
Mkize, Saul 197
mobility 19, 33, 51, 55, 85, 89, 96–7, 132, 151, 182–3, 188, 195, 228
Moodie, T. Dunbar 141
Moore, Barrington 164
Moshoeshoe 22
Mozambique 26, 30–1, 44–5, 53, 61, 64–7, 98, 150, 191, 215, 225–6, 241, 253
Mpanza, James 127–8, 184
Mpetha, Oscar 232
Mpondo people 6, 11, 16, 129, 158
Mugabe, Robert 226
Murray, M. 201, 243
Mzamane, Mbulelo 221

Natal 11, 18, 20, 23, 30, 32, 63, 65, 70–1, 96, 100–1, 104, 107, 156, 158, 161, 163, 165, 186, 193, 196, 222–3, 248, 256
amalaita 105
Bambatha Rebellion 68, 86, 91, 94, 95
economic and social change in 43–51
Indians 90–1, 125, 131
Limehill 199
Msinga 96
strike (1973) 212
Natal Indian Congress 90, 148, 233
Nathan, L. 247
National Education Crisis Committee (NECC) 243
National Union of South African Students (NUSAS) 218, 233
nationalism 35, 110, 128, 138, 143, 230, 256, 260
African 87, 89, 92, 94, 101–2, 108, 120, 125, 155–6, 158, 160, 182
Afrikaner 38, 40, 50, 58, 62, 75, 79, 89, 116–7, 131, 180
Nationalist Party 109, 111–2, 132–3, 137–46, 150, 153, 156, 161–3, 172, 176, 179, 186, 188, 209, 212, 227, 229–30, 236, 244, 250–2, 254–5
Native Administration Act (1927) 107
Native Affairs Department (NAD) 107, 119–20, 129, 142, 153, 156
Native Economic Commission (NEC) (1930–2) 117–8, 129, 155, 157
Native Labour Regulation Act (1911) 67
Native Recruiting Corporation (NRC) 67
Native Representation Act (1936) 118, 132
Native Service Contract Act (1932) 132
Native Trust and Land Act (1936) 10, 55, 118–19, 130, 196
Natives Land Act (1913) 10, 34, 54–5, 86–8
Nattrass, J. 165
Naude, Beyers 217
Nazarites 186

Ndzundza Ndebele people 97, 202
Newcastle 72
New Zealand (Aotearoa) 39, 214
Ninevites 106
Nkomati Accord (1984) 241
Nkrumah, Kwame 157
Nxumalo, Henry 195
Nyagumbo, Maurice 183

Ohlange Institution 87, 91
oil 165, 167, 169
OK Bazaars 175
O'Meara, D. 110, 112
Oppenheimer, Ernest 167
Oppenheimer, Harry 167-8
oppression, racial 16, 20, 47, 58, 63,
    70, 91-3, 108-9, 141, 165, 178,
    181, 188, 220, 229, 246, 252,
    258-9
Orange Free State 11, 20, 22, 46, 48,
    51, 54-5, 87-8, 90, 131-2,
    167-70, 196, 199, 201, 230
Ossewabrandwag (OB) 131, 177
ox-wagons 2, 21, 23, 40, 48-9, 116,
    131, 139, 260

Pan Africanist Congress (PAC)
    159-60, 180, 213, 215, 217, 248
    Azanian People's Liberation Army
    (APLA) 257
    Poqo 212
passes, urban 33, 55, 88-9, 99, 121,
    125, 127, 152, 157, 159, 192, 238,
    247
Paton, Alan 122-3
patriarchy 18, 32, 46, 103, 141, 175,
    179
peasantries 14-15, 19-25, 32-3, 37,
    46-7, 51-2, 56, 93, 102, 129,
    158, 214
Pedi people 14, 26, 28, 30, 97, 105,
    156
Pegging Act (1943) 146
Peregrino, F. Z. S. 86
Peterson, Hector 221
Pick and Pay 175
Pietermaritzburg 72, 256
    Edenvale 249
Pietersburg 186

Plaatje, Solomon 54, 55, 84-5, 87,
    88, 92, 93
plough 11, 19, 21, 23
Pondoland 31, 129, 158, 162
population increase 47, 118, 129,
    138, 172, 189, 203, Tables
Population Registration Act (1950)
    141, 143, 254
Port Elizabeth 10, 30, 39-40, 74,
    100, 121, 151, 232
Portuguese imperialism 45-6, 61,
    64, 165, 219, 225-6
Posel, D. 152
potatoes 194-5
Potchefstroom 108, 225
Poto, Chief 158, 207
poverty 31, 66, 77-8, 83, 118, 123,
    125, 138, 153, 164, 190, 203-206,
    210-11, 239, 259-60
    poor whites 54-6, 77-8, 110, 164
pregnancy 190
Pretoria 72-3, 78, 105, 137, 152,
    194, 199, 202, 204, 207-8, 226
    Hammanskraal 217
Prevention of Illegal Squatting Act
    (1951) 147
Price, Robert M. 241
Progressive Party 179-80
Prohibition of Improper Political
    Interference Act (1967) 145
Putco (Public Utility Transport
    Corporation) 202

Queenstown 39, 72
Qwaqwa 201, 211

race 68, 71, 162, 208
    classification 142, 189
racism 24, 56-8, 89, 92, 110, 116,
    120, 137-9, 141-3, 149, 179, 216,
    232
radicalism 99-101, 103, 107-8,
    222-3, 235
railways 48-9, 78, 82, 94, 110, 116,
    120, 131, 145, 148, 255
rainfall 10-11, 16-17, 36, 39
Ramaphosa, Cyril 243, 254
Ramphele, Mamphela 206, 219

Rand 25, 30, 32, 44, 48, 71, 73, 79,
   98, 105, 107, 114, 116, 121,
   131–2, 151, 159, 167, 170, 184,
   238–9, 256
   boycott (1922) 102
   gold mining 26–7, 31, 59, 66, 72,
      82
   Revolt (1922) 99
   strike (1913) 88
   strike (1946) 128
   strike (1981) 232
Reeves, Jim 175
reform, political 225–37, 239, 242,
   244–6, 250–5
religion 24–5, 78–9, 84, 95, 97–8,
   103, 115–16, 128, 179, 182–3,
   186–7, 216–19, 258
Relly, Gavin 242
Rembrandt van Rijn 177
Renamo organization 226
rents 238–9
Reservation of Separate Amenities
   Act (1953) 146, 254
reserves 10–11, 14–15, 18–19, 31,
   33–4, 37, 41, 48, 51, 53, 55, 57,
   88, 96–7, 107–8, 117–18, 121,
   129–30, 150–1, 153–6, 192,
   198–9, 203, 206, 209
resistance, African 15, 42, 57,
   84–108, 128–31, 148, 160, 165,
   206, 210, 241–2, 246, 252, 259
   passive 89–91
   religious 97–8
   women 102, 108, 152, 157–8
   see also Bambatha Rebellion; riots
Rhodes, Cecil 20, 26, 27, 38, 59–60,
   63, 73, 84, 85, 137, 167
Richardson, P. 79
Riekert Commission (1979) 228
rights:
   African 19, 23, 34, 50, 61, 67, 73,
      96, 110, 117–8, 125–6, 151–2,
      216, 228, 230, 233, 237, 247, 258
   coloured 86, 143
   racial 90, 142
   urban 88
   workers 101
Riotous Assemblies Act (1914) 80
riots 86, 96, 98, 101, 104–5, 128, 152

Roosevelt, Franklin D. 113
Rose-Innes, Lady 110
Rubusana, Walter 85–6
rugby 177–8, 185, 214, 260
Rupert, Anton 173, 177

sabotage 212–13, 233, 246
Sachs, Solly 116
Sampson, A. 148
sanctions 164, 241, 243, 249, 254
sanitation syndrome 74
Sasol Corporation 169, 255
Schreiner, Olive 40, 63
Sebatakgomo movement 157
Sebokeng 239
Second World War 117, 120, 124,
   131, 134
Seekings, J. 237
segregation 27, 34–5, 44–5, 53–5,
   57–8, 70, 73–4, 78, 81–3, 85,
   87–8, 93, 96–7, 99–100, 107–9,
   112, 117–24, 127, 129, 133,
   137–8, 140, 143, 145, 149, 155–7,
   163–4, 173, 175, 180, 187, 214,
   218, 235, 239
   spatial 142, 146–9, 154, 229, 252
   see also apartheid
Seme, P. 87
Separate Representation of Voters
   Act (1951) 143, 145
settler farmlands, see agriculture,
   white
settler state in depression and war
   109–34
Shabalala, Thomas 248
Shangaan people 99, 156
sharecropping 35, 51–5, 57
Sharpeville 159–62, 239
sheep 21–2, 37, 39–43, 48, 111, 114,
   129, 193, 205
Shepstone, Sir T. 137
Sigcau, Botha 129, 158
Simkins, C. 197
Sisulu, Albertina 234
Sisulu, Walter 160, 234, 253
Sisulu, Zwelakh 243
Skosana, Simon 248
Slovo, Joe 253
slums 98, 121–3, 198–9

smoking 176–7, 182
Smuts, Jan 44, 62, 74–5, 76–80, 91,
    100, 103, 109, 112, 116, 120–1,
    124–6, 137, 244
  demise of 131–4
Sobukwe, Robert 159, 248
Social Darwinism 57, 68
Social and Economic Planning
    Council 125
socialism 81, 107, 116–7, 215, 223,
    229, 236, 254
Sofasonke movement 127–8
Soil Erosion Act (1932) 113
solidarity 99, 106, 126, 131, 139,
    222, 242
Solomon ka Dinuzulu 107
sorghum 17, 47, 104, 185
Sotho people 11, 16, 22–3, 51, 199,
    201, 206
South Africa Act (1909) 75
South Africa Congress of Trade
    Unions (SACTU) 150, 159, 222,
    224
South Africa Development Trust
    198
South Africa Native Congress
    (SANC) 85–6
South Africa Native National
    Congress (SANNC) 84, 87–8
South African Agricultural Union
    (SAAU) 194–5
South African Allied Workers'
    Union (SAAWU) 224, 231, 232
South African Council of Churches
    217, 221
South African Native Affairs
    Commission (SANAC) 69–70,
    87, 117
South African Party 63, 75, 109, 112
South African Railways 110
South African Spectator 86
South African Students Movement
    (SASM) 219–20
South African Students Organization
    (SASO) 218
South African War 27, 46, 61–2, 64,
    77, 84, 90–1, 97, 137
South West Africa People's

Organization (SWAPO) 226,
    250
Southall, R. 208
Soweto 52, 122, 128, 165, 186, 202,
    205, 212, 219–21, 224–5, 227,
    237, 239
sport 177–8, 214–5, 252, 259
springbok 41, 49, 177, 260
squatters 53, 69, 122, 127–8, 131,
    184, 239, 256
Stadler, A. 128
state intervention 41, 44, 50, 54, 56,
    58, 67, 70, 82, 96–8, 108, 110,
    112, 114, 117, 120–1, 124–5,
    127–30, 142, 158, 161, 164, 168
State Security Council 250
Stellenbosch University 38, 115, 140,
    177
stokvel 184, 222
Streek, B. 210
strikes 79–81, 91, 99–101, 104, 106,
    126–8, 131, 149, 159, 222–4,
    231, 243–4
Strydom, J. G. 140, 145
suffrage movement 110
sugar 30, 43–4, 66, 91, 94, 193–4,
    196, 209
Sundkler, B. 103
Suppression of Communism Act
    (1950) 149
Surplus People Project (SPP) 196–7
Suzman, Helen 180
Swazi people 87, 92, 97

Tambo, Oliver 128, 160, 214
taxation 20, 45, 63, 87, 91, 93–5,
    111–2, 114, 130, 169
taxis, microbus 202, 256
Taylor, Jeremy 174, 183
technology 11, 21, 35, 113, 132, 193,
    203, 235
tenancy 14–15, 19, 35, 45–7, 51–8,
    94, 97, 101, 119, 127, 130, 193,
    195–6
Thaba Nchu 199, 201, 211
Thembu people 11, 160
Thompson, L. 70, 74
Tlokoa people 87

Tomlinson Commission (1956)
    154–5
'total strategy' 245
Transvaal Native Congress 85
trade 20–3, 90, 114, 128, 138, 164–7,
    169, 171–2, 175, 208, 249
Trade Union Congress of South
    Africa (TUCSA) 150, 222
trade unionism 71, 78–81, 99–102,
    106, 116, 125–7, 132, 149, 219,
    222–4, 228, 231–3, 243–4,
    253–4
traditionalism 15, 23, 96–7, 99, 181,
    206
Transkei 16, 18, 21, 23, 33, 44, 86,
    90, 156–7, 160, 177, 203–5,
    207–10, 257
    Butterworth 198
Transkei National Independence
    Party (TNIP) 207–8
transport 21, 47–8, 127, 208, 210,
    256
Transvaal 10–11, 18, 20–1, 23, 26,
    40, 50, 64, 72–3, 75, 77, 83, 90,
    92, 97, 99, 101, 104–5, 130–2,
    169–70, 186, 193, 197, 230, 239
    amalaita 105
    Bethal 195
    imperialism 62–3, 74, 80
    Jameson Raid 59
    Lydenburg 130
    mining 29–30, 61, 65–6
    Pietersburg 186
    settlers 46, 49, 51
    tenancy 53, 55–6, 196
    Zeerust 157
Transvaal British Indian Association
    90
Transvaal Labour Commission 65
Trapido, S. 47, 164, 223
trekkers 44–5, 49
Treurnicht, Dr A. 230
tribe, idea of 117–9, 154–5, 203,
    216, 248
Tswana people 11, 16, 22, 156, 199
Tumahole 239
Turrell, R. 26, 29
Tutu, Archbishop Desmond 234

Umlazi 198, 248
unemployment 195, 211, 220,
    239–41, 254
Union 12–13, 75, 80, 86, 88, 107,
    124, 137, 244
United Democratic Front (UDF)
    234, 237, 241–3, 248, 253
United Nations 214
United South African Nationalist
    Party (UP) 112, 116, 120,
    131–3, 143–5, 180
United States of America 25, 35, 87,
    99, 113, 166, 175, 216–7, 250
Unity movement (NEUM) 144–5
university 38, 172, 174, 177, 218–9,
    223, 258
University Christian Movement 217
Urban Advisory Council 236
Urban Areas Act (1923) 121
Urban Areas Act (1952) 151
Urban Foundation 228, 242
urbanization:
    African 33, 37, 55, 138, 142,
        148–50, 152–3, 155, 181, 187–8,
        190–2
    Afrikaner 78, 115, 188–9
    displaced 196–203, 205–6,
        209–11, 220, 225, 236–9
    in reconstruction era 67–74
    rural life and African 122–30
    segregation and 117–22
Usuthu 94–5, 105, 222

Vaal dam 170
van den Bergh, General 213
van Onselen, C. 57, 59, 105
van Rensburg, prophet 77
Venda people 14, 207
Vereeniging, Peace Treaty of (1902)
    46, 74, 85
Verwoerd, Hendrik F. 71, 138, 140,
    153, 155, 157, 161, 171, 178, 209,
    214, 244
vigilantes 247–8, 256–7
Vilakazi, A. 181
villagization 129–30
violence 58, 117, 161, 212–13,
    218–21, 242–4, 247–8, 255–7

Vorster, Johannes Balthazar 165,
171, 213–4, 221, 225–6

Walker, C. 110
Wall Street Crash (1929) 111
war 2, 20, 23, 46, 226, 245, 249
see also First World War; Second
World War; South African War
War Veterans' Torch Commando
144
Washington, Booker T. 87
water 16–17, 170, 193, 205
Webster, D. 246
Webster, E. 224
Welkom 201
Wernher, Beit and Eckstein 64
wheat 22, 36, 38, 193
white workers 71, 79–81, 110–11,
132, 149, 164, 172, 194, 230
Wicksteed, R. 210
Wiehahn Report (1979) 228
Wilson, F. 206
windmills 11, 41
Winterveld 199, 202
Witwatersrand, *see* Rand
Witwatersrand Native Labour
Association (WNLA) 64, 67,
150
Wolpe, H. 150, 223

women 70, 73, 88–9, 103, 105, 121,
141, 151, 153, 177, 179, 186, 190
brewing beer 104–5, 122–3
division of labour 18, 21, 32, 52,
103, 114, 172–3
franchise 110, 115, 119
resistance 102, 108, 152, 157–8
role 115, 206
wool, *see* sheep
workers, working class, *see* diamond
mining, gold, labour,
manufacturing, migrancy, trade
unionism, white workers

Xhosa people 11, 16, 84, 95, 140,
156, 199, 206, 256
Xuma, Dr A. 128, 147–9, 152

Yudelman, D. 64, 79, 81

Zeerust 157
Zimbabwe (Rhodesia) 27, 161, 183,
214
Zimbabwe African National Union
(ZANU) 226
Zion Christian Church 186
Zulu people 11, 16, 44, 93–5, 100–1,
105–7, 141, 156–7, 206, 208,
249, 256
Zululand 23, 94
see also KwaZulu
Zwelithini, Goodwill 222

OXFORD

MORE OXFORD PAPERBACKS

This book is just one of nearly 1000 Oxford Paperbacks currently in print. If you would like details of other Oxford Paperbacks, including titles in the World's Classics, Oxford Reference, Oxford Books, OPUS, Past Masters, Oxford Authors, and Oxford Shakespeare series, please write to:

UK and Europe: Oxford Paperbacks Publicity Manager, Arts and Reference Publicity Department, Oxford University Press, Walton Street, Oxford OX2 6DP.

Customers in UK and Europe will find Oxford Paperbacks available in all good bookshops. But in case of difficulty please send orders to the Cash-with-Order Department, Oxford University Press Distribution Services, Saxon Way West, Corby, Northants NN18 9ES. Tel: 0536 741519; Fax: 0536 746337. Please send a cheque for the total cost of the books, plus £1.75 postage and packing for orders under £20; £2.75 for orders over £20. Customers outside the UK should add 10% of the cost of the books for postage and packing.

USA: Oxford Paperbacks Marketing Manager, Oxford University Press, Inc., 200 Madison Avenue, New York, N.Y. 10016.

Canada: Trade Department, Oxford University Press, 70 Wynford Drive, Don Mills, Ontario M3C 1J9.

Australia: Trade Marketing Manager, Oxford University Press, G.P.O. Box 2784Y, Melbourne 3001, Victoria.

South Africa: Oxford University Press, P.O. Box 1141, Cape Town 8000.

Oxford Reference

The Oxford Reference series offers authoritative and up-to-date reference books in paperback across a wide range of topics.

Abbreviations
Art and Artists
Ballet
Biology
Botany
Business
Card Games
Chemistry
Christian Church
Classical Literature
Computing
Dates
Earth Sciences
Ecology
English Christian
  Names
English Etymology
English Language
English Literature
English Place-Names
Eponyms
Finance
Fly-Fishing
Fowler's Modern
  English Usage
Geography
Irish Mythology
King's English
Law
Literary Guide to Great
  Britain and Ireland
Literary Terms

Mathematics
Medical Dictionary
Modern Quotations
Modern Slang
Music
Nursing
Opera
Oxford English
Physics
Popes
Popular Music
Proverbs
Quotations
Sailing Terms
Saints
Science
Ships and the Sea
Sociology
Spelling
Superstitions
Theatre
Twentieth-Century Art
Twentieth-Century
  History
Twentieth-Century
  World Biography
Weather Facts
Word Games
World Mythology
Writer's Dictionary
Zoology

THE STRUGGLE FOR THE MASTERY OF EUROPE 1848–1918

A. J. P. Taylor

The fall of Metternich in the revolutions of 1848 heralded an era of unprecedented nationalism in Europe, culminating in the collapse of the Hapsburg, Romanov, and Hohenzollern dynasties at the end of the First World War. In the intervening seventy years the boundaries of Europe changed dramatically from those established at Vienna in 1815. Cavour championed the cause of *Risorgimento* in Italy; Bismarck's three wars brought about the unification of Germany; Serbia and Bulgaria gained their independence courtesy of the decline of Turkey—'the sick man of Europe'; while the great powers scrambled for places in the sun in Africa. However, with America's entry into the war and President Wilson's adherence to idealistic internationalist principles, Europe ceased to be the centre of the world, although its problems, still primarily revolving around nationalist aspirations, were to smash the Treaty of Versailles and plunge the world into war once more.

A. J. P. Taylor has drawn the material for his account of this turbulent period from the many volumes of diplomatic documents which have been published in the five major European languages. By using vivid language and forceful characterization, he has produced a book that is as much a work of literature as a contribution to scientific history.

'One of the glories of twentieth-century writing.' *Observer*

LAW FROM OXFORD PAPERBACKS

INTRODUCTION TO ENGLISH LAW
Tenth Edition

William Geldart

Edited by D. C. M. Yardley

'Geldart' has over the years established itself as a standard account of English law, expounding the body of modern law as set in its historical context. Regularly updated since its first publication, it remains indispensable to student and layman alike as a concise, reliable guide.

Since publication of the ninth edition in 1984 there have been important court decisions and a great deal of relevant new legislation. D. C. M. Yardley, Chairman of the Commission for Local Administration in England, has taken account of all these developments and the result has been a considerable rewriting of several parts of the book. These include the sections dealing with the contractual liability of minors, the abolition of the concept of illegitimacy, the liability of a trade union in tort for inducing a person to break his/her contract of employment, the new public order offences, and the intent necessary for a conviction of murder.

PAST MASTERS

General Editor: Keith Thomas

SHAKESPEARE

Germaine Greer

'At the core of a coherent social structure as he viewed it lay marriage, which for Shakespeare is no mere comic convention but a crucial and complex ideal. He rejected the stereotype of the passive, sexless, unresponsive female and its inevitable concommitant, the misogynist conviction that all women were whores at heart. Instead he created a series of female characters who were both passionate and pure, who gave their hearts spontaneously into the keeping of the men they loved and remained true to the bargain in the face of tremendous odds.'

Germaine Greer's short book on Shakespeare brings a completely new eye to a subject about whom more has been written than on any other English figure. She is especially concerned with discovering why Shakespeare 'was and is a popular artist', who remains a central figure in English cultural life four centuries after his death.

'eminently trenchant and sensible . . . a genuine exploration in its own right' John Bayley, *Listener*

'the clearest and simplest explanation of Shakespeare's thought I have yet read' Auberon Waugh, *Daily Mail*

OPUS

General Editors: Walter Bodmer,
Christopher Butler, Robert Evans,
John Skorupski

CLASSICAL THOUGHT

Terence Irwin

Spanning over a thousand years from Homer to Saint Augustine, *Classical Thought* encompasses a vast range of material, in succinct style, while remaining clear and lucid even to those with no philosophical or Classical background.

The major philosophers and philosophical schools are examined—the Presocratics, Socrates, Plato, Aristotle, Stoicism, Epicureanism, Neoplatonism; but other important thinkers, such as Greek tragedians, historians, medical writers, and early Christian writers, are also discussed. The emphasis is naturally on questions of philosophical interest (although the literary and historical background to Classical philosophy is not ignored), and again the scope is broad—ethics, the theory of knowledge, philosophy of mind, philosophical theology. All this is presented in a fully integrated, highly readable text which covers many of the most important areas of ancient thought and in which stress is laid on the variety and continuity of philosophical thinking after Aristotle.

POPULAR SCIENCE FROM
OXFORD PAPERBACKS

THE AGES OF GAIA

A Biography of Our Living Earth

James Lovelock

In his first book, *Gaia: A New Look at Life on Earth*, James Lovelock proposed a startling new theory of life. Previously it was accepted that plants and animals evolve on, but are distinct from, an inanimate planet. Gaia maintained that the Earth, its rocks, oceans, and atmosphere, and all living things are part of one great organism, evolving over the vast span of geological time. Much scientific work has since confirmed Lovelock's ideas.

In *The Ages of Gaia*, Lovelock elaborates the basis of a new and unified view of the earth and life sciences, discussing recent scientific developments in detail: the greenhouse effect, acid rain, the depletion of the ozone layer and the effects of ultraviolet radiation, the emission of CFCs, and nuclear power. He demonstrates the geophysical interaction of atmosphere, oceans, climate, and the Earth's crust, regulated comfortably for life by living organisms using the energy of the sun.

'Open the cover and bathe in great draughts of air that excitingly argue the case that "the earth is alive".' David Bellamy, *Observer*

'Lovelock deserves to be described as a genius.' *New Scientist*

PHILOSOPHY IN OXFORD PAPERBACKS
THE GREAT PHILOSOPHERS

Bryan Magee

Beginning with the death of Socrates in 399, and following the story through the centuries to recent figures such as Bertrand Russell and Wittgenstein, Bryan Magee and fifteen contemporary writers and philosophers provide an accessible and exciting introduction to Western philosophy and its greatest thinkers.

Bryan Magee in conversation with:

A. J. Ayer	John Passmore
Michael Ayers	Anthony Quinton
Miles Burnyeat	John Searle
Frederick Copleston	Peter Singer
Hubert Dreyfus	J. P. Stern
Anthony Kenny	Geoffrey Warnock
Sidney Morgenbesser	Bernard Williams
Martha Nussbaum	

'Magee is to be congratulated . . . anyone who sees the programmes or reads the book will be left in no danger of believing philosophical thinking is unpractical and uninteresting.' Ronald Hayman, *Times Educational Supplement*

'one of the liveliest, fast-paced introductions to philosophy, ancient and modern that one could wish for' *Universe*

WORLD'S CLASSICS SHAKESPEARE

'*not simply a better text but a new conception of Shakespeare. This is a major achievement of twentieth-century scholarship.*' Times Literary Supplement

Hamlet
Macbeth
The Merchant of Venice
As You Like It
Henry IV Part I
Henry V
Measure for Measure
The Tempest
Much Ado About Nothing
All's Well that Ends Well
Love's Labours Lost
The Merry Wives of Windsor
The Taming of the Shrew
Titus Andronicus
Troilus & Cressida
The Two Noble Kinsmen
King John
Julius Caesar
Coriolanus
Anthony & Cleopatra

WORLD'S CLASSICS SHAKESPEARE
AS YOU LIKE IT
Edited by Alan Brissenden

As You Like It is Shakespeare's most light-hearted comedy, and its witty heroine Rosalind has his longest female role.

In this edition, Alan Brissenden reassesses both its textual and performance history, showing how interpretations have changed since the first recorded production in 1740. He examines Shakespeare's sources and elucidates the central themes of love, pastoral, and doubleness. Detailed annotations investigate the allusive and often bawdy language, enabling student, actor, and director to savour the humour and the seriousness of the play to the full.